Family Favorites

A Collection of Recipes from Our Associates
Celebrating the 125th Anniversary of
The Kroger Co.

Family Favorites

A Collection of Recipes from Our Associates
Celebrating the 125th Anniversary of The Kroger Co.

Published by The Kroger Co., Inc.
Copyright © 2008 by The Kroger Co., Inc.

Photography © by The Kroger Co., Inc.
Photographs on cover and on pages 25, 59, 93, 127, 161, 211, 245, and 279 by Mike Rutherford
Food Stylist: Mary Ann Fowlkes

This cookbook is a collection of favorite recipes, which are not necessarily original recipes.

ISBN: 978-0-6152271-0-8

Edited, Designed, and Produced by
Favorite Recipes® Press
an imprint of

FRP.

a wholly owned subsidiary of Southwestern/Great American, Inc.
P. O. Box 305142
Nashville, Tennessee 37230
800-358-0560

Art Direction: Steve Newman
Book Design: Steve Newman and Travis Rader
Project Editors: Georgia Brazil, Linda Jones, Mary Spotswood Underwood,
    Debbie Van Mol, and Tanis Westbrook
Project Coordinator: Julee Hicks
Test Kitchens: Mary Ann Fowlkes and Charlene Sproles

Manufactured in the United States of America
First Printing: 2008
25,000 copies

Table of Contents

Foreword

Dear Colleagues:

This cookbook is a celebration. It celebrates our people, our company's 125th anniversary, and the joy of sharing a meal with family and friends.

The 300-plus recipes in this cookbook were chosen from the nearly 4,000 that were submitted by associates across the country. The entries were as interesting and varied as the people who work with us in our company. The cookbook experts we hired to produce this collection sorted, tested, and tasted recipes to ensure this book reflected the great diversity and exceptional talent of our people.

This cookbook is also a celebration of our community. By purchasing this book, you are making a contribution to your local Helping Hands Fund, which provides modest financial support for associates facing catastrophic medical bills and other unexpected emergencies. Our company is underwriting the cost of producing this cookbook, so your entire purchase price goes directly into the Helping Hands Fund to help us continue this important work in your area.

There aren't many companies that are still around after 125 years. Kroger is among a special group. We believe we have not just survived, but thrived because we have been dedicated to listening to our associates and our customers, and responding to their ever-changing needs.

Thank you for purchasing this book and for sharing in our celebration of our company's 125th anniversary. Thank you, especially, for all you do every day to serve our customers as a member of the Kroger family.

Happy cooking!

David B. Dillon
Chairman and CEO

Helping Hands Fund

When a personal emergency turns into a financial hardship for one of our associates, the Helping Hands Fund is ready to help.

The program—funded by the company and by donations from associates—provides financial support to help with unexpected expenses in times of crisis such as the loss of your home because of fire, flood, or storm; the death or serious illness of a spouse or child; or major medical expenses beyond what insurance will pay.

The Helping Hands Fund can often help eligible associates with rent or mortgage payments, utilities, medical bills, food, and clothing.

Associates of the Fred Meyer division recieve similar support from that division's Gold Star Fund.

If you or someone you know needs assistance due to an emergency, contact your division's Human Resources department or talk with your supervisor for more information.

Acknowledgments

Thank you to the more than 3,000 associates who sent in nearly 4,000 recipes for this 125th anniversary cookbook. We wish we could include all of the delicious creations that you shared. The final three hundred recipes included in this book were selected by a team of professionals from our cookbook publishing company, FRP—Favorite Recipes® Press, Nashville, Tennessee.

A project like this takes a team of people to move from an idea to the book you hold in your hands. Thank you to Dave Dillon, Kroger's Chairman and CEO; Don McGeorge, President and COO; and Rodney McMullen, Kroger Vice-Chair, for their support of the idea of this cookbook from the beginning. The Kroger Co. is funding the cost of this cookbook—all of the $12.50 you contributed goes to your local Helping Hands Fund. These funds will assist our fellow co-workers in times of need. All the money—every penny—will be deposited into the Helping Hands Fund for your local division.

Thank you to the following people at Kroger who played a role in bringing this together:

Evan Anthony	Tim Houston
Janet Ausdenmoore	Pauline Lutmer
Mark Belleville	Denise Osterhues
Bill Boehm and Corporate Brands team	Cathy Owen
Tammy Bottcher	Angela Rose
Brenda Bruns	Dave Rustad
Deborah Bryant	Matt Sander
Jeff Burt	Linda Severin
Meghan Glynn	Rod Taylor
Kathy Hanna	Ross Thomas and team at CB&S
Lisa Holsclaw	

Advertising and Public Affairs Managers in all divisions

I hope you will enjoy this book and the recipes from our great associates for many years. Thank you for being a member of the Kroger family.

Lynn Marmer

Lynn Marmer
Group VP, Corporate Affairs

Division Histories

Atlanta Division

Kroger's Atlanta Division is one of the southeast's largest retail grocers, with 218 stores in Georgia, Alabama, eastern Tennessee, and South Carolina. More than 27,000 associates work in the division's stores and at its main office in Atlanta, Georgia.

In 1935 Kroger purchased twenty-five Piggly Wiggly stores in Atlanta, and the company opened its first Kroger store there the following year. By 1960 the Atlanta Division had fifty-eight stores in Georgia, and business continued to grow through the years. The division currently focuses its charitable efforts on hunger relief, K–12 education, women's health initiatives, and local organizations in the communities it serves.

Kroger operated this store at 527 Moreland Avenue in Atlanta, Georgia. (circa 1952)

Central Division

Kroger's Central Division operates stores under the banners of Kroger, Hilander, Owen's, Pay Less, and Scott's in Illinois, Indiana, Michigan, Missouri, and Ohio. The division's offices are in Indianapolis, Indiana. More than 15,000 associates work at 154 grocery stores and 49 fuel centers in the Central Division.

In 1924 Barney Kroger purchased seventy stores from the Childs Grocery Company. These stores in Indianapolis formed the foundation for what would eventually become the Central Division. In 1932 Kroger opened its first drive-in store in Indianapolis featuring its own parking lot.

In 1937 Kroger operated five stores in Anderson, Indiana.

Cincinnati/Dayton Division

Today, more than 15,000 associates work in 109 Kroger stores and 42 fuel centers in Cincinnati, northern Kentucky, and Dayton. The division's offices are in Cincinnati.

In 1883 Barney Kroger opened his first grocery store at 66 East Pearl Street in Cincinnati, Ohio. By 1908, 200 horses and wagons were making regular deliveries to 136 Kroger stores serving customers in Cincinnati, Dayton, Columbus, and northern Kentucky. The company continued to grow and expand in Cincinnati and beyond.

In the 1970s, Kroger introduced ultra-modern stores—based on customer input from extensive market research—featuring old-fashioned values and trend-setting specialty shops featuring cheese, deli and bakery items, flowers, and other items.

The new face of Kroger's Cincinnati/Dayton Division: Grand Opening Day at a Monroe, Ohio, store.

Division Histories

Columbus Division

The Columbus Division's Kroger stores are located mostly in Ohio, with a few locations in West Virginia's panhandle region. More than 16,000 associates work at 125 stores in the region. The Columbus Division offices are in Westerville, Ohio.

    The first Kroger store in Columbus opened in 1907. In 1928 Kroger acquired thirty-one Columbus-area Piggly Wiggly stores, and the division continued to grow through the years with new stores. The format for most locations is the traditional food and drug; in addition, there are six MarketPlace and two Fresh Fare stores.

The Columbus Division's first store opened in 1907 in Columbus, Ohio, at the intersection of North High and Spruce Streets.

Delta Division

The Delta Division, headquartered in Memphis, Tennessee, operates more than one hundred Kroger stores in western Tennessee, Mississippi, Arkansas, western Kentucky, and southern Missouri. More than 12,000 associates serve customers in these stores and in a 550,000-square-foot distribution center in Memphis.

    The first store in the division opened in 1928 in Paris, Arkansas. The current Delta Division was formed when the Little Rock and Memphis Divisions merged in 1974.

This Kroger store in the Delta Division opened in 1956 in North Little Rock, Arkansas.

Michigan Division

More than 16,000 associates in Kroger's Michigan Division serve customers in 137 stores and 20 fuel centers throughout the state's 97,000 square miles. The division's offices are in Novi.

  The first Kroger store in Michigan opened in 1917 in Ypsilanti. Kroger's presence grew with new stores and the acquisition of grocery chains such as Great Scott! and Kessel Food Markets.

In 2004 the Michigan Division and Columbus Divisions merged to form the Great Lakes Division. After acquiring twenty Farmer Jack stores in 2007, the company separated the division again into Michigan and Columbus Divisions.

Inside an early store in Detroit, Michigan.

Mid-Atlantic Division

More than 14,000 associates work in Kroger's Mid-Atlantic division, which serves customers in central and southwest Virginia, West Virginia, North Carolina, northeast Tennessee, eastern Kentucky, and Ohio. Mid-Atlantic operates 126 stores and 38 fuel centers throughout the region, and its division offices are in Roanoke, Virginia.

The division has grown since Kroger opened its first store in Charleston, West Virginia, in 1926. In 1929 Kroger acquired ninety-two stores from the Roanoke Grocery & Milling Co. in West Virginia, Virginia, Tennessee, and North Carolina. More recently, Kroger has acquired several Harris Teeter stores in Virginia as well as twenty Hannaford Brothers stores in Richmond and Virginia Beach, Virginia.

A newly remodeled store in Roanoke, Virginia.

Mid-South Division

The Mid-South Division operates Kroger stores in Kentucky, central Tennessee, southern Illinois, and southern Indiana. The division's main offices are in Louisville, Kentucky, with a satellite office in Nashville, Tennessee. More than 20,000 Mid-South associates work at 162 grocery stores and 90 fuel centers in the region.

In 1928 Kroger bought 108 stores from the Piggly Wiggly Valley Co. and entered the Kentucky market. Shortly after, the company opened stores in Tennessee. The Mid-South Division more recently acquired Randall's Food Stores, E. W. James, J & J Foods, and Beuhler's Market in Kentucky.

Mid-South operated this store in Winchester, Kentucky, in 1934.

Southwest Division

The Southwest Division operates 209 grocery stores in Texas and Louisiana that employ more than 25,000 people. The division's main office is in Shenandoah, Texas, near Houston, with a satellite office in Dallas. Southwest Division got its start in 1955, when Kroger merged with Henke & Pilot, Inc., a twenty-six–store food chain, and Childs Big Chain in the eastern Texas and Shreveport/Bossier City, Louisiana, areas. In 1994 Southwest launched its Signature

Store concept, which incorporates feedback from residents about the products and services they value most. Today nearly three quarters of Southwest's locations are Signature Stores.

One of Southwest's newest Signature Stores in Houston.

Dillon Stores

Dillon Stores, with headquarters in Hutchinson, Kansas, manages ninety-six stores in Kansas, Missouri, and Nebraska under the Dillons, Gerbes, Bakers, and Food 4 Less banners.

John S. Dillon first sold groceries at a general store in Sterling, Kansas, in the 1890s, and he opened the J. S. Dillon Cash Food Market in Hutchinson in 1913. In 1957 his son, Ray, added stores in Wichita. By 1968 J. S. Dillon and Sons had grown into Dillon Companies, Inc., and began acquiring regional banners, including City Market, Fry's, Gerbes, and King Soopers. Dillon Companies joined The Kroger Co. family in 1983. The company's current chairman and CEO, Dave Dillon, is the great-grandson of John S. Dillon.

Inside an earlier Dillons produce department.

Division Histories

Food 4 Less

The Food 4 Less Division operates 145 supermarkets under the Food 4 Less banner in southern California, Nevada, Illinois, and Indiana, and the Foods Co. banner in central and northern California. In addition, Food 4 Less operates three supermarkets in San Francisco under the Cala Foods and Bell Markets names. The division's office is in Compton, California, with a satellite Midwest office in Burbank, Illinois. In 1988 the first two Food 4 Less stores opened in San Bernardino and Moreno Valley, California. Food 4 Less expanded to the Greater Las Vegas area in 1997 and opened its first stores in the greater Chicago area in 2002. Today more than 8,500 associates work in the division, which is a recognized low-price leader in the communities it serves.

Fred Meyer

FredMeyer This division operates Fred Meyer stores in Alaska, Idaho, Oregon, and Washington, and its main office is in Portland, Oregon. Smaller format stores are Fred Meyer Marketplaces and Fred Meyer Northwest Best, an upscale "new concept" store. In 1922 Fred G. Meyer opened his first public market in downtown Portland. By the 1940s, general merchandise and apparel were added to the original food and drug selection. In May 1999, The Kroger Co. merged with Fred Meyer Inc.; today, more than 30,000 associates work at 129 Fred Meyer stores.

Fred Meyer's flagship store opened in 1922 at Fifth and Yamhill in Portland, Oregon.

Division Histories

Fry's Food Stores

Fry's Food Stores serve more than two million customers each week in Arizona. Its division offices are in Tolleson, Arizona, west of Phoenix. More than 16,000 associates work at 118 grocery stores, including Fry's Food and Drug Stores, Fry's Marketplace, Fry's Mercado, and Fry's Signature Stores.

In 1954 Chuck and Don Fry opened the first Fry's Food Store in Oakland, California, and later opened their first store in Phoenix in 1960. Fry's established itself as the low-price leader through the years and continued building on the brothers' legacy of great service. In 1972 Fry's merged with Dillon Companies and then joined The Kroger Co. when Kroger and Dillon Stores merged in 1983.

Division Histories

Jay C Food Stores

More than 2,100 associates work in 30 stores in the lower third of Indiana under the banners of Jay C and Ruler Foods. The division's offices are in Seymour, Indiana. Swiss immigrant John C. Groub founded the company in 1863 with a grocery store in Rockford, Indiana, making Jay C Stores the oldest division of our company. The first store under the Jay C banner opened in 1928. Jay C Food Stores was owned and operated by successive generations of the founder until it became part of The Kroger Co. in 1999.

Jay C opened this store in Seymour, Indiana, in 1953.

Division Histories

King Soopers

Part of the King Soopers/City Market Division, King Soopers' operations are based in Denver. The stores are located along the Rocky Mountains from Cheyenne, Wyoming, to Pueblo, Colorado. More than 15,000 associates serve customers at the 103 King Soopers stores in the region.

King Soopers is consistently ranked as the leading retail grocery chain in Colorado. Founder Lloyd King opened the first King Soopers store in 1947 in Arvada, Colorado. King Soopers was purchased by Dillon Companies in 1957 and joined The Kroger Co. after Kroger and Dillons merged in 1983. In 2001 King Soopers and City Market were consolidated into one division.

Lloyd King opened his first store in 1947 at 57th and Webster in Arvada, Colorado, a Denver suburb.

City Market

City Market is part of the King Soopers/City Market Division. Its retail operations are managed in Grand Junction, Colorado, and its marketing operations are based in Denver. More than 3,700 associates in 38 stores serve customers throughout central and western Colorado as well as Shiprock, New Mexico; Rawlins, Wyoming; and Moab, Utah.

Joseph Prinster, an Austrian immigrant, was City Market's founder. He and his four sons opened the first City Market store in Grand Junction in 1924. In 1969 City Market merged with Dillon Companies in Hutchinson, Kansas, and then joined The Kroger Co. after Kroger and Dillons merged in 1983.

City Market's newest store opened in Granby, Colo., in 2005.

QFC

QFC (Quality Food Centers) was founded in Seattle in 1956 with a commitment to provide quality products, excellent variety, and superior customer service. Today, more than 5,800 QFC associates work in 75 neighborhood markets in Western Washington and Portland, Oregon.

Founder Jack Croco opened the first QFC store in 1956 in Bellevue, Washington. In the mid-1990s, QFC expanded to Southern California by acquiring Hughes Family Markets, many of which were later sold to Ralphs and ultimately to Portland-based Fred Meyer. QFC merged with Fred Meyer, Inc., in 1997 and joined The Kroger Co. with the Kroger-Fred Meyer merger in 1999.

Division Histories

Ralphs

Ralphs, is the oldest supermarket chain in the western United States, is also older than Kroger. When one-time bricklayer George Albert Ralphs opened his first store in downtown Los Angeles in 1873, there were fewer people in the entire city (7,200) than there are Ralphs associates today (21,000).

Today 266 Ralphs stores serve customers throughout southern California, and the division's offices are in Los Angeles, California. In 1998 Ralphs merged with Fred Meyer and then joined The Kroger Co. after Kroger and Fred Meyer, Inc., merged in 1999. Ralphs has come a long way from its modest beginnings in 1873.

Ralphs' classic stores reflected the rich architecture of the Los Angeles area. This art deco-inspired Ralphs store served residents of Long Beach, California, in the 1930s.

Division Histories

21

Smith's Division

Smith's Food & Drug Stores operates 133 stores in the southwestern and intermountain states of Arizona, Idaho, Montana, New Mexico, Nevada, Utah, and Wyoming. Nearly 15,000 associates work in the Smith's Division, and its offices are in Salt Lake City, Utah. In 1932 Lorenzo J. Smith opened a grocery store in Brigham City, Utah. He and his son, Dee, later formed a partnership, and their business grew and focused on providing friendly service, quality, and value for every customer. In 1998 Smith's merged with Fred Meyer Stores and then joined The Kroger Co. when Kroger and Fred Meyer, Inc., merged in 1999.

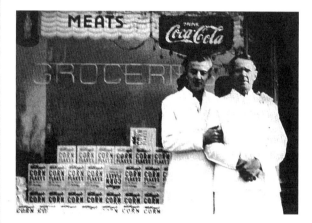

Dee Smith, left, and his father, Lorenzo, managed the first Smith's store in Brigham City, Utah.

Division Histories

Kroger Manufacturing

In 1901, Kroger became the first grocery company to operate its own bakeries. State Avenue, which still produces a wide range of grocery products, opened in 1925. Since those early days, the manufacturing division has grown to 42 facilities in 17 states and nearly 7,900 associates. The plants produce 55 percent of the corporate brand items sold in the Kroger family of stores coast to coast.

Convenience Store Group

Combining the timesaving and personalized service of a small store and the operational efficiency of a supermarket, the company's first convenience store—a Kwik Shop—opened in 1960. Today, the convenience store division includes more than 780 stores under five banners— Kwik Shop, Loaf N' Jug, Quik Stop Markets, Tom Thumb Food Stores, and Turkey Hill Minit Markets—as well as Turkey Hill Dairy in Pennsylvania. Based in Hutchinson, Kansas, the group employs more than 7,500 associates.

*The first Kwik Shop was located at
30th and Plum in Hutchinson, Kansas.*

Division Histories

Appetizers & Beverages

Appetizers & Beverages

Dinah O'Dell
Kroger
Westfield, Indiana

Roasted Cinnamon Almonds

1/2 cup sugar	1 egg white
1/2 teaspoon cinnamon	1 teaspoon water
1/4 teaspoon salt	4 cups whole almonds

Mix the sugar, cinnamon and salt in a bowl. Beat the egg white and water in a mixing bowl until frothy. Add the almonds and stir to coat. Spread in a 10x15-inch baking pan. Sprinkle with the sugar mixture and mix well. Pat the almonds into a single layer. Roast at 250 degrees for 1 hour, stirring occasionally; watch carefully to prevent overbrowning. Remove to a platter to cool; the almonds will be slightly soft. Store in an airtight container.

Serves 10

I needed a dish to take to a food day at work. I forgot about it until late the evening before. I used basic ingredients found in most kitchens to create these deviled eggs, and they were a hit.

Sandra McLendon
Kroger
Cincinnati, Ohio

Spicy Deviled Eggs

12 hard-cooked eggs	1/4 cup mayonnaise-type salad dressing
1 envelope ranch salad dressing mix	1/4 cup bottled ranch salad dressing
1/2 teaspoon cayenne pepper	1 teaspoon prepared yellow mustard
2 tablespoons sweet pickle relish	

Slice the eggs lengthwise into halves. Carefully scoop the yolks into a bowl and mash with a fork until of a grainy consistency. Stir in the salad dressing mix and then the cayenne pepper. Add the pickle relish and mix well. Stir in the mayonnaise-type salad dressing, ranch salad dressing and mustard.

Mound the egg yolk mixture in the egg white halves and arrange on a serving platter. Chill, covered, until serving time.

Makes 2 dozen

Spinach Pinwheels

2 (10-ounce) packages frozen chopped spinach,
    thawed and squeezed dry
1 (8-ounce) can water chestnuts, drained and chopped
1 (4-ounce) package real bacon bits
1 envelope ranch salad dressing mix
Chopped green onions to taste
8 ounces cream cheese, softened
1 cup (or more) sour cream
1 cup (or more) mayonnaise
8 (10-inch) flour tortillas

Combine the spinach, water chestnuts, bacon, salad dressing mix and green onions in a bowl and mix well. Add the cream cheese, sour cream and mayonnaise and mix until of a spreading consistency, adding sour cream and mayonnaise as needed.

Spread the spinach mixture evenly on the tortillas and roll tightly to enclose the filling. Wrap individually in plastic wrap and chill until firm. Line two of the rolls side by side on a hard surface and cut off the ends using an electric knife. Cut each roll into approximately eight slices using the electric knife. Arrange cut side up on a serving platter. Repeat the process with the remaining tortilla rolls.

Makes about 64 pinwheels

Brenda Fowler
Kroger
Benton, Arkansas

This past Thanksgiving everyone ate the dip and chips until it was gone. We had to pack up the turkey and send it home with everyone.

Jane Platt
Scott's
Fort Wayne, Indiana

Buffalo Chicken Dip

2 pounds Private Selection boneless skinless
   chicken breasts
1 (12-ounce) bottle hot red pepper sauce
16 ounces cream cheese or light cream cheese
1 (16-ounce) bottle ranch salad dressing or
   light ranch salad dressing
8 to 12 ounces Colby Jack cheese, shredded

Combine the chicken with enough water to cover in a saucepan and bring to a boil. Reduce the heat and simmer until the chicken is cooked through; drain. Let cool slightly. Shred the chicken in a 9x13-inch baking dish or baking pan. Pour the hot sauce over the chicken.

Heat the cream cheese in a microwave-safe dish until softened and of a spreading consistency. Add the salad dressing and mix well. Spread over the prepared layers with a spatula. Bake at 350 degrees for 30 minutes. Sprinkle with the Colby Jack cheese and bake for 10 minutes or until the cheese melts. Serve hot with tortilla chips.

Serves 10 to 12

Amber's Buffalo Chicken Dip

2 (10-ounce) cans white chicken, drained
3/4 cup hot red pepper sauce
16 ounces cream cheese, softened

1 cup ranch salad dressing
1 1/2 cups (6 ounces) shredded
   Cheddar cheese

Heat the chicken and hot sauce in a skillet over medium heat, stirring to separate the chicken chunks. Add the cream cheese half at a time, mixing until combined after each addition. Stir in the salad dressing and Cheddar cheese.

Cook until the Cheddar cheese melts and the dip is heated through. Spoon into a slow cooker set on Low to keep warm. Serve with celery sticks and tortilla chips.

Serves 12 to 15

Joe Grieshaber
Kroger
Cincinnati, Ohio

Shrimp Dip

32 ounces cream cheese
1 1/2 pounds cooked shrimp, peeled,
   deveined and chopped
8 ounces imitation crab meat, flaked
   or chopped
4 to 6 pickled hot yellow chiles, seeded
   and chopped

4 to 6 pickled banana peppers, seeded
   and chopped
2 tomatoes, chopped
1 large sweet onion, chopped
1 teaspoon crushed garlic

Heat the cream cheese in a large saucepan over low heat until melted, stirring frequently. Add the shrimp and crab meat and stir until combined. Stir in the yellow chiles, banana peppers, tomatoes, onion and garlic.

Cook over low heat until hot, stirring frequently. Serve hot with tortilla chips and/or assorted party crackers. Keep warm in a slow cooker set on Low, if desired. The amount of chiles may be adjusted to achieve the desired level of spiciness.

Serves 25

Chuck Ackerman
Ralphs
Compton, California

Avocado, Tomato and Feta Cheese Appetizer

2 avocados, chopped
4 Roma tomatoes, chopped
1 small red onion, chopped
1 bunch cilantro, trimmed and chopped
4 ounces feta cheese, crumbled
1/4 cup olive oil
1 tablespoon red wine vinegar
1 tablespoon ground cumin
1 teaspoon kosher salt

Combine the avocados, tomatoes and onion in a bowl. Mix gently. Stir in the cilantro. Add the cheese, olive oil, vinegar, cumin and salt and mix until combined. Chill, covered, in the refrigerator. Serve with warm pita wedges, tortilla chips or crostini.

For a variation, use the avocado mixture to make a flatbread appetizer. Roll out prepared pizza dough. Prick the dough four to five times with a fork. Bake according to the package directions until golden brown. Spread the avocado mixture on top and slice into wedges. Serve warm.

Serves 20

Black Bean Dip

1 (15-ounce) can black beans, drained
  and rinsed
1 (12-ounce) can white chicken
1 (10-ounce) package frozen creamed
  spinach, thawed

8 ounces sharp Cheddar cheese, shredded
1 cup salsa
4 ounces sharp Cheddar cheese, shredded

Combine the beans, chicken, spinach, 8 ounces cheese and the salsa in a bowl and mix well. Spread in a baking dish lined with foil. Sprinkle with 4 ounces cheese.

Bake at 350 degrees for 30 to 35 minutes or until the cheese melts and the dip is bubbly around the edges. Serve warm with tortilla chips.

Serves 10

Kip Selby
Kroger
Louisville, Kentucky

Black Bean and Feta Cheese Salsa

1/4 cup apple cider vinegar
1/4 cup vegetable oil
1/4 cup sugar
2 teaspoons garlic salt
1 (15-ounce) can black beans, drained
  and rinsed

1 (11-ounce) can white Shoe Peg
  corn, drained
8 ounces crumbled feta cheese
1 bunch scallions, chopped

Whisk the vinegar, oil, sugar and garlic salt in a bowl until blended. Add the beans, corn, cheese and scallions and mix well. Serve with tortilla chips.

Serves 10

Lauren Storer
Kroger
Cincinnati, Ohio

Chris Reyes
Kroger
Houston, Texas

Spicy Mango Salsa

2 cups chopped peeled mangoes
2 cups chopped peeled peaches or nectarines
2 garlic cloves, minced
2 tablespoons chopped fresh ginger
1/4 cup chopped fresh cilantro or basil
2 serrano chiles, chopped
Lime juice to taste

Combine the mangoes, peaches, garlic, ginger and cilantro in a bowl and mix well. Stir in the chiles and lime juice. Chill, covered, for 2 hours or longer. Serve with tortilla chips.

Serves 8 to 10

Pico de Gallo ("Beak Of The Rooster")

6 to 8 large tomatoes, cored and chopped
1 green bell pepper
1 large red onion, chopped
1 large cucumber, seeded and chopped
2 or 3 jalapeño chiles, seeded and finely chopped
1 bunch fresh cilantro, finely chopped
1/4 to 1/2 cup lime juice
Salt to taste

Combine the tomatoes, bell pepper, onion, cucumber, 2 jalapeño chiles, the cilantro and 1/4 cup lime juice in a bowl. Season with salt. Add additional lime juice and jalapeño chile, if desired. Serve as an appetizer with corn chips or use as a condiment with tacos, eggs or grilled meat and fish.

Serves 24

Trash Can Salsa

1 very ripe pineapple, chopped, or 4 very ripe
   peaches, chopped
1 poblano chile, chopped
1 green bell pepper, chopped
1 yellow bell pepper, chopped
4 jalapeño chiles, seeded and chopped
1/2 onion, chopped
1/2 bunch cilantro, trimmed and chopped
Chopped green chiles to taste
Chopped jicama to taste

Combine the pineapple, poblano chile, bell peppers, jalapeño chiles, onion, cilantro, green chiles and jicama in a bowl and mix well. Serve with tortilla chips or as an accompaniment to fish. Decrease the amount of chiles for a less spicy salsa.

Serves 10

I observed the produce manager throwing out overripe fruits and vegetables. I had just seen a T.V. commentary about "good food being thrown out," so I took the fruits and vegetables, washed them, chopped them, and served them. Everyone loved the hot and fruity salsa.

B. J. MacDonald
City Market
Grand Junction,
  Colorado

A neighbor taught me to make this salsa when I was attending Drake University in Des Moines, Iowa. She had spent a lot of time in Texas and was a fantastic cook. Thanks, Cathy!

Angie Klopp
Kroger
Lincoln, Illinois

Cathy's Fresh Salsa

5 jarred mild banana peppers
1/2 cup white vinegar
6 to 8 medium to large tomatoes, coarsely chopped
1 large green bell pepper, cut into chunks

1/2 large yellow onion, cut into chunks
2 tablespoons fresh cilantro
1 jalapeño chile (optional)
Salt to taste
1 garlic clove, minced

Drain the banana peppers, reserving 1/2 cup of the liquid. Combine the banana peppers, reserved banana pepper liquid, the vinegar, half the tomatoes, the bell pepper, onion, cilantro, jalapeño chile, salt and garlic in a blender or food processor. Process to the desired consistency. Mix with the remaining tomatoes in a bowl.

Chill, covered, for 4 to 8 hours to allow the flavors to blend. Serve with tortilla chips. You may serve immediately, but the flavor improves if chilled. Store in glass containers in the refrigerator for up to 7 days.

Serves 6 to 10

Amy Woody
Dillons
Derby, Kansas

White Queso

1 1/2 cups (6 ounces) grated Parmesan cheese
1 cup (4 ounces) shredded Monterey Jack cheese

1 cup mayonnaise
2 (4-ounce) cans chopped green chiles
1/4 teaspoon cumin
1/8 teaspoon chili powder

Mix the Parmesan cheese, Monterey Jack cheese, mayonnaise, green chiles, cumin and chili powder in a bowl. Spoon into a 1-quart casserole dish. Bake at 350 degrees for 20 minutes or until the top begins to turn golden brown. Serve hot with tortilla chips.

Serves 8 to 10

Garlic Cheese Fondue

1/2 cup dry white wine (riesling, chablis, chenin blanc)
2 teaspoons garlic powder
1 teaspoon onion powder
Dash of nutmeg
2 tablespoons butter
12 ounces Swiss cheese, cut into cubes
8 ounces Colby cheese, cut into cubes

8 ounces Monterey Jack cheese, cut into cubes
1/2 cup Cheez Whiz
1/2 cup (about) dry white wine (riesling, chablis, chenin blanc)
1 loaf crusty dark, sourdough or roasted garlic bread, cubed or torn

Mix 1/2 cup wine, the garlic powder, onion powder and nutmeg in a bowl. Melt the butter in a 2 1/2-quart saucepan over medium heat. Add the cheese and cook until the cheese begins to blend, stirring constantly. Add the Cheez Whiz and the wine mixture gradually, stirring constantly until incorporated.

Cook over medium-low heat for 10 minutes or until hot and of the desired consistency, stirring frequently to prevent the fondue from sticking to the bottom of the pan. Add 1/2 cup wine as needed for a thinner consistency.

Pour into a fondue pot or warming dish. Serve with the bread. Substitute minced fresh garlic for the garlic powder and minced fresh onion for the onion powder for a chunky texture. Add your favorite hot sauce for a little zip.

Serves 4

Hearty, dark, or whole grains breads tend to work best. Cube the bread a few hours before serving to allow the bread to dry out and toughen up, making it more sturdy and apt to absorb the cheese.

Jason Anderson
Kroger
Portland, Oregon

Black Bean Hummus

Kristin Woods
Kroger
Cincinnati, Ohio

1 (15-ounce) can black beans, drained and rinsed
2 tablespoons olive oil
2 tablespoons lemon juice
2 tablespoons tahini
1 tablespoon minced garlic

1 teaspoon cumin
$1/2$ teaspoon salt
$1/4$ teaspoon cayenne pepper
12 kalamata olives, thinly sliced
Paprika to taste

Combine the beans, olive oil, lemon juice, tahini, garlic, cumin, salt and cayenne pepper in a food processor or blender. Process until mixed or of the desired consistency, scraping the side of the bowl as needed.

Spoon the hummus into a bowl and sprinkle with the olives and paprika. Serve with pita chips or bagel chips.

Serves 6 to 8

Hummus

To yield the best flavor, use fresh lemon juice, sea salt and olive oil with a low acidity.

Alethea Morden
CB&S Advertising
Portland, Oregon

1 (15-ounce) can garbanzo beans, drained
4 garlic cloves
3 tablespoons tahini
$1 1/2$ tablespoons olive oil
2 to 3 tablespoons fresh lemon juice
Sea salt to taste

Combine the beans, garlic, tahini, olive oil, lemon juice and salt in a food processor. Process for 1 minute or until smooth. Serve with assorted party crackers or pita wedges.

Serves 4

Drunken Shrimp Bruschetta

1 1/2 cups olive oil
2 to 3 cups white wine
1 large red onion, finely chopped
2 poblano chiles, finely chopped
1 yellow bell pepper, finely chopped
1 orange bell pepper, finely chopped
2 red jalapeño chiles, finely chopped
6 garlic cloves, sliced

Salt and pepper to taste
20 ounces frozen peeled deveined small
    shrimp, thawed
80 (1/2-inch-thick) slices French baguette
    (about 2 1/2 loaves)
16 ounces Pepper Jack cheese or Swiss
    cheese, sliced to fit baguettes

Jen Anticoli
Kroger
Cincinnati, Ohio

Whisk the olive oil and wine in a large bowl and add the onion, poblano chiles, bell peppers, jalapeño chiles and garlic. Season with salt and pepper. Add the shrimp and stir to coat. Marinate, covered, in the refrigerator for 2 to 10 hours, stirring occasionally.

Heat a sauté pan until hot. Add the shrimp with a small amount of the marinade in batches. Cook until the vegetables are tender and the shrimp turn pink, stirring frequently; drain. Let stand until cool.

Spoon about 1 tablespoon of the shrimp mixture on each baguette slice and top with a slice of cheese. Arrange the bruschetta in a single layer on a baking pan. Bake at 350 degrees for 5 to 7 minutes or until the cheese melts. Serve immediately.

Makes about 80 appetizers

Good-For-You Poppers

1 pound fresh jalapeño chiles

8 ounces cream cheese, softened

1 cup (4 ounces) shredded mozzarella cheese

1 cup (4 ounces) shredded Cheddar cheese

6 slices bacon, crisp-cooked and crumbled

1/4 teaspoon salt

1/4 teaspoon chili powder

1/2 cup cracker crumbs or bread crumbs

Slice the jalapeño chiles into halves lengthwise wearing gloves. Discard the seeds and veins and rinse. Combine the cream cheese, mozzarella cheese, Cheddar cheese, bacon, salt and chili powder in a bowl and mix well.

Stuff each jalapeño chile with approximately 1 teaspoon of the cream cheese mixture, rounding the top. Coat with the cracker crumbs and arrange cheese side up in a single layer on a baking sheet. Bake at 300 degrees for 20 minutes for hot poppers, 30 minutes for medium-hot poppers and 40 minutes for mild poppers.

Serves 6 to 10

Patrick Miller

Kroger

Muncie, Indiana

David's Stuffed Jalapeños

1 dozen jalapeño chiles

8 ounces cream cheese, softened

2 pounds bulk breakfast sausage

Split the jalapeño chiles lengthwise into halves. Discard the seeds and veins. Fill level with the cream cheese. Wrap the stuffed jalapeño chiles completely with the sausage.

Arrange in a single layer on a baking sheet. Bake at 350 degrees for 40 minutes or until brown. Remove to a wire rack to drain. Cool slightly before serving.

Makes 1 dozen

You will find that they are not very "jalapeño" hot, but they do have a good flavor. Great for parties.

David Himsel

Kroger

Pasadena, Texas

Cheesy Greek Swirls

1 (17-ounce) package frozen puff pastry
8 ounces cream cheese, softened
1 cup crumbled feta cheese
1 cup sliced kalamata olives
1 cup chopped marinated artichoke hearts
1 cup frozen chopped spinach, thawed and
    squeezed dry
1 cup chopped sweet hot red piquanté chiles
2 cups (8 ounces) shredded Gruyère cheese or
    Swiss cheese
1/2 teaspoon salt
1/2 teaspoon pepper
1/2 teaspoon garlic powder

Thaw the puff pastry using the package directions. Arrange one sheet of the puff pastry on a hard surface and spread with one-half of the cream cheese. Layer with half the feta cheese, half the olives, half the artichokes, half the spinach, half the piquanté chiles and half the Gruyère cheese. Sprinkle with 1/4 teaspoon of the salt, 1/4 teaspoon of the pepper and 1/4 teaspoon of the garlic powder. Roll tightly as for a jelly roll.

Cut the roll into 1/2-inch-thick slices. Arrange the slices 2 inches apart in a single layer on a baking sheet. Repeat the process with the remaining puff pastry and the remaining ingredients. Bake at 400 degrees for 15 minutes or until golden brown. Serve warm or at room temperature.

Makes about 20 swirls

These swirls are always a hit. Must be the gooey cheese, salty olives, and a little heat from the piquanté chiles— all wrapped up in a warm flaky pastry. This recipe was adapted from a stromboli recipe made famous by my Aunt Rhnae.

Sheila Lowrie
Dillons
Hutchinson, Kansas

My mom made these egg rolls at all our family functions. They always went a long way.

Barbara Hughes

Food 4 Less

Santa Clarita, California

Mom's Miniature Egg Rolls

2 pounds extra-lean ground beef

2 cups bean sprouts, finely chopped

2 cups mushrooms, finely chopped

1 cup finely chopped onion

3/4 cup finely chopped celery

1/2 cup raisins, finely chopped

1/4 cup soy sauce

1/2 teaspoon garlic powder

3 packages small won ton wrappers

2 cups peanut oil or vegetable oil

Brown the ground beef in a large skillet, stirring until crumbly; drain. Sauté the bean sprouts, mushrooms, onion, celery and raisins in a skillet until tender. Add to the ground beef and mix well. Stir in the soy sauce and garlic powder.

Lay one won ton wrapper on a hard surface and brush the edges with water. Spoon approximately 1 teaspoon of the ground beef filling in the center of the wrapper. Fold one point over to within 1/2 inch of the opposite point, forming a triangle. Fold the two outside points to the center so they just meet. Roll up snugly from the center toward the remaining point. Press lightly to seal. Repeat the process with the remaining won ton wrappers and the remaining ground beef filling. Arrange the egg rolls between sheets of waxed paper to prevent sticking.

Heat the peanut oil in a deep skillet or wok to 350 degrees. Fry the egg rolls in the hot oil until light brown; drain. Do not overcook. The egg rolls will look dark and the wrappers will become transparent. Serve with sweet-and-sour sauce, plum sauce and/or hot mustard. You may freeze the uncooked egg rolls for future use. Fry just before serving.

Makes 135 egg rolls

Portobello Quesadillas with Cashews and Asiago

2 large portobello mushrooms
1 teaspoon olive oil
2 tablespoons balsamic vinegar
1/4 teaspoon allepo pepper flakes, chili
   pepper flakes or dried chives
1/8 teaspoon shallot pepper
2 large flour tortillas

1 cup (4 ounces) plus 2 teaspoons shredded
   asiago cheese
3 tablespoons chopped sun-dried tomatoes
1/4 cup cashew halves
Olive oil for brushing
2 teaspoons grated Parmesan cheese
6 blades of garlic chives

The fun crunch of toasted cashews, the chewy smokiness of melted asiago cheese, and the dense meatiness of the portobello mushrooms makes for a wonderful combination of texture and taste. For those allergic to nuts, top with avocado slices instead of cashews.

Royce Waxenfelter
Fred Meyer
Portland, Oregon

Cut the mushrooms into 1/2-inch slices. Heat 1 teaspoon olive oil in a skillet and add the mushrooms, vinegar, pepper flakes and shallot pepper. Sauté for 2 to 3 minutes.

Arrange the tortillas on a hard surface. Layer each with 1/2 cup of the asiago cheese, 1 tablespoon of the sun-dried tomatoes, 1 tablespoon of the cashews and half the mushroom mixture. Fold the tortillas over to cover the filling and arrange on a baking sheet. Lightly brush the tops with olive oil.

Arrange the baking sheet on the top oven rack and broil or bake at 450 degrees for about 2 minutes. Turn the quesadillas using a wide spatula. Lightly brush with olive oil and sprinkle each with 1 tablespoon of the remaining cashews and 1 1/2 teaspoons of the remaining sun-dried tomatoes. Sprinkle each with 1 teaspoon of the remaining asiago cheese. Broil for 1 to 2 minutes or until the cheese melts. Watch carefully to prevent the quesadillas from burning. Remove from the oven and sprinkle with the Parmesan cheese.

Let stand for 2 minutes to absorb any excess oil. Cut each quesadilla into three wedges and garnish each wedge with one blade of the garlic chives. Serve with your favorite berry fruit drink or favorite wine. You may substitute a mixture of a pinch of pepper and 1/8 teaspoon minced shallot for shallot pepper.

Makes 2 quesadillas

Paxton-MacKenna Meatballs

I named these meatballs for my grandchildren who love them. They get something different from chicken nuggets and ranch dressing when they visit grandma.

Stacy Arellano

Dillons

Hutchinson, Kansas

Paxton's Meatballs

2 pounds frozen meatballs
1 (16-ounce) can jellied cranberry sauce
1 (12-ounce) bottle chili sauce

MacKenna's Meatballs

2 pounds frozen meatballs
1 (18-ounce) jar apricot preserves
1 (18-ounce) jar salsa or picante sauce

For the Paxton's Meatballs, combine the meatballs, cranberry sauce and chili sauce in a slow cooker. Cook on Low for 3 to 4 hours, stirring at least once every hour. Serve warm.

For MacKenna's Meatballs, combine the meatballs, apricot preserves and salsa in a slow cooker. Cook on Low for 3 to 4 hours, stirring at least once every hour. Serve warm.

Serves 10

Chicken Lettuce Wraps with Peanut Sauce

Vince Front
Tamarack Farms
  Dairy
Westerville, Ohio

Peanut Sauce

1/4 cup creamy or chunky peanut butter

1/4 cup mayonnaise-type salad dressing

2 tablespoons honey

2 tablespoons soy sauce

2 tablespoons warm water

1 teaspoon ginger

Lettuce Wraps and Assembly

4 small boneless skinless chicken breasts

12 large Bibb lettuce leaves

3/4 cup bean sprouts

3/4 cup grated carrots

1/4 cup chopped green onions or scallions (optional)

To prepare the sauce, combine the peanut butter, salad dressing, honey, soy sauce, water and ginger in a saucepan. Cook over medium heat until blended and heated through, stirring occasionally. Cover to keep warm.

To prepare the wraps, arrange the chicken in a single layer in a baking pan. Bake at 350 degrees for 20 to 30 minutes or until cooked through. Slice the chicken into thin strips and cover to keep warm. Pour the warm peanut sauce into a bowl and place in the center of a serving platter. Surround the sauce with the lettuce leaves, bean sprouts, carrots and green onions.

To assemble, arrange the chicken strips in the lettuce leaves and drizzle with some of the peanut sauce. Top with the bean sprouts, carrots and green onions and wrap the lettuce leaves to enclose the filling. Serve immediately. Substitute leftover turkey for the chicken for variety.

Makes 12

Mike Weaver
Kroger
Keller, Texas

Mike's Hot Wings

1 to 2 pounds chicken wings
1 (8-ounce) bottle Italian salad dressing
2 tablespoons vegetable oil
1 (12-ounce) bottle mild to hot Tabasco sauce or
    favorite hot red pepper sauce
1/4 cup honey or teriyaki sauce
1/2 white or yellow onion, finely chopped
1 to 3 jalapeño chiles, or 1 to 2 habanero chiles,
    finely chopped
1 to 2 tablespoons cracked black pepper

Disjoint the wings and discard the tips. Pour the dressing over the chicken wings in a sealable plastic bag and seal tightly. Turn to coat. Marinate in the refrigerator for 1 to 10 hours, turning occasionally; drain.

Heat the oil in a skillet and add the chicken. Cook for 5 minutes or until light brown. Mix the Tabasco sauce, honey, onion, jalapeño chiles and pepper in a bowl. Reserve one-fourth of the sauce for dipping and add the remaining sauce to the chicken.

Cook for about 5 to 8 minutes or until the sauce thickens, stirring frequently. Serve hot or chilled with the reserved sauce, blue cheese salad dressing and/or ranch salad dressing. Add finely chopped peppers and/or onions, if desired.

Serves 4 to 8

Frito Misto

16 (3/4-inch) cubes provolone cheese

16 slices mortadella

1 1/2 cups all-purpose flour

1 1/4 teaspoons garlic powder

1 1/4 teaspoons white pepper

1 1/4 teaspoons salt

1 1/2 cups (6 ounces) grated
   Parmesan cheese

1 1/2 cups water

3 eggs, beaten

Canola oil or peanut oil

1 1/2 cups bite-size pieces cauliflower

1 1/2 cups bite-size pieces broccoli

1 1/2 cups small fresh mushrooms

1 cup artichoke hearts, drained

This is my favorite appetizer. The vegetables, artichoke hearts, and cheese cubes offer a nice variety of flavors and textures.

Jim Fraker
QFC
Bellevue, Washington

Wrap each provolone cheese cube with a mortadella slice and secure with wooden picks. Mix the flour, garlic powder, white pepper and salt in a bowl. Add the Parmesan cheese and water and mix until blended. Stir in the eggs.

Heat the canola oil to 325 degrees in a deep-fat fryer. Dip the cauliflower, broccoli, mushrooms and artichokes in the batter. Add the vegetables and wrapped cheese cubes to the hot oil in batches; do not crowd. Fry for 3 to 5 minutes or until light brown, shaking the fryer occasionally to keep the vegetables separate. Drain on paper towels and remove to a heated serving platter. Garnish with additional grated Parmesan cheese and finely chopped flat-leaf parsley. Serve immediately with warmed marinara sauce. Be careful not to overcook the cheese cubes as all the cheese will seep out.

Serves 8

Baked Jalapeño Won Tons

Denise Danekas
Smith's
Las Vegas, Nevada

1 bunch green onions, finely sliced
8 ounces cream cheese, softened
2 jalapeño chiles, seeded and chopped
1 package won ton wrappers, or 1 package
   egg roll wraps, cut into quarters
3 tablespoons soy sauce
1 teaspoon sugar
1 teaspoon crushed red pepper
1/4 teaspoon sesame oil

Reserve 1 teaspoon of the green onions. Mix the remaining green onions, the cream cheese and jalapeño chiles in a bowl until combined. Arrange eight or nine won ton wrappers on a hard surface. Place 1 teaspoon of the cream cheese mixture in the center of each wrapper. Moisten the edges with water and fold each into a triangle; seal tightly. Repeat the process with the remaining won ton wrappers and the remaining cream cheese mixture.

Arrange the won tons on a baking sheet sprayed with nonstick cooking spray. Bake at 350 degrees for 10 to 12 minutes or until brown. Mix the reserved green onion, the soy sauce, sugar, red pepper and sesame oil in a bowl. Serve with the won tons.

Makes 45 won tons

Strawberryaki Beef Jerky

1/2 cup strawberry purée mix or puréed
   fresh strawberries
1/3 cup teriyaki sauce or teriyaki marinade
1/3 cup sugar
1 teaspoon garlic powder
1 teaspoon cayenne pepper
1/2 teaspoon black pepper
3 pounds petite sirloin, cut into 1/4-inch-thick slices

Combine the purée mix, teriyaki sauce, sugar, garlic powder, cayenne pepper and black pepper in a large nonreactive bowl and stir until the sugar dissolves. Add the sirloin and mix to coat. Marinate, covered, in the refrigerator for 24 hours, stirring occasionally; drain.

Place the top oven rack approximately 81/2 inches from the heat source. Cover the bottom oven rack with foil to catch any drippings. Arrange the sliced sirloin on the top rack. Prop the oven door open approximately 2 inches at the top with a small piece of wood to allow the moisture to escape. Bake at 200 degrees for about 51/2 hours or until the sirloin is dark and opaque.

Serves 6 to 8

For generations the Native Americans prepared a high-energy food made of dried meat, berries, and spices call *pemmican*. This later became known as jerky by the frontiersmen who "jerked" the meat in order to tear it apart.

Mark Etnire
Fred Meyer
Bend, Oregon

My father used caribou meat in this recipe while living in Anchorage, Alaska, from 1965 to 1969. He has continued to use this recipe with deer, elk, and freshwater duck ever since.

Bryce Baker
QFC
Bothell, Washington

Easy Wild Game Jerky

3 pounds boneless meat, partially frozen
1 1/2 cups red wine
1 cup soy sauce
1 cup teriyaki sauce
1 1/2 tablespoons liquid smoke
2 teaspoons garlic salt
1 1/2 to 2 teaspoons pepper
1/2 to 1 1/2 tablespoons liquid smoke, or to taste
3 to 4 cups red wine

Cut the meat into 2- to 3-inch strips, 1/4 inch wide. Combine 1 1/2 cups wine, the soy sauce, teriyaki sauce, 1 1/2 tablespoons liquid smoke, the garlic salt and pepper in a nonreactive bowl and mix well. Add the meat and mix to coat. Marinate, covered, in the refrigerator for 8 to 10 hours, stirring occasionally. Drain on a wire rack or on paper towels for about 30 minutes.

Use a smoker or dehydrator or bake the meat in the oven for 4 to 8 hours or to the desired degree of doneness. Brush with 1/2 to 1 1/2 tablespoons liquid smoke. Share 3 to 4 cups wine with your friends while testing the jerky during the cooking process.

Makes 18 to 24 pieces

Black-Eyed Pea and Ham Bites with Cranberry Dipping Sauce

John Waters
Kroger
Angleton, Texas

Cranberry Dipping Sauce

1 (16-ounce) can whole cranberry sauce

1 tablespoon maple syrup

1 teaspoon garlic powder

Black-Eyed Pea and Ham Bites

1 (16-ounce) can black-eyed peas, drained
   and coarsely mashed

1 cup finely chopped cooked ham

2 shallots, finely chopped

1/2 red bell pepper, finely chopped

1 cup cornstarch

4 egg whites, lightly beaten

Salt and freshly ground pepper to taste

Vegetable oil

To prepare the sauce, combine the cranberry sauce, syrup and garlic powder in a saucepan. Cook until heated through, stirring occasionally. Cover to keep warm.

To prepare the bites, combine the black-eyed peas, ham, shallots and bell pepper in a bowl and mix well. Stir in the cornstarch. Add the egg whites, salt and pepper and mix well.

Heat the oil in a Dutch oven to 325 degrees. Working in batches, carefully slide the black-eyed pea batter in 2 teaspoonful portions into the hot oil. The batter is soft so be sure to slide, not drop, the batter portions into the oil. Deep-fry for 3 to 5 minutes or until golden brown and crisp. Drain on a baking sheet lined with paper towels. Serve with the warm sauce.

Serves 8

I was never fond
of spinach until
my mother made
these—delicious.

A. J. Taulbee
Tara Foods
Albany, Georgia

Spinach Balls

1 (10-ounce) package frozen spinach, cooked and squeezed dry
1 (6-ounce) package stove-top stuffing mix
3/4 cup (1 1/2 sticks) butter or margarine, melted
1/2 cup (2 ounces) grated Parmesan cheese
3 eggs, lightly beaten
1 onion, chopped

Combine the spinach and stuffing mix in a bowl and mix well. Stir in the butter, cheese, eggs and onion.

Shape the spinach mixture into golfball-size balls and arrange in a single layer on an ungreased baking sheet. Bake at 350 degrees for 14 to 16 minutes or until light brown.

Makes 34 to 36 balls

Diane Swiatkowski
Kroger
LaPorte, Indiana

Holiday Punch

3/4 cup sugar
6 cups (48 ounces) cranberry juice cocktail
1/2 cup lemon juice
2 cups orange juice
3 1/2 cups (28 ounces) ginger ale
2 pints raspberry sherbet

Dissolve the sugar in the cranberry juice cocktail, lemon juice and orange juice in a punch bowl. Spoon the sherbet over the top. Pour the ginger ale over the sherbet. Chill for 30 minutes.

Serves 10

Brownie's Swamp Water

1 pint rainbow sherbet
3 (12-ounce) cans lemon-lime soda
3 (12-ounce) cans orange soda
3 (12-ounce) cans grape soda

Let the sherbet stand at room temperature to soften. Pour the lemon-lime soda, then the orange soda and then the grape soda into a large clear punch bowl. Add the sherbet 1 tablespoon at a time to the soda mixture. Within one minute of adding the sherbet, the punch will begin to bubble making iridescent bubbles. Ladle into punch cups.

Serves 18

I created this recipe for my cub scout troop. Half the fun is watching the scouts making it look like "swamp water." Also, it really tastes good.

Kelly Brown
Kroger
Shelbyville, Indiana

Grandma Christy's Cranberry Tea

1 gallon water
1 (12-ounce) bag cranberries
1 cup orange juice
2 cinnamon sticks
1 small handful whole cloves
1 1/2 to 2 cups sugar

Combine the water, cranberries, orange juice, cinnamon sticks and cloves in a large saucepan. Bring to a boil over high heat. Reduce the heat to medium-low and simmer for 20 minutes or until the cranberries burst and the liquid turns red. Remove from the heat and strain, pressing on the solids to release the excess liquid in the cranberries. Discard the solids. Stir in the sugar. Serve hot or cold.

Makes 1 gallon

Sarah McCormick
Kroger
Marietta, Georgia

This recipe was shared with me by my Aunt Judi. She was a checker at King Soopers until she retired to go into catering.

Kari McNinch
King Soopers
Fort Collins, Colorado

Crowd Pleasin' Punch

1 (12-ounce) can frozen lemonade concentrate
1 (12-ounce) can frozen grape juice concentrate
8 to 9 lemonade cans water
Lemon slices, sliced strawberries, cranberries
    and/or raspberries (optional)

Combine the lemonade concentrate, grape juice concentrate and water in a punch bowl or large pitcher and mix well. Float lemon slices, strawberries, cranberries and/or raspberries on the top. Ladle into punch cups.

Serves 20

This makes your home smell great!

Trinity Bess
Kroger
Blacksburg, Virginia

Hot Buttered Cider

1 lemon
4 (1-inch-long) cinnamon sticks
1 teaspoon whole allspice
1 teaspoon whole cloves

8 cups apple cider or apple juice
2 tablespoons brown sugar
2 tablespoons butter, or as needed

Cut the zest from the lemon. Remove and discard any pith from the lemon zest. Slice the lemon zest into strips. Place the lemon zest, cinnamon sticks, allspice and cloves in the center of two layers of a 6x6-inch piece of cotton cheesecloth. Bring the corners together and tie with kitchen string, sealing well. Combine the spice bag, apple cider and brown sugar in a 3 1/2- or 4-quart slow cooker. Cook, covered, on Low for 4 to 6 hours or on High for 2 to 3 hours. Discard the spice bag. Ladle the cider into mugs and top each serving with 1/2 teaspoon butter. Garnish with additional strips of lemon zest, if desired.

Serves 8 to 12

Hot Buttered Rum Batter

2 cups (4 sticks) butter
1 (1-pound) package brown sugar
1 (1-pound) package confectioners' sugar
1 quart vanilla ice cream, softened

1 tablespoon cinnamon
1 teaspoon nutmeg
Rum
Nutmeg to taste

Melt the butter in a large saucepan over medium heat. Add the brown sugar and confectioners' sugar and cook until blended, stirring frequently. Remove from the heat and whisk in the ice cream, cinnamon and 1 teaspoon nutmeg. Pour into freezer containers and seal tightly. Freeze until firm.

To serve, place 1 tablespoon of the frozen butter mixture and 2 tablespoons rum in a coffee mug. Fill the mug with boiling water and stir. Sprinkle with nutmeg to taste and serve immediately.

Serves 100

Great for gift-giving. Omit the rum and stir into coffee for a nonalcoholic beverage.

Brenda Jaime
Fred Meyer
Bellingham,
*   Washington*

Perfect Mai Tai

1 cup pineapple juice
1 cup orange juice
1/2 cup light rum
1/2 cup dark rum
1/4 cup grenadine

Combine the pineapple juice, orange juice, rum and grenadine in a large pitcher and mix well. Pour over ice in glasses. Serve immediately.

Serves 6

Dan Oldenkamp
Payless
West Lafayette,
*   Indiana*

Brandy Slush

7 cups water
2 cups sugar
2 cups water
4 black tea bags
1 (12-ounce) can frozen orange juice concentrate
1 (12-ounce) can frozen lemonade concentrate
1 to 2 cups brandy
Lemon-lime or citrus soda

Great summer drink!

Carol Briggs
Kroger
Bluffton, Indiana

Combine 7 cups water and the sugar in a saucepan and bring to a boil. Boil until the sugar dissolves. Let stand until cool. Bring 2 cups water to a boil in a saucepan and add the tea bags. Let steep until cool.

Squeeze the tea bags to remove any remaining tea and pour the tea into the sugar mixture. Add the orange juice concentrate, lemonade concentrate and brandy and mix well. Pour into a freezer container and freeze for 3 to 4 days.

To serve, place two or three scoops of the slush mixture into a glass and fill with soda. Omit the brandy, if desired.

Serves 10 to 12

Yogurt Latte

1 cup fat-free vanilla yogurt
1/2 cup skim milk
4 ice cubes
3 tablespoons confectioners' sugar
1 tablespoon instant espresso powder
2 tablespoons whipped topping (optional)
Baking cocoa to taste (optional)

Combine the yogurt, milk, ice cubes, confectioners' sugar and espresso powder in a blender and process until smooth. Pour evenly into two glasses. Top with the whipped topping and sprinkle with baking cocoa. Serve immediately.

Serves 2

Robert Garrett
Dillons
Winfield, Kansas

Chocolate Punch

1/2 cup sugar
1/4 cup instant coffee granules
1 cup boiling water
2 quarts milk
1 quart vanilla ice cream, softened
1 quart chocolate ice cream, softened

Dissolve the sugar and coffee granules in the boiling water in a heatproof bowl. Chill, covered, in the refrigerator. Pour the chilled coffee mixture into a 1-gallon punch bowl just before serving. Stir in the milk. Add the ice cream in scoops and stir until melted. Serve immediately in punch cups.

Serves 12

You may need to double the recipe— it goes fast.

Juaneta Phelps
Kroger
Martinsville, Indiana

Brunch & Breads

SERVING CUSTOMERS for 125 Years
1883 Kroger 2008

Brunch & Breads

Baked Oatmeal

1 cup packed brown sugar
2 teaspoons baking powder
1 teaspoon salt
3 cups prepared oatmeal

1 cup milk
2 eggs, beaten
1/4 cup (1/2 stick) butter, melted
1 (6-ounce) package diced mixed dried fruit

Mix the brown sugar, baking powder and salt in a bowl. Add the oatmeal, milk, eggs and butter and mix well. Stir in the fruit.

Spread the oatmeal mixture in a greased 8x8-inch baking pan. Bake at 350 degrees for 30 minutes; the top will be golden brown. Serve in bowls with additional milk, if desired. Prepare the night before and store, covered, in the refrigerator. Bake just before serving.

Serves 6

I was given this recipe by a customer who comes in the store all the time.

Kim Burnett
Kroger
Dayton, Ohio

Old-Fashioned German Goetta

2 pounds pinhead or steel-cut oats
8 cups water
1 pound ground beef
1 pound bulk breakfast sausage
2 onions, finely chopped

2 tablespoons parsley
1 tablespoon salt
2 bay leaves
1 teaspoon thyme
Vegetable oil for frying

Place the oats in a large bowl and add enough water to cover by 1 inch. Let stand for 4 to 10 hours or until the water is absorbed and the oats swell.

Bring 8 cups water, the ground beef, sausage, onions, parsley, salt, bay leaves and thyme to a boil in a stockpot, stirring occasionally. Reduce the heat and simmer for 30 minutes, stirring occasionally. Stir in the soaked oats. Cook for 1 hour, stirring every 20 minutes. Remove from the heat and discard the bay leaves. Divide between two loaf pans sprayed with nonstick cooking spray. Bake at 350 degrees for 1 hour. Cool in the pans on a wire rack. Chill, covered with foil, in the refrigerator. Remove the loaf to a platter and cut into 1/2-inch slices. Fry the slices in hot oil in a skillet; drain.

Serves 20

Jim Scheeler
Kroger
Cincinnati, Ohio

Meat-Stuffed Breakfast Burritos

1 pound bulk breakfast sausage

8 ounces kielbasa, coarsely chopped

8 ounces bacon

1 (32-ounce) package O'Brien southwest
  hash brown potatoes

12 extra-large eggs

1/2 cup milk

1/2 cup chopped bell pepper, mushrooms
  and/or onion

16 ounces cheese, shredded

15 (10-inch) flour tortillas

Great for camping, fishing, and hunting trips. Even better when served with salsa.

Tonja Tinker
Fred Meyer
Anchorage, Alaska

Brown the breakfast sausage and kielbasa in a skillet, stirring until the breakfast sausage is crumbly; drain. Cook the bacon in a skillet until brown and crisp. Let cool slightly and then crumble. Cook the potatoes using the package directions.

Whisk the eggs and milk in a bowl until blended. Stir in the sausage, bacon, potatoes and bell pepper. Pour into a large skillet and cook until the eggs are set. Combine the egg mixture and cheese in a bowl and mix well.

Heat each tortilla just until warm in a lightly greased skillet. Spoon approximately 1 cup of the egg filling on the lower half of each tortilla. Roll to enclose the filling Serve immediately.

Serves 10

Meat-Lovers Breakfast Casserole

1 pound bulk breakfast sausage

8 ounces bacon

8 ounces cooked ham, coarsely chopped

1 (30-ounce) package frozen shredded potatoes

1/2 cup chopped green onions (optional)

1/2 cup chopped green bell pepper (optional)

1 1/2 cups (6 ounces) shredded cheese

6 eggs

1/2 cup milk

1/2 cup sour cream

Salt and pepper to taste

1/2 cup (2 ounces) shredded cheese

You may prepare the casserole ahead of time and store, covered, in the refrigerator. Bake just before serving. Great for a crowd.

Tammy Ridgeway

Kroger

Monticello, Indiana

Brown the sausage in a skillet, stirring until crumbly; drain. Cook the bacon in a skillet until brown and crisp; drain. Let cool slightly and then crumble. Lightly brown the ham in a skillet; drain. Layer the potatoes, sausage, bacon, ham, green onions, bell pepper and 2 cups cheese in a 9x13-inch baking pan sprayed with nonstick cooking spray or coated with butter.

Whisk the eggs, milk, sour cream, salt and pepper in a bowl until blended. Pour over the prepared layers. Bake at 350 degrees for 40 minutes. Sprinkle with 1/2 cup cheese and cook for 5 minutes or until the cheese melts. Serve warm with toast.

Serves 12

Sausage and Egg Casserole

1 pound bulk breakfast sausage

2 1/2 cups milk

10 eggs

2 1/2 cups seasoned croutons

1 1/2 cups (6 ounces) medium-sharp Cheddar cheese

1 teaspoon dry mustard

Brown the sausage in a skillet, stirring until crumbly; drain. Whisk the milk and eggs in a bowl until blended. Stir in the sausage, croutons, cheese and dry mustard.

Pour the sausage mixture into a greased 9x13-inch baking dish. Bake at 350 degrees for 50 to 60 minutes or until set. Let stand for 5 to 10 minutes before serving.

Serves 8 to 10

Perfect for a special brunch with friends and neighbors, when the children come home for the weekend from college, or any time you have people staying overnight.

John Hackett
Kroger
Louisville, Kentucky

Add anything you like to the omelets. My husband likes lots of jalapeño chiles in his, and since the omelets are cooked in individual bags there is no danger of flavors transferring. Everyone will have a custom omelet that can be eaten at the same time.

Susan Luna
Kroger
Fort Wayne, Indiana

Slumber Party Omelets

1 pound bacon
1 pound bulk breakfast sausage
12 eggs
1/2 cup 2% milk
1 teaspoon salt
1 teaspoon pepper
5 quarts water
8 ounces Mexican cheese blend, shredded
8 ounces cooked ham, chopped

Cook the bacon in a skillet over medium heat until brown and crisp; drain. Let cool and then crumble. Place the bacon in a covered container. Brown the sausage in a skillet, stirring until crumbly; drain. Place the sausage in a covered container. Chill the sausage and bacon for 8 to 10 hours. Whisk the eggs and milk in a bowl until blended. Stir in the salt and pepper and pour into a pitcher. Chill, covered, for 8 to 10 hours.

Bring the water to a boil in a 6-quart stockpot. Pour 1/2 cup of the egg mixture into each of six sealable sandwich-size plastic bags. Instruct each guest to add the desired amount of bacon, sausage, cheese and/or ham to their bag. Seal the bags tightly, pushing out any air.

Drop the bags into the boiling water and boil for 15 minutes or until set. Remove the bags from the water carefully. Open the bags and slide the omelets onto individual serving plates. Serve immediately.

Serves 6

Spinach-Stuffed Omelet

3 or 4 slices bacon, chopped
1/4 cup finely chopped onion
3 ounces fresh spinach, trimmed
4 eggs
1/2 cup milk
1/4 cup (1 ounce) shredded Colby Jack cheese

Greg Folck
Scott's
Angola, Indiana

Sauté the bacon and onion in a skillet until the onion is tender. Add the spinach and stir until wilted; drain on paper towels. Whisk the eggs and milk in a bowl until blended.

Pour the egg mixture into a nonstick skillet sprayed with nonstick cooking spray, tilting the skillet to ensure even coverage. Cook, lifting the edge of the omelet gently with a spatula as the eggs set to allow the uncooked eggs to flow underneath; do not stir. When the egg mixture is almost set, spoon the spinach filling over half the omelet and sprinkle with the cheese. Cook until the cheese melts.

Loosen the omelet with a spatula and fold over. Slide onto a plate and cut into two equal portions. Serve immediately.

Serves 2

Hash Brown Potato Quiche

Rebecca Werner
King Soopers
Centennial, Colorado

3 cups frozen hash brown potatoes, thawed
1/3 cup butter, melted
1 cup chopped cooked ham
1 cup (4 ounces) shredded Cheddar cheese
1/4 cup chopped green, yellow or red bell pepper
1/4 cup finely chopped onion (optional)
1 jalapeño chile, finely chopped (optional)
2 eggs
1/2 cup milk
1/2 teaspoon salt
1/4 teaspoon black pepper

Spread the potatoes on paper towels and press out any remaining moisture. Pat the potatoes over the bottom and up the side of an ungreased 9-inch pie plate. Drizzle the butter over the potatoes, making sure the edge is totally covered. Bake at 425 degrees for 25 minutes. Reduce the oven temperature to 350 degrees.

Layer the ham, cheese, bell pepper, onion and jalapeño chile over the baked crust. Whisk the eggs, milk, salt and pepper in a bowl until blended and pour over the prepared layers. Bake for 25 minutes or until a knife inserted in the center comes out clean.

Serves 8

Spinach Quiches

1 pound mild bulk breakfast sausage
1 (16-ounce) package frozen chopped spinach
1/4 cup frozen chopped onion
1 teaspoon chicken bouillon granules, or to taste
2 eggs
8 ounces Cheddar cheese, shredded
3 dashes of hot sauce (optional)
2 ounces Cheddar cheese, shredded

Line muffin cups with foil liners and spray with nonstick cooking spray. Brown the sausage in a skillet, stirring until crumbly; drain. Add the spinach and onion and cook until all of the liquid evaporates, stirring occasionally. Stir in the bouillon granules; the drier the mixture, the better the texture. Let stand until cool.

Whisk the eggs in a bowl until blended and mix in 8 ounces cheese. Gently stir in the spinach mixture and hot sauce. Spoon about 1/4 cup of the spinach mixture into each prepared muffin cup. Sprinkle with 2 ounces cheese. Bake at 350 degrees for 20 minutes or until set.

Serves 8

Add chopped mushrooms and/or chopped scallions with the spinach, if desired. Or, add chopped tomatoes to the cooled spinach mixture. Easy to serve, and the flavor is even better the following day.

Sonya Marsh
Kroger
Glen Allen, Virginia

The strata can easily be made the night before and stored in the refrigerator until baking time. Substitute hot salsa and hot pork sausage to spice it up a bit. Take to a Sunday brunch and share with friends.

Jill Wilson

Kroger

Indianapolis, Indiana

Southwestern Breakfast Strata

1 loaf thickly sliced white bread
1 pound bulk pork sausage
8 ounces cooked ham, chopped
8 ounces Cheddar cheese, shredded
1 cup mild salsa
1 tablespoon butter or margarine, melted
1/4 teaspoon salt
1/4 teaspoon pepper
12 eggs
1 cup milk
8 ounces Cheddar cheese, shredded

Tear the bread into bite-size pieces and place in a large mixing bowl. Brown the sausage in a skillet, stirring until crumbly; drain. Add the sausage, ham, 8 ounces cheese, the salsa, butter, salt and pepper to the bread and mix well.

Whisk the eggs and milk in a bowl until blended. Add to the bread mixture and mix well. Pour into a greased 9x13-inch baking pan and sprinkle with 8 ounces cheese. Bake, covered with foil, for 35 minutes. Remove the foil and bake for 15 minutes or until a wooden pick inserted in the center comes out clean.

Serves 12

Perfect Brunch Cheese Strata

12 slices bread
8 ounces Cheddar cheese or cheese of
   choice, shredded
1 (10-ounce) package frozen chopped broccoli,
   cooked and drained
2 cups finely chopped cooked ham or crumbled
   cooked sausage
8 eggs, lightly beaten
3 cups milk
1 small onion, finely chopped
1 tablespoon mustard
1/2 teaspoon salt
8 ounces Cheddar cheese or cheese of
   choice, shredded

This recipe may be modified to fit your family's preferences. It is our family's traditional Christmas morning favorite. The holiday is not complete without it.

Carol Lillich
Kroger
Cincinnati, Ohio

Using a doughnut cutter, cut twelve doughnuts and holes from the bread slices. Arrange the remaining bread scraps over the bottom of a 9x13-inch baking dish. Layer 8 ounces cheese, the broccoli and ham in the baking dish. Top with the bread doughnuts and doughnut holes.

Combine the eggs, milk, onion, mustard and salt in a bowl and mix well. Pour over the prepared layers. Chill, covered, for 6 to 10 hours. Bake at 325 degrees for 50 minutes. Sprinkle with 8 ounces cheese and bake for 10 minutes longer. Let stand for 10 minutes before serving.

Serves 12

Matt Partin
Kroger
Liberty Township, Ohio

Blue Cheese Biscuit Hash

1/2 cup fresh corn kernels

1/4 cup chopped red bell pepper

1/4 cup chopped seeded jalapeño chiles

2 tablespoons butter

3 eggs

4 cups crumbled buttermilk biscuits

2 cups heavy whipping cream

1 cup crumbled blue cheese

Salt and pepper to taste

Sauté the corn, bell pepper and jalapeño chiles in the butter in a skillet until tender. Let stand until cool. Whisk the eggs in a bowl until blended and then stir in the biscuits, cream, cheese, salt and pepper.

Add the vegetables to the biscuit mixture and mix well. Pour into a 2-quart baking dish sprayed with nonstick cooking spray. Bake at 350 degrees for 25 to 35 minutes or until set. Serve immediately.

Serves 8

Ultimate French Toast

French Toast

1 loaf French bread

3 tablespoons honey

2 tablespoons vanilla extract

2 tablespoons grated high-quality chocolate
 or baking cocoa

8 eggs

1 cup half-and-half

5 cups frosted flake cereal, crushed

Butter

Custard Sauce and Assembly

8 egg yolks

1/2 cup sugar

2 cups heavy cream

1/2 teaspoon vanilla extract

2 or 3 bananas, sliced

Whipped cream

Grated chocolate

This recipe is time consuming, extremely fattening, somewhat expensive for a single dish, and will make a mess out of your kitchen. Because of this, I only make it for special occasions like Christmas morning or when we have certain out-of-town guests staying at our home who specifically request this dish and have completed outlandish favors and chores for me. Once you have tried it, you will realize it is well worth all the effort!

Sandra Klein
Kroger
Cincinnati, Ohio

To prepare the French toast, cut the bread loaf into twelve 1- to 1 1/2-inch slices. Mix the honey, vanilla and chocolate in a microwave-safe dish. Microwave on High for 10 to 15 seconds or until blended. Whisk the eggs and half-and-half in a bowl and stir in the chocolate mixture.

Soak the bread slices in the egg mixture on one side for 30 to 60 seconds. Turn and soak for 30 to 60 seconds on the remaining side. Coat both sides of the bread slices with the cereal, making sure they are completely covered. Arrange the slices on a rack over a baking sheet. Let stand for 3 to 5 minutes.

Melt butter in a large skillet and add the coated bread slices in batches. Cook until golden brown and crisp on both sides, turning once. Arrange the French toast on a clean rack over a baking sheet. Place in a 350-degree oven while preparing the sauce.

To prepare the sauce, mix the egg yolks and sugar in a bowl until smooth and pale yellow . Heat the cream in a saucepan until almost simmering. Add 1/2 cup of the warm cream 1 tablespoon at a time to the egg yolk mixture, stirring constantly. Stir the egg yolk mixture into the warm cream. Add the vanilla and mix well. Cook over medium heat until thickened and of a custard consistency, stirring frequently. Remove from the heat.

Arrange two slices of the French toast on each plate and top each serving with 1/2 sliced banana. Drizzle with the desired amount of sauce and top each with a dollop of whipped cream and a sprinkling of chocolate. Serve immediately.

Serves 4 to 6

Orange Pecan Waffles

1 1/2 cups cake flour
2 1/2 teaspoons baking powder
2 tablespoons sugar
1/2 teaspoon salt
2 egg yolks
1/2 cup milk
1/2 cup orange juice
1/3 cup butter, melted
1/2 cup chopped pecans
2 egg whites

For a different twist, substitute your favorite fruit juice for the orange juice and/or walnuts for the pecans.

Bobbi Jo Brandon
King Soopers
Longmont, Colorado

Sift the cake flour, baking powder, sugar and salt together. Whisk the egg yolks, milk and orange juice in a bowl until blended. Add the flour mixture and stir until smooth. Blend in most of the butter. Stir in the pecans.

Beat the egg whites in a small mixing bowl until stiff peaks form. Fold the egg whites into the batter using a rubber spatula. Brush a preheated waffle iron with some of the remaining butter or coat with nonstick cooking spray. Add about 1 1/2 cups of the batter and bake using the manufacturer's directions. Repeat the process with the remaining butter and remaining batter.

Makes 2 large waffles, or 6 small waffles

Rocky Mountain Waffles

Waffles

1 cup whole wheat flour

1/2 cup cornmeal

2 teaspoons baking powder

1 teaspoon cinnamon

1 3/4 cups milk

2 eggs

3 tablespoons vegetable oil

2 tablespoons agave nectar or honey

1 banana

3/4 cup chopped walnuts

Fruit Topping

1 cup frozen or fresh raspberries or
   blackberries

2 tablespoons agave nectar, honey or
   maple syrup

A good waffle is one that tastes great before any syrup or toppings are added. These hearty waffles are sweet and nutty and taste great right off the griddle...like a freshly baked muffin.

David Stevenson
King Soopers
Denver, Colorado

To prepare the waffles, mix the whole wheat flour, cornmeal, baking powder and cinnamon in a bowl. Whisk the milk, eggs, oil and agave nectar in a bowl until blended. Mash the banana in a bowl until very smooth and then whisk into the milk mixture. Add the flour mixture and whisk until combined.

Pour the desired amount of batter onto a preheated waffle iron lightly sprayed with nonstick cooking spray and sprinkle with the walnuts. Bake using the manufacturer's directions; these hearty waffles may require a longer baking time. Repeat the process with the remaining batter and remaining walnuts.

To prepare the topping, combine the berries and agave nectar in a microwave-safe dish. Microwave until the berries are thawed and the mixture is slightly bubbling. Mash until puréed. Serve warm with the waffles. Each cup of berries makes enough topping for two waffles.

The banana and agave nectar can cause waffles to stick, so be sure to use nonstick cooking spray on the waffle iron. Any berry can be used for the fruit topping. Raspberries and blackberries work best because they mash and blend well. Blueberries, strawberries, and cherries also make good toppings. This recipe can also be used to make hearty pancakes.

Serves 6

Black-Eyed Pea Corn Bread

Jim Hardcastle
Kroger
Memphis, Tennessee

1 pound bulk pork sausage
1 onion, chopped
1 cup white cornmeal
1/2 cup all-purpose flour
1 teaspoon salt
1/2 teaspoon baking soda
1 cup buttermilk
1/2 cup vegetable oil
3 eggs, lightly beaten
1 (15-ounce) can black-eyed peas, drained and rinsed
2 cups (8 ounces) shredded Cheddar cheese
1 (4-ounce) can chopped green chiles, drained
1/4 cup cream-style corn

Brown the sausage with the onion in a skillet, stirring until the sausage is crumbly and the onion is tender; drain. Mix the cornmeal, flour, salt and baking soda together. Whisk the buttermilk, oil and eggs in a bowl until blended. Add the cornmeal mixture and stir just until moistened; the batter does not have to be smooth. Fold in the sausage mixture, peas, cheese, green chiles and corn.

Spread the batter in a greased 9x13-inch baking pan. Bake at 350 degrees for 50 to 55 minutes or until golden brown. Cut into small squares and serve as an appetizer, or cut into larger squares and serve as a main dish or side dish. Serve warm.

Serves 12

Beignets

1 cup (or more) all-purpose flour
1 tablespoon baking powder
1/2 teaspoon salt
1/2 teaspoon nutmeg
1/2 teaspoon cinnamon

3 eggs
1/2 cup sugar
Peanut oil for deep-frying
Confectioners' sugar

Sift 1 cup flour, the baking powder, salt, nutmeg and cinnamon in a bowl and mix well. Beat the eggs in a mixing bowl until blended. Add the sugar and beat until light and fluffy. Add the flour mixture and mix until smooth. If the batter is too thin, add additional flour 1/4 cup at a time until of the desired consistency.

Heat peanut oil in a deep fryer to 375 degrees. Using a 1-ounce scoop or a teaspoon, drop the batter into the hot oil. Fry for 1 to 2 minutes per side or until light golden brown. Drain on paper towels and sprinkle with confectioners' sugar. Serve warm.

Makes 2 dozen beignets

Beignets are excellent with hot cocoa on a cold day.

Jason Wright
Kroger
Louisville, Kentucky

Buñuelos

2 cups all-purpose flour
1/4 cup milk
2 eggs, lightly beaten
All-purpose flour for sprinkling

Vegetable oil for frying
1 cup sugar
1 to 4 tablespoons cinnamon

Combine 2 cups flour, the milk and eggs in a bowl and mix until a dough forms. Let stand for 5 minutes. Shape the dough into twelve balls, sprinkling additional flour over the balls to prevent the dough from becoming sticky.

Roll the balls as if making tortillas into the desired shape on a hard surface. Fry one at a time in the hot oil in a deep heavy skillet over high heat until light brown and crisp on both sides, using tongs to turn. Remove the buñuelos with tongs and immediately coat with a mixture of the sugar and cinnamon. Cool for 5 minutes before serving.

Makes 1 dozen buñuelos

Sylvia Saenz
Kroger
Cypress, Texas

Prepared regularly by my mother, Kathy Ginther, this is easily my favorite breakfast/ brunch dish as I grew up. Even great for dessert, I often had my fill. Dad and I usually finished off a pan in one day.

Chris Ginther

Kroger

Indianapolis, Indiana

Blockbuster Blueberry Buckle

2 cups sifted all-purpose flour
2 teaspoons baking powder
1/2 teaspoon salt
3/4 cup sugar
1/4 cup (1/2 stick) butter, melted
1 egg
1/2 cup milk
2 cups fresh blueberries
1/2 cup sugar
1/3 cup all-purpose flour
1/4 cup (1/2 stick) butter, softened
1/2 teaspoon cinnamon

Mix 2 cups flour, the baking powder and salt together. Beat 3/4 cup sugar and 1/4 cup melted butter in a mixing bowl until light and fluffy. Add the egg and beat until blended. Add the flour mixture alternately with the milk, beating until smooth after each addition. Fold in the blueberries. Spoon the batter into a greased 9x9-inch baking pan.

Combine 1/2 cup sugar, 1/3 cup flour, 1/4 cup softened butter and the cinnamon in a bowl and mix until crumbly. Sprinkle over the prepared layer. Bake at 375 degrees for 35 minutes. Serve warm.

Serves 9

Organic Whole Wheat Banana Bread

1 1/2 cups organic whole wheat flour
3 1/2 teaspoons baking powder
1 teaspoon sea salt
5 organic bananas
1 1/2 cups organic evaporated cane juice (sucanant)
1 cup quinoa
1 cup organic walnuts or pecans
1 cup plain unsalted sunflower seeds (optional)
1/4 cup organic vegetable oil
1/3 cup organic milk
1/3 cup organic sour cream

This recipe is from a high altitude and may need adjusting for lower altitudes.

Sharon Lind
City Market
Gunnison, Colorado

Mix the whole wheat flour, baking powder and salt together. Mash the bananas in a bowl until smooth. Add the flour mixture, cane juice, quinoa, walnuts, sunflower seeds, oil, milk and sour cream and mix for 30 seconds.

Grease the bottom of a 4x8-inch loaf pan. Spoon the batter into the prepared pan and bake at 350 degrees until a wooden pick inserted in the center comes out clean. Cool in the pan for 10 minutes. Remove to a wire rack and cool completely before slicing.

Makes 10 slices

Sarah Hritz
Kroger
Crossville, Tennessee

Cranberry Pumpkin Bread

2^1/4 cups all-purpose flour
1 tablespoon pumpkin pie spice
2 teaspoons baking powder
^{1}/2 teaspoon sea salt
2 cups sugar
1 (15-ounce) can pumpkin purée
^{1}/2 cup vegetable oil
2 eggs, beaten
1 cup dried cranberries
^{1}/2 cup chopped walnuts

Mix the flour, pumpkin pie spice, baking powder and salt together. Combine the sugar, pumpkin purée, oil and eggs in a bowl and mix well. Add the flour mixture and mix well. Fold in the cranberries and walnuts.

Spoon the batter into two greased and floured 5x9-inch loaf pans. Bake at 350 degrees for 55 minutes or until wooden picks inserted in the centers come out clean. Cool in the pans for 20 minutes. Remove to a wire rack to cool completely.

Makes 2 dozen slices

Fresh Strawberry Bread

2 cups all-purpose flour
1 cup quick-cooking oats
1 tablespoon cinnamon
1 teaspoon baking soda
1 teaspoon salt
1/2 teaspoon baking powder
2 cups sugar
3 eggs
1 cup vegetable oil
1 tablespoon vanilla extract
2 cups crushed strawberries
1 cup chopped nuts (optional)

Bake extra loaves and freeze for future use. Makes great holiday gifts. This is an old Michigan recipe from a local strawberry farmer.

Donald Famiano
Kroger
Cincinnati, Ohio

Mix the flour, oats, cinnamon, baking soda, salt and baking powder in a bowl. Beat the sugar and eggs in a mixing bowl until blended. Add the oil and vanilla and beat until smooth. Stir in the flour mixture and then fold in the strawberries and nuts.

Spoon the batter evenly into two greased and floured loaf pans. Bake at 350 degrees for 1 hour. Cool in the pans for 30 minutes. Remove the loaves to a wire rack. Slice and serve warm topped with ice cream or chilled.

Makes 16 slices

I personally favor the carrots, but for raisin lovers this is a great opportunity to enjoy a healthy bread.

Brian Lawhorn
Kroger
Cincinnati, Ohio

Zucchini Bread

3 cups all-purpose flour
2 teaspoons baking soda
1 1/2 teaspoons cinnamon
1 teaspoon salt
3/4 teaspoon nutmeg
1/2 teaspoon baking powder
1 cup chopped nuts
1 cup grated carrots or raisins
3 eggs
2 cups sugar
1 cup vegetable oil
1 teaspoon vanilla extract
2 cups grated zucchini
1 cup drained crushed pineapple

Combine the flour, baking soda, cinnamon, salt, nutmeg and baking powder in a bowl and mix well. Stir in the nuts and carrots. Beat the eggs in a mixing bowl until blended. Add the sugar, oil and vanilla and beat until thickened. Stir in the zucchini and pineapple. Add the flour mixture and mix well.

Spoon the batter evenly into two 5x9-inch loaf pans. Bake at 350 degrees for 1 hour. Cool in the pans for 10 minutes. Remove to a wire rack to cool completely.

Makes 16 slices

Prize-Winning Zucchini Bread

3 cups sugar

3 cups all-purpose flour

3 tablespoons cinnamon

1 teaspoon salt

1 teaspoon baking soda

$1/4$ teaspoon baking powder

3 eggs

$2^1/2$ cups grated zucchini

1 cup canola oil

2 teaspoons vanilla extract

1 cup chopped walnuts

We grow our own zucchini. I grate the zucchini and store in $2^1/2$-cup measurements in the freezer so I can make the bread all winter. The past two years I won a blue ribbon with this recipe at the Jackson County Fair.

Marilyn Williamson
Kroger
Concord, Michigan

Combine the sugar, flour, cinnamon, salt, baking soda and baking powder in a bowl and mix well. Beat the eggs in a mixing bowl until light and fluffy. Add the zucchini, canola oil and vanilla and mix gently until combined.

Add the zucchini mixture one-third at a time to the sugar mixture, mixing well after each addition. Stir in the walnuts. Spoon the batter evenly into two greased and floured 5x9-inch loaf pans or six miniature loaf pans. Bake at 350 degrees for 1 hour. Cool in the pans for 10 minutes. Remove to a wire rack to cool completely. Bake in muffin cups, if desired.

Makes 2 (5x9-inch) loaves, or 6 miniature loaves

Breakfast Muffins

These muffins are high in complex carbohydrates, protein, and Omega-3 fatty acids. I freeze them to have on hand for my daughter's breakfast on school days. These nutrient-packed muffins sustain her all morning.

John Chenney
King Soopers
Arvada, Colorado

2 cups whole wheat pastry flour
1/4 cup ground flax seeds
2 teaspoons pumpkin pie spice
1 1/2 teaspoons baking soda
1 teaspoon baking powder
1 teaspoon cinnamon
1/4 teaspoon salt
1 (15-ounce) can pumpkin
1/2 cup packed brown sugar
1/2 cup honey
1/4 cup soy milk
1/4 cup vanilla nonfat yogurt
3 tablespoons canola oil
1 egg, lightly beaten
1 egg white, lightly beaten
1 1/4 cup frozen blueberries (do not thaw)
3/4 cup finely chopped walnuts

Whisk the whole wheat flour, flax seeds, pumpkin pie spice, baking soda, baking powder, cinnamon and salt in a bowl. Combine the pumpkin, brown sugar, honey, soy milk, yogurt, canola oil, egg and egg white in a bowl and mix well. Add the flour mixture and mix until moistened. Fold in the blueberries and walnuts.

Spoon the batter evenly into twelve muffin cups coated with nonstick cooking spray. Bake at 375 degrees for 28 minutes. Let cool for 2 minutes and then remove to a wire rack.

Makes 1 dozen muffins

Good-For-You Fruit and Nut Muffins

1 1/2 cups oat bran
1 cup wheat bran
1 cup all-purpose flour
1 cup ground flax seeds
1/2 teaspoon salt
Sections of 3 navel oranges
1 1/2 cups packed light brown sugar
1 cup buttermilk
1/2 cup canola oil
2 eggs
1 teaspoon baking soda
1 teaspoon vanilla extract
2 cups fresh cranberries
1 cup chopped pecans or walnuts
1 cup fresh or frozen blueberries

Combine the oat bran, wheat bran, flour, flax seeds and salt in a bowl and mix well. Combine the orange sections, brown sugar, buttermilk, canola oil, eggs, baking soda and vanilla in a food processor or blender. Process until blended. Add to the oat bran mixture and mix until moistened. Fold in the cranberries, pecans and blueberries.

Spoon the batter evenly into eighteen muffin cups sprayed with nonstick cooking spray. Bake at 375 degrees for 40 to 45 minutes or until the tops are firm and a wooden pick inserted in the centers comes out clean. Cool for 2 minutes and remove to a wire rack. You may bake in miniature muffin cups, reducing the baking time as needed. Blackberries, cherries, raisins or your favorite fruits may be substituted.

Makes 1 1/2 dozen muffins

I found a healthy muffin recipe to use as a base and then developed it into what I liked—plus, they're good for me. I purchase fresh cranberries and blueberries in season and freeze them to have all year long.

Stephanie Boehle
Kroger
Cincinnati, Ohio

Healthy Honey Bran Muffins

I have always loved the honey bran muffins at the Carrows Restaurant. I set out to make muffins like theirs, but with healthier ingredients. These come pretty close.

Kathy Crimo
Ralphs
Glendale, California

1 1/2 cups raisin bran cereal
1/3 cup boiling water
1 cup whole wheat flour
1 teaspoon baking soda
1 teaspoon baking powder
1/2 teaspoon salt
1 cup packed brown sugar
1/3 cup unsweetened applesauce
1 egg
1 cup buttermilk
1/4 cup chopped nuts (optional)
1/4 cup honey

Combine the cereal and boiling water in a heatproof bowl and mix well. Let stand until cool. Mix the whole wheat flour, baking soda, baking powder and salt together. Beat the brown sugar, applesauce and egg in a mixing bowl until creamy. Add the dry ingredients, cereal mixture and buttermilk and mix just until moistened. Fold in the nuts.

Fill twelve jumbo muffin cups or twenty-four standard muffin cups sprayed with nonstick cooking spray three-fourths full. Drizzle each jumbo muffin with 1 teaspoon of the honey, or each standard muffin with 1/2 teaspoon of the honey. Bake at 375 degrees for 18 to 20 minutes or until a wooden pick inserted in the centers comes out clean.

Makes 1 dozen jumbo muffins, or 2 dozen standard muffins

Thanksgiving Muffins

1/4 cup (1/2 stick) butter, softened
2 tablespoons olive oil
5 ribs celery, chopped
1 large yellow onion, chopped
1 bay leaf
3 red apples, chopped
2 tablespoons poultry seasoning
2 teaspoons sage
Salt and pepper to taste
8 cups cube stuffing mix
1/4 cup chopped parsley
2 to 3 cups chicken broth
1/4 cup (1/2 stick) butter, softened

Heat 1/4 cup butter and the olive oil in a large skillet over medium-high heat until the butter melts. Stir in the celery, onion, bay leaf and apples. Sprinkle with the poultry seasoning, sage, salt and pepper.

Cook for 7 minutes or until the vegetables and apples begin to soften, stirring frequently. Discard the bay leaf. Add the stuffing mix and parsley and mix well. Add just enough of the broth to soften but not saturate the stuffing mix and mix well.

Coat the bottoms and sides of twelve jumbo muffin cups or twenty-four standard muffin cups with 1/4 cup butter. Fill the prepared muffin cups with the stuffing mixture. Bake at 375 degrees for 10 to 15 minutes or until the muffins test done. Let cool for 2 minutes and then remove to a wire rack.

Makes 1 dozen jumbo muffins, or 2 dozen standard muffins

This is a favorite during the holidays.

Cindy Campbell
Kroger
Snellville, Georgia

Mark Henshaw
King Soopers
Denver, Colorado

Swedish Rye Bread

1 cup dark molasses
3/4 cup shortening
1/2 cup sugar
1 tablespoon salt
3 1/2 cups water, at room temperature
3 envelopes dry yeast
1/2 cup warm water
Pinch of sugar
4 cups rye flour
7 cups (about) all-purpose flour
Shortening for coating

Combine the molasses, 3/4 cup shortening, 1/2 cup sugar and the salt in a mixing bowl and beat until blended. Add 3 1/2 cups water and mix until smooth. Mix the yeast, 1/2 cup warm water and a pinch of sugar in a bowl. Let stand for 3 minutes or until bubbly. Add to the molasses mixture and mix well.

Add the rye flour 1 cup at a time to the molasses mixture, mixing well after each addition with a mixer fitted with a bread hook. Add 4 cups of the all-purpose flour and mix until blended. Turn the dough onto a lightly floured surface and knead in enough of the remaining all-purpose flour 1/2 cup at a time until a stiff dough forms. Knead for 10 to 15 minutes or until the dough pushes back.

Place the dough in a greased bowl, turning to coat the surface. Let rise, covered with a tea towel, for 2 to 3 hours or until doubled in bulk. Turn the dough onto a nonfloured surface and punch down. Lightly coat six 5x9-inch loaf pans with shortening. Coat your hands with shortening and shape the dough into six loaves. Arrange the loaves in the prepared pans. Let rise, covered with tea towels, for 1 hour or until doubled in bulk. Bake at 325 degrees for 30 to 35 minutes or until the loaves test done. Remove to a wire rack and position the loaves on their sides. Let stand until cool. Serve with butter or use to make sandwiches.

Makes 6 loaves

Butterfly Rolls

3/4 cup warm water
2 tablespoons dry yeast
1 tablespoon sugar
1 1/2 cups milk
1/2 cup sugar
1 teaspoon salt
2 eggs, beaten
4 1/2 cups (about) all-purpose flour
Shortening
Melted butter

These are a tradition in our family and you can guarantee that someone will make them during the holiday season.

Holly Whiting
Smith's
Chubbuck, Idaho

Mix the warm water, yeast and 1 tablespoon sugar in a bowl and let stand until bubbly. Scald the milk in a saucepan until bubbles appear. Combine the scalded milk, 1/2 cup sugar and the salt in a heatproof bowl and mix well. Let cool slightly and then stir in the eggs and yeast mixture. Add just enough of the flour until the dough is no longer sticky, mixing until blended after each addition. Knead for 5 minutes or until smooth.

Roll the dough 1/2 inch thick on a lightly floured surface. Spread the surface of the dough with shortening and shape into a ball. Repeat the process two more times, spreading the dough with shortening each time. Roll 1/2 inch thick and cut into 2 1/2-inch rounds with a round cutter. Using a butter knife, lightly score a line in the center of each round. Dip the rounds in melted butter and fold over.

Arrange the rolls close together in a baking pan. Let rise, covered with a tea towel, for 2 hours or until doubled in bulk. Bake at 375 degrees for 6 to 10 minutes or until light brown.

Makes about 4 dozen rolls

My-My was my great grandmother. The recipe originated before 1886. The family traditionally makes these rolls at least once a year. The butter-flavor shortening is the only modern revision. They are very rich tasting, and this recipe is so easy that even a beginner cook can make them.

Lynne Rudd
Kroger
Cincinnati, Ohio

My-My's Rich-and-Easy Dinner Rolls

1 cup milk
1/2 cup butter-flavor shortening
5 tablespoons sugar
3 1/2 teaspoons salt
1 cup water, at room temperature
2 1/2 envelopes fast-rising yeast
2 jumbo eggs, beaten
6 cups sifted bread flour or unsifted unbleached flour

Scald the milk in a saucepan. Pour into a large heatproof bowl. Add the shortening, sugar and salt and mix well. Cool to lukewarm by stirring in the water. Add the yeast and gently stir until the yeast dissolves. Blend in the eggs.

Add the bread flour 1 cup at a time, mixing well after each addition. Do not knead; the dough will be soft. At this point the dough may be stored in the refrigerator for use at a later date. Place the dough in a greased bowl, turning to coat the surface. Let rise in a warm place (85 degrees or warmer) for 2 hours or until doubled in bulk. Punch the dough down and shape into rolls.

Arrange the rolls in greased muffin cups. Let rise for 1 1/2 hours or until doubled in bulk. If the dough has been chilled, this time will increase. Bake on the middle oven rack at 400 degrees for 18 minutes.

If you prepare these rolls when the temperature is cold, add a pan of boiling water to the bottom rack of your oven and place the dough in the cold oven with the door closed to rise. Or, they rise well in a utility room when the furnace is operating.

Makes 2 dozen rolls

Squash Rolls

1/2 cup sugar
2 tablespoons yeast
1 tablespoon cornstarch
1/2 cup warm water
6 1/2 cups unbleached white flour
1 (16-ounce) package frozen yellow squash,
    thawed and drained
1 cup milk
1/2 cup (1 stick) butter
1 teaspoon salt
1/2 cup (1 stick) butter, melted

You can makes these in advance and let rise, covered with plastic wrap sprayed with nonstick cooking spray, in the refrigerator for 10 to 24 hours. Let the rolls stand at room temperature for 1 hour before baking.

Barbara Beach
Fred Meyer
Portland, Oregon

Combine the sugar, yeast and cornstarch in a large mixing bowl and mix well. Stir in the warm water. Let stand for 10 minutes. Add the flour, squash, milk and 1/2 cup butter and mix for 5 minutes. Add the salt and knead for 5 minutes or until the dough is smooth and elastic. Let rise in a warm place for 1 hour. Punch the dough down and knead again.

Shape the dough into twenty-four rolls on two large baking sheets. Drizzle 1/2 cup melted butter over the rolls. Let rise for 1 hour. Snip each roll top with kitchen shears. Bake at 375 degrees for 18 to 20 minutes or until light brown.

Makes 2 dozen rolls

Soups & Salads

SERVING CUSTOMERS
for 125 Years
1883 Kroger 2008

Soups & Salads

This is a family favorite that I prepare every Christmas.

Alice Nuhring
Kroger
Batesville, Indiana

Alice's Reuben Soup

12 ounces shaved deli corned beef

6 cups chicken broth or chicken bouillon

2 cups refrigerator sauerkraut

1 large or 6 baby carrots, thinly shredded

$1/2$ small onion, chopped

1 teaspoon garlic powder

$1/2$ teaspoon thyme, crushed

$1/4$ teaspoon white or black pepper

$1/4$ teaspoon tarragon, crushed

1 bay leaf

3 tablespoons cornstarch

$1/3$ cup water

12 ounces processed Swiss cheese slices

8 ounces natural Swiss cheese, shredded

2 (12-ounce) cans evaporated milk

Combine the corned beef, broth, sauerkraut, carrot, onion, garlic powder, thyme, pepper, tarragon and bay leaf in a stockpot and mix well. Bring to a boil and then reduce the heat.

Simmer, covered, for 30 minutes. Remove from the heat and remove the cover. The soup will have an unpleasant odor, but do not be concerned. Mix the cornstarch and water in a bowl until blended and stir into the soup. Cook for 2 minutes, stirring occasionally. Reduce the heat and stir in the cheese and evaporated milk.

Cook until heated through, stirring occasionally. Discard the bay leaf. Ladle into soup bowls and serve with croutons or rye crackers. The flavor is enhanced if prepared one day in advance and stored, covered, in the refrigerator. Reheat the soup in a slow cooker on Low to allow the flavors to blend.

Serves 8

Albóndigas Meatball Soup

1 pound frozen meatballs, thawed
6 cups water
1 (8-ounce) can tomato sauce
1/2 onion, finely chopped
1 teaspoon vinegar
1 garlic clove, minced

1 large potato, cut into 1/2-inch chunks
1 large carrot, diagonally cut into
    1/4-inch slices
2 teaspoons chicken bouillon granules or salt
1/2 teaspoon each oregano and thyme
1/4 cup finely chopped cilantro.

Cook the meatballs using the package directions; drain. Bring the water to a boil in a large saucepan and add the meatballs, tomato sauce, onion, vinegar and garlic. Stir in the potato and carrot and return to a boil. Add the bouillon, oregano and thyme and mix well. Simmer for 3 to 5 minutes or until the carrot and potato are tender. Stir in the cilantro. Ladle into soup bowls and serve with warm corn tortillas.

Serves 6

This is the simplified version of my mother's traditional Mexican meal and a favorite of my family.

Monica Castaneda
La Habra Bakery
La Habra, California

Spicy Chicken Curry Soup

2 or 3 boneless skinless chicken breasts,
    cut into bite-size pieces
1 tablespoon olive oil
1 tablespoon curry powder
1 tablespoon garlic salt
1 tablespoon poultry seasoning

1 tablespoon kosher salt
1 tablespoon freshly ground pepper
1 onion, cut into strips
1 tomato, cut into strips
1 red or yellow bell pepper, cut into strips
2 cups quick-cooking brown rice

Brown the chicken in the olive oil in a large saucepan over medium heat. Stir in the curry powder, garlic salt, poultry seasoning, salt and pepper. Cook for 2 to 3 minutes, stirring frequently. Mix in the onion, tomato and bell pepper. Add enough water to cover and bring to a boil. Reduce the heat to low. Simmer, covered, for 45 minutes or until the vegetables are tender. Stir in the rice. Remove from the heat and let stand, covered, for 10 minutes or until the rice is tender. Ladle into soup bowls and serve with potato rolls or crusty bread. Add water to the soup to reduce the spiciness, if desired.

Serves 6

Tara Lopez
King Soopers
Fort Collins, Colorado

Grandma's Chicken Soup

Grandma believed chicken soup could cure any ailment. It is good for the soul.

Michael Marx
Kroger
Houston, Texas

1 (2¹/₂- to 3-pound) chicken
2 (8-ounce) cans chicken broth
3 large carrots, chopped
3 green onions, chopped
1 teaspoon chopped garlic
Pinch of nutmeg
Salt and pepper to taste
8 ounces fine egg noodles

Discard the gizzard and liver from the chicken. Place the chicken and broth in a stockpot and add enough water to cover. Add the carrots, green onions, garlic, nutmeg, salt and pepper. Bring to a boil and then reduce the heat.

Cook until the chicken is tender. Remove the chicken to a platter using a slotted spoon, reserving the broth and vegetables. Chop the chicken into bite-size pieces, discarding the skin and bones.

Return the chicken to the broth mixture. Stir in the pasta and cook until the pasta is tender. Ladle into soup bowls.

Serves 8

Chicken, Black Bean and Rice Soup

6 cups water

2 whole chicken breasts

2 tablespoons chicken base with parsley

1 teaspoon garlic powder

1 teaspoon seasoned salt

1 teaspoon Italian seasoning

1 teaspoon sage

1 1/2 cups long grain brown rice

1 (15-ounce) can black beans

1 (14-ounce) can diced tomatoes with jalapeños

1/2 cup salsa

1/2 teaspoon cumin seeds

1/2 teaspoon ground cumin

1/8 teaspoon cayenne pepper

Combine the water, chicken, chicken base, garlic powder, seasoned salt, Italian seasoning and sage in a large stockpot and bring to a boil. Boil for 30 minutes or until the chicken is cooked through. Remove the chicken to a platter using a slotted spoon, reserving the broth mixture. Chop the chicken, discarding the skin and bones and store in the refrigerator until needed.

Add the brown rice to the reserved broth mixture. Bring to a boil over medium-high heat and then reduce the heat to low to medium. Cook, with the lid ajar to allow steam to escape, for 1 hour, stirring occasionally to prevent the rice from sticking. Stir in the chicken, beans, tomatoes, salsa, cumin seeds, ground cumin and cayenne pepper. Cook over low heat for 20 minutes or until heated through. Ladle into soup bowls.

Serves 12

Since I was diagnosed with high cholesterol, I make this soup about every two weeks. It has become a family favorite and my signature dish. My daughter, Sara, likes to dip sliced French bread into the soup.

Larry Arnold
Kroger
Monroe, Indiana

Roasted Bell Pepper Bisque with Crab Meat

Allison Tartt

Kroger

Atlanta, Georgia

10 ounces jumbo lump crab meat

Zest and juice of 1 lemon

2 tablespoons fresh basil leaves, julienned

Salt and freshly ground white pepper
   to taste

2 or 3 large yellow bell peppers

3 large orange bell peppers

3 tablespoons butter

4 shallots, minced

1/2 cup chardonnay

8 cups chicken broth

1/4 cup heavy cream

1 cup crème fraîche

Place the crab meat in a small bowl. Add the lemon zest and half the lemon juice. Add the basil, salt and white pepper and toss gently to combine. Set aside.

Using tongs, roast the bell peppers over an open flame until the skin is blistered and charred on all sides, turning frequently. Place the bell peppers in a bowl and cover tightly. Chill for 15 minutes or until cool enough to handle. Remove the seeds, stems and charred skin by scraping gently with a paring knife. Chop the bell peppers into 1-inch pieces.

Combine the butter and shallots in a medium saucepan. Sweat the shallots over low heat for 2 to 3 minutes. Stir in the roasted peppers and cook for 2 to 3 minutes, stirring frequently to prevent browning. Stir in the wine and cook until most of the liquid evaporates. Mix in the broth and simmer over low heat for 15 minutes.

Process the bell pepper mixture in batches in a blender until puréed. Return the purée to the saucepan and whisk in the cream. Add the remaining lemon juice and season with salt and white pepper. Simmer just until heated through; do not boil. Ladle into soup bowls and top each serving with a dollop of the crème fraîche and some of the crab meat mixture. Serve immediately. The bisque may be served hot or chilled as a main entrée or as an appetizer.

Serves 8

Chunky Fall Chili

1 pound lean ground beef
2 garlic cloves, crushed (optional)
1 Vidalia onion, coarsely chopped
1 large red bell pepper, coarsely chopped
1 large green bell pepper, coarsely chopped
1 cup coarsely chopped peeled butternut squash
1 (10-ounce) package frozen corn
2 (14-ounce) cans stewed tomatoes
1 (15-ounce) can chili hot beans
1 (14-ounce) can beef broth
1 1/2 teaspoons chili powder
1 teaspoon ground cumin

Brown the ground beef in a Dutch oven or small stockpot, stirring until crumbly; drain. Add the garlic, onion, bell peppers and squash and mix well. Stir in the corn, tomatoes, beans, broth, chili powder and cumin. Simmer for 30 minutes. Ladle into chili bowls.

Serves 8

My cousin and I have been passing a version of this recipe back and forth for six years and finally agree this is the best version. It is a beautiful, colorful, and flavorful twist on traditional chili.

Stacey Nash
Kroger
Gallatin, Tennessee

Linda's Secret Chili

I have been making this chili for years and everyone always wonders what gives this chili a different flavor. It's baking cocoa, which mellows out the heat and makes for a wonderful flavor.

Diana Van
Clackamas Bakery
Clackamas, Oregon

2 large onions, chopped
1 green bell pepper, chopped
1 red bell pepper, chopped
1 yellow bell pepper, chopped
5 garlic cloves, chopped
Vegetable oil for browning
1 pound beef steak tips, chopped
2 pounds bulk pork sausage
1 (21-ounce) can diced tomatoes
2 (10-ounce) cans tomatoes with
 green chiles
1 (15-ounce) can kidney beans

1 (15-ounce) can black beans
2 (4-ounce) cans diced green chiles
1 (6-ounce) can tomato paste
5 tablespoons chile powder
1/4 cup baking cocoa
1 to 2 teaspoons thyme
1 to 2 teaspoons oregano
1 to 2 teaspoons rosemary
1 to 2 teaspoons marjoram
1 teaspoon cayenne pepper
Salt and black pepper to taste
1 (15-ounce) can baked beans

Sauté the onions, bell peppers and garlic in the oil in a large stockpot until the onions are tender. Remove to a bowl using a slotted spoon, reserving the pan drippings. Brown the steak and sausage in the reserved pan drippings, stirring frequently; drain. Return the sautéed vegetables to the stockpot. Stir in the tomatoes, kidney beans, black beans, green chiles, tomato paste, chili powder, baking cocoa, thyme, oregano, rosemary, marjoram, cayenne pepper, salt and black pepper and mix well.

Simmer for 1 hour, stirring occasionally. Add the baked beans and simmer over very low heat for 3 hours or longer or until of the desired consistency and flavor. The longer the chili simmers, the better the flavor will be. Ladle into chili bowls and serve with shredded Cheddar cheese, chopped onions, sour cream or any of your favorite toppings. This chili is extremely spicy.

Serves 16

Lillie's Triple-Threat Tailgate Chili

1 pound ground turkey

1 onion, chopped

4 garlic cloves, chopped, or equivalent
   amount of garlic paste

6 bratwurst, sliced

5 (15-ounce) cans assorted beans, such as
   red kidney, black, garbanzo, chili beans
   in red sauce and white kidney beans

2 (15-ounce) cans chicken broth

1 (15-ounce) can corn

1 (15-ounce) can diced tomatoes

1 (15-ounce) can Italian-style tomato sauce

1 (6-ounce) can tomato paste

3 tablespoons chili powder, or to taste

3 tablespoons Cajun seasoning

1 tablespoon sugar

3 dashes of hot red pepper sauce

3 dashes of red pepper flakes

2 dashes of Penzey Spices Seasoned Pepper

1/2 teaspoon cumin

1/2 teaspoon curry powder

Dash of cinnamon

Brown the ground turkey in a nonstick skillet, stirring until crumbly. Remove the turkey to a large stockpot using a slotted spoon, reserving the pan drippings. Sauté the onion and garlic in the reserved drippings until the onion is tender. Add to the turkey. Stir in the bratwurst, beans, broth, corn, tomatoes, tomato sauce, tomato paste, chili powder, Cajun seasoning, sugar, hot sauce, red pepper flakes, seasoned pepper, cumin, curry powder and cinnamon and mix well.

Bring to a boil and then reduce the heat. Simmer, covered, for 1 to 2 hours or until of the desired consistency, stirring occasionally. Ladle into chili bowls. You can combine all the ingredients in a slow cooker and cook on Low for 8 to 10 hours. This chili is very spicy.

Serves 15

I created this chili for the 2007 United Way Kroger Great Lakes Chili Cook-Off. I won first place in two categories: Most Bizarre Chili and Best Overall Chili.

Lillie Teeters
Kroger
Westerville, Ohio

Debbie Goulding
Kroger
Cincinnati, Ohio

Chicken Cashew Chili

4 pounds chicken breasts and thighs, roasted
2 chipotle chiles in adobo sauce
2 cups chicken stock
1 cup raw or roasted cashews
3 tablespoons olive oil
3 white onions, coarsely chopped
7 garlic cloves, finely chopped
2 tablespoons cumin
1 tablespoon chili powder
2 teaspoons kosher salt
3 tablespoons cilantro, chopped
2 cups chopped tomatoes with juice
4 cups cannellini beans, soaked and drained
2 cups chicken stock
2 cups white wine
1 cup cashews, roasted
3 tablespoons cilantro, chopped
1/2 to 1 ounce semisweet chocolate

Shred the chicken, discarding the skin and bones. Process the chipotle chiles, 2 cups stock and 1 cup cashews in a blender until puréed. Heat the olive oil in a heavy stockpot over medium heat until hot. Add the onions and garlic and cook until the onions are tender. Stir in the cumin, chili powder and salt. Add the chipotle chile purée, 3 tablespoons cilantro and the tomatoes and mix well.

Simmer, covered, for 25 minutes, stirring occasionally. Stir in the chicken, beans, 2 cups stock and the wine. Simmer for 1 hour, stirring occasionally. Stir in 1 cup roasted cashews, 3 tablespoons cilantro and the chocolate. Cook over medium heat for 45 to 60 minutes or until of the desired consistency. Ladle into chili bowls. The chili may be prepared up to 2 days in advance and stored, covered, in the refrigerator. Reheat before serving.

Serves 14 to 16

White Chicken Chili

2 onions, chopped
1 tablespoon olive oil
2 (4-ounce) cans chopped green chiles
2 tablespoons chopped garlic
2 tablespoons cumin
1 1/2 teaspoons oregano

1/4 teaspoon red pepper
3 (16-ounce) cans Great Northern beans
6 cups chicken broth
4 cups chopped cooked chicken
3 cups (12 ounces) shredded
   Cheddar cheese

Sauté the onions in the olive oil in a stockpot until tender. Stir in the green chiles, garlic, cumin, oregano and red pepper. Sauté for 2 minutes. Add the beans and broth and bring to a boil. Reduce the heat. Stir in the chicken and cheese and cook until the cheese melts, stirring occasionally. Ladle into chili bowls. Serve with sour cream.

Serves 16 to 20

A welcome and healthy change from the typical chili. Great for football Sundays.

Dawn Olson
Kroger
Nokomis, Illinois

Black Bean Chili

4 cups chopped onions
4 garlic cloves, minced
1 cup water
2 tablespoons cumin
2 tablespoons coriander
2 cups salsa
2 red bell peppers, chopped
2 green bell peppers, chopped

4 (15-ounce) cans black beans, drained
   and rinsed
2 (28-ounce) cans diced tomatoes
3 cups frozen or canned corn
1/2 cup chopped cilantro
2 tablespoons brown sugar
Salt and pepper to taste
Tabasco sauce to taste

Combine the onions, garlic and water in a stockpot and cook for 10 minutes. Stir in the cumin and coriander. Add the salsa and bell peppers and cook over medium heat for 10 minutes. Stir in the beans and tomatoes. Cook over medium to low heat for 10 minutes, stirring occasionally. Add the corn, cilantro, brown sugar, salt, pepper and Tabasco sauce and simmer for 10 to 15 minutes or until heated through. Ladle into chili bowls and serve with cornbread and fat-free sour cream.

Serves 12

Easy to prepare in one pot, this is my favorite dish for a quick meal during the week.
It's low fat and tasty.
Serve "Cincinnati-style" over cooked spaghetti with shredded Cheddar cheese.

Lynn Marmer
Kroger
Cincinnati, Ohio

Steve Henn
Kroger
Franklin, Indiana

Carrot and Ginger Soup

1/2 cup (1 stick) unsalted butter
1 cup chopped sweet onion
1/2 cup grated fresh ginger
4 garlic cloves, minced
2 pounds baby carrots
7 cups chicken broth

1 cup Private Selection white
   cooking wine
Juice of 1 lemon
Pinch of cayenne pepper
1/4 teaspoon curry powder
1/4 teaspoon nutmeg

Melt the butter in a large stockpot and add the onion, ginger and garlic. Sauté for 20 minutes. Stir in the carrots, broth and wine and bring to a boil. Reduce the heat to medium. Simmer for 45 minutes, stirring occasionally. Process with an immersion blender or in several batches in a blender until puréed. Stir in the lemon juice, cayenne pepper, curry powder and nutmeg. Ladle into soup bowls. Serve hot or chilled garnished with chopped fresh parsley or chives and a dollop of sour cream..

Serves 6

Suzie Haberman
Ralphs
Compton, California

Creamy Cilantro Soup

1 bunch cilantro
1 cup chicken broth
2 tablespoons butter
3 to 4 tablespoons all-purpose flour
3 cups chicken broth

8 ounces cream cheese, cut into cubes
1 cup sour cream
1 garlic clove, minced
1/2 teaspoon ground red pepper
1/4 teaspoon cumin

Remove the cilantro leaves from the stems and coarsely chop the leaves, discarding the stems. Process the cilantro and 1 cup broth in a food processor until blended.

Melt the butter in a Dutch oven over medium heat. Whisk in the flour until smooth. Cook until bubbly, stirring constantly. Gradually add 3 cups broth, whisking constantly until blended. Bring to a boil and boil for 1 minute, whisking frequently. Add the cilantro mixture, cream cheese, sour cream, garlic, red pepper and cumin and mix well. Simmer for 15 minutes. Ladle into soup bowls. You may purée the soup in a food processor for a creamier consistency.

Serves 4

Pozole Blanco (Golden Hominy Soup)

1 pound boneless lean pork, cut into 1-inch pieces

6 chicken thighs

1/2 onion, cut into 2 portions

2 garlic cloves

2 teaspoons salt

12 peppercorns

6 cups water

1 (29-ounce) can golden hominy, drained and rinsed

Salt to taste

Salsa

1/2 onion, chopped

6 to 8 radishes, sliced

1/2 head lettuce, shredded

1 avocado, sliced

2 tablespoons dried oregano leaves

6 small limes, cut into halves

Leonor Lopez
Kroger
Houston, Texas

Place the pork and chicken in separate saucepans. Add 1 onion portion, 1 garlic clove, 1 teaspoon salt, 6 peppercorns and 3 cups water to each saucepan. Bring to a boil and then reduce the heat. Skim any foam from the surface. Simmer the pork, covered, for 1 hour. Simmer the chicken, covered, for 45 minutes.

Remove the pork and chicken to a large saucepan using a slotted spoon, reserving the broth. Cut the chicken from the bones, discarding the bones. Return the chicken and pork to the saucepan. Strain the broth and add to the pork mixture. Stir in the hominy and bring to a boil. Reduce the heat and simmer, covered, for 30 minutes. Season with salt to taste. Ladle into soup bowls and top with salsa, chopped onion, radishes, lettuce, avocado, oregano and/or limes.

Serves 6

Garden Vegetable Beef Soup

This recipe makes a large amount of soup. It freezes or cans well for future. I eat this all winter, and I always have a list of friends who want a bowl or quart for later.

Carol Ross

Kroger

Galveston, Indiana

2 pounds beef short ribs
12 ounces rib-eye steak
1 1/2 pounds potatoes, cut into
    bite-size pieces
6 ounces baby carrots, cut into
    bite-size pieces
1 large onion, cut into bite-size slivers
1 small head cabbage, cut into
    bite-size pieces
1 bundle fresh asparagus, trimmed and
    cut into bite-size pieces
1 cup frozen cut okra
1 cup frozen baby lima beans
1/2 cup barley
2 or 3 (15-ounce) cans French-style
    green beans
1 (6-ounce) can sliced water chestnuts
1 (8-ounce) can mushroom pieces
    and stems

1 (6-ounce) can sliced bamboo shoots
1 (15-ounce) can corn
1 (15-ounce) can garbanzo beans
1 (15-ounce) can dark red kidney beans
1 (15-ounce) can black beans
1 (15-ounce) can small red beans
1 (15-ounce) can black-eyed peas
1 (15-ounce) can spinach
3 (28-ounce) cans diced tomatoes
2 (46-ounce) cans tomato juice
1 or 2 (15-ounce) cans beef broth
1 (5-inch) zucchini, sliced
1 (5-inch) yellow squash, sliced
1 cup small cauliflower florets
1/2 cup small broccoli florets
1/2 cup frozen peas
2 tablespoons dried Italian seasoning
1 1/2 tablespoons dried oregano
2 to 3 tablespoons garlic salt

Cook the short ribs and steak in a slow cooker until tender. Store the beef and pan juices in the refrigerator for 48 before making the soup. Discard the fat and bones from the ribs and place the rib meat in a 20-quart stockpot. Cut the steak into dime-size pieces and place in the stockpot. Add the reserved pan juices, potatoes, carrots, onion, cabbage, asparagus, okra, lima beans and barley and mix well.

Cook for 10 to 15 minutes. Stir in the green beans, water chestnuts, mushrooms, bamboo shoots, corn, garbanzo beans, kidney beans, black beans, red beans, peas, spinach and tomatoes; do not drain the canned vegetables. Add the tomato juice and broth and mix well. Stir in the zucchini, yellow squash, cauliflower, broccoli and peas. Cook until heated through, stirring frequently. Mix in the Italian seasoning, oregano and garlic salt. Bring to a boil and then reduce the heat. Cook for 2 hours, stirring occasionally. Turn off the heat and allow the soup to finish cooking. Ladle into soup bowls.

Makes 18 quarts

Spicy Potato Soup

1 pound Italian sausage, casings removed
1/3 cup bread crumbs
1 egg, lightly beaten
2 cups water
3 cubes beef bouillon
6 cups water
1 (15-ounce) can diced tomatoes, drained
2 cups chopped celery

1 cup chopped carrots
1 white onion, chopped
2/3 cup chopped green bell pepper
1 bay leaf
1 garlic clove, crushed
3 cups chopped potatoes
1/2 head cabbage, shredded
Salt and pepper to taste

Tom Mueller
King Soopers
Firestone, Colorado

Combine the sausage, bread crumbs and egg in a bowl and mix well. Shape into 3/4-inch balls and arrange in a single layer on a baking sheet. Bake at 350 degrees for 20 minutes or until cooked through; drain. Bring 2 cups water to a boil in a stockpot and add the bouillon cubes. Stir until dissolved. Add the meatballs, 6 cups water, the tomatoes, celery, carrots, onion, bell pepper, bay leaf and garlic. Simmer for 2 hours. Stir in the potatoes and cabbage. Cook, covered, until the potatoes are tender. Discard the bay leaf and season the soup with salt and pepper. Ladle into soup bowls and serve with saltine crackers or warm bread.

Serves 6

Grilled Steak Salad

1 (8- to 10-ounce) steak
2 cups spring salad mix
1/2 Bartlett pear, sliced
1/3 red onion, thinly sliced
3 tablespoons pine nuts, toasted

1/4 cup Italian salad dressing or dressing
   of choice
2 ounces Gorgonzola cheese or blue
   cheese, crumbled

Timothy Kennedy
Kroger
Cincinnati, Ohio

Grill the steak over hot coals to the desired degree of doneness. Toss the salad greens, pear, onion and pine nuts in a bowl. Add the salad dressing and mix to coat. Divide the salad mixture equally between two serving plates. Cut the steak into 1/2-inch strips and arrange over the salad greens. Sprinkle with the cheese. Serve immediately.

Serves 2

Brian King
Kroger
Knoxville, Tennessee

Chicken Salad

3 large chicken breasts, cooked and
   chopped
1/4 cup chopped onion
1/4 cup chopped green bell pepper
1/4 cup sliced or slivered almonds

1/4 cup drained crushed pineapple
1/4 cup sweet pickle salad cubes
1/4 cup chopped celery
1 cup (about) mayonnaise
Salt and pepper to taste

Combine the chicken, onion, bell pepper, almonds, pineapple, pickle salad cubes and celery in a bowl and mix well. Add the mayonnaise and mix to coat. Chill, covered, until serving time.

Serves 6

A friend brought this chicken salad to me after the birth of my first child. This is healthy, refreshing, and easy to prepare.

Janel Brandstoettner
Dillons
Topeka, Kansas

Gourmet Chicken Salad

3 cups chopped cooked chicken
1 (5-ounce) can water chestnuts, sliced
3/4 cup sliced celery
3/4 cup chopped macadamia nuts or toasted
   slivered almonds
1 (8-ounce) can pineapple chunks, drained
1 (8-ounce) can mandarin
   oranges, drained

8 ounces seedless red or green grapes
   (about 1 1/2 cups)
1 cup mayonnaise
1 1/2 teaspoons soy sauce
1/4 teaspoon curry powder
Lettuce leaves
1/4 cup chopped macadamia nuts or toasted
   slivered almonds.

Combine the chicken, water chestnuts, celery and 3/4 cup macadamia nuts in a bowl and mix well. Stir in the pineapple, mandarin oranges and grapes. Mix the mayonnaise, soy sauce and curry powder in a bowl. Add to the chicken mixture and mix to coat. Chill, covered, in the refrigerator.

Mound the chicken salad on a lettuce-lined serving platter and sprinkle with 1/4 cup macadamia nuts. Garnish with additional pineapple chunks, mandarin oranges and grape clusters. Serve with croissants.

Serves 6

Black-Eyed Steak Salad

Lime Chili Vinaigrette

1/2 cup fresh lime juice
1/2 cup olive oil
1 teaspoon ground cumin
1 teaspoon chili powder
1 teaspoon salt
1 teaspoon sugar
1/2 teaspoon minced garlic

Salad

1 pound dried black-eyed peas
1/4 cup red wine vinegar
1 1/2 pounds Private Selection top
    sirloin steak
1 cup chopped water chestnuts
1 red or green bell pepper, julienned
1 (4-ounce) can diced green chiles, drained
1/2 cup sliced green onions
1/2 cup black olives
1/4 cup chopped fresh cilantro
Romaine leaves

Vickie Konecny
Kroger
Fremont, Ohio

To prepare the vinaigrette, combine the lime juice, olive oil, cumin, chili powder, salt, sugar and garlic in a jar with a tight-fitting lid and seal tightly. Shake to combine.

To prepare the salad, sort and rinse the peas. Cook using the package directions; drain. Whisk 1/4 cup of the vinaigrette with the vinegar in a bowl. Pour over the steak in a large sealable plastic bag and seal tightly; turn to coat. Marinate in the refrigerator for 1 hour, turning twice. Drain, discarding the marinade. Arrange the steak on a broiler pan 3 inches from the heat source. Broil for 12 to 15 minutes or to the desired degree of doneness, turning once.

Combine the remaining vinaigrette, the black-eyed peas, water chestnuts, bell pepper, green chiles, green onions and olives in a large skillet. Simmer, covered, over medium-low heat for 5 minutes or until heated through. Stir in the cilantro.

Line a serving platter with romaine. Spoon the black-eyed pea mixture over the romaine. Cut the steak diagonally across the grain into thick slices. Arrange the slices over the black-eyed pea mixture. Garnish with cherry tomatoes and additional cilantro.

Serves 4 to 6

Heidi's Shredded Pork Salad and Dressing

Colleen Wolters
Smith's
Salt Lake City, Utah

Pork

1 (6-pound) pork roast
1 (16-ounce) jar salsa
1 (12-ounce) can soda
2 cups packed brown sugar

Lime Cilantro Rice

2 tablespoons vegetable oil
1 pound long grain rice
1 bunch cilantro, trimmed and chopped
4 garlic cloves, minced
4 cups water
Juice of 2 limes

Black Beans

2 garlic cloves, minced
1 teaspoon ground cumin
1 1/2 tablespoons olive oil
1 (15-ounce) can black beans,
    drained and rinsed
1 1/3 cups tomato juice
1 1/2 teaspoons salt
2 tablespoons chopped fresh cilantro

To prepare the pork, place the pork in a slow cooker and cover with water. Cook on High for 6 hours; drain. Remove the bone and fat from the pork and return the meat to the slow cooker. Mix the salsa, soda and brown sugar in a bowl and spoon over the top of the pork. Cook on High for 3 hours. Drain, reserving the sauce. Shred the pork using two forks. Return the shredded pork to the slow cooker and mix with enough of the reserved sauce to moisten. Keep warm on Low.

To prepare the rice, heat the oil in a skillet and add the rice, cilantro and garlic. Sauté for 3 to 5 minutes. Combine the water and lime juice in a rice cooker. Add the rice mixture and cook using the manufacturer's directions. If a rice cooker is not available, combine the rice mixture, water and lime juice in a 3-quart saucepan and bring to a boil. Reduce the heat and simmer until all the liquid is absorbed.

To prepare the beans, cook the garlic and cumin in the olive oil in a skillet over medium heat until fragrant. Stir in the beans, tomato juice and salt. Cook until heated through, stirring frequently. Stir in the cilantro just before serving.

Creamy Tomatillo Salad Dressing

1 cup buttermilk

1 cup mayonnaise

3/4 cup cilantro

3 tomatillos, peeled and chopped

1 envelope ranch salad dressing mix

2 garlic cloves

1 teaspoon cayenne pepper

Crispy Corn Strips and Assembly

10 soft corn tortillas, cut into thin strips

Salt to taste

14 soft corn tortillas, heated

Shredded lettuce

To prepare the dressing, process the buttermilk, mayonnaise, cilantro, tomatillos, salad dressing mix, garlic and cayenne pepper in a blender until combined. Chill for 1 hour or longer before serving.

To prepare the corn strips, arrange the tortilla strips in a single layer on a baking sheet. Sprinkle with water or spray with nonstick cooking spray and sprinkle lightly with salt. Bake at 400 degrees for 10 minutes or until crisp.

To serve, top each warm tortilla with equal portions of the rice, beans, lettuce and pork. Top with corn strips. Drizzle each with some of the salad dressing or serve on the side.

Serves 14

Pasta Salad with Ginger Peanut Butter Dressing

Any combination of vegetables may be used for the salad. Tomatoes are not recommended because the acid will affect the peanut butter.

Michelle Vandeput
Kroger
Cincinnati, Ohio

Salad
16 ounces pasta
2 spring onions, sliced
1 large red bell pepper, julienned
2 carrots, julienned
1 (10-ounce) package frozen green peas or snow peas, thawed

Ginger Peanut Butter Dressing and Assembly
1 bottle ginger salad dressing
1/4 to 1/2 cup peanut butter
Grated fresh ginger (optional)
Cayenne pepper (optional)
2 tablespoons rice wine vinegar or white vinegar (optional)
2 tablespoons canola oil (optional)
Salt to taste
Crushed peanuts

To prepare the salad, cook the pasta using the package directions; drain. Let stand until cool. Reserve some of the spring onions for garnish. Toss the remaining spring onions, the bell pepper, carrots and peas with the pasta in a bowl until combined.

To prepare the dressing, mix the salad dressing and 1/4 cup of the peanut butter in a bowl. Taste and add additional peanut butter if desired for a stronger peanut flavor. Season with ginger and cayenne pepper. For a thinner consistency, add the vinegar and canola oil.

Add the dressing to the pasta mixture and toss to coat Season with salt. Chill, covered, in the refrigerator. Sprinkle with the reserved spring onions and peanuts just before serving.

Serves 20

Ambria's Pasta Salad

16 ounces rotini
1 orange bell pepper, chopped
1 pound cherry tomatoes, chopped
2 small zucchini, chopped
8 radishes, chopped
8 baby carrots, chopped
1/2 cup chopped celery
1 (2-ounce) can sliced black olives, drained and chopped
1/4 cup sliced green olives, chopped
10 ounces hard salami, julienned
1/2 (16-ounce) bottle creamy Caesar salad dressing
1/2 (16-ounce) bottle zesty Italian salad dressing
4 ounces feta cheese, crumbled

Cook the pasta using the package directions; drain. Let stand until cool. Combine the bell pepper, tomatoes, zucchini, radishes, carrots, celery and olives in a bowl and mix well. Stir in the salami. Add the salad dressings and pasta and toss to coat Sprinkle with the cheese. Chill, covered, in the refrigerator. Stir before serving.

Serves 8

Whenever we have a family get-together, I always have to bring my pasta salad. Add more or less of the salad dressings depending on how you like it. You can make it lower in calories by using fat-free salad dressings and low-fat salami. For variety add artichoke hearts, green bell pepper, or any crisp vegetable.

Ambria Day
Fred Meyer
Sandy, Oregon

Garden Bow Tie Pasta Salad

Patty Freeman
Peyton
Portland, Tennessee

16 ounces bow tie pasta
2 cups broccoli florets
1 large red onion, chopped
1 large red bell pepper, chopped
1 large yellow bell pepper, chopped
8 ounces grape tomatoes, cut into halves
1 (16-ounce) bottle sun-dried tomato vinaigrette
1 (3-ounce) package real bacon bits
Grated Parmesan cheese to taste

Cook the pasta using the package directions, adding the broccoli 3 minutes before the end of the cooking process. Drain and rinse with cold water; drain again. Combine the pasta mixture, onion, bell peppers and tomatoes in a bowl and mix gently. Add the vinaigrette and toss to coat. Chill, covered, for 8 hours or longer. Stir before serving and sprinkle with the bacon bits and cheese.

Serves 10

Corn Bread Salad

Cindy Andrews
Kroger RASC
Nashville, Tennessee

1 (6-ounce) package Mexican corn bread mix
1 envelope ranch salad dressing mix
1 small head romaine, shredded
2 large tomatoes, chopped
1 (15-ounce) can black beans, drained and rinsed
1 (15-ounce) can Mexican corn, drained
2 cups (8 ounces) shredded Mexican four-cheese blend
6 slices bacon, crisp-cooked and crumbled
5 green onions, chopped

Prepare the corn bread using the package directions. Let stand until cool and then crumble. Prepare the dressing mix using the package directions.

Layer the corn bread, romaine, tomatoes, beans, corn, cheese, bacon, green onions and salad dressing one-half at a time in a large bowl. Chill, covered, for 2 hours or longer before serving.

Serves 15

Mediterranean White Bean Salad

2 (15-ounce) cans Great Northern beans,
   drained and rinsed
2 (6-ounce) jars Private Selection marinated
   artichoke quarters, drained and chopped
1 cup chopped tomatoes
1 cup chopped seeded peeled cucumber
1/2 cup sliced celery
1/4 cup finely chopped roasted red pepper
1/2 cup kalamata olives, coarsely chopped
1 (16-ounce) bottle olive oil and vinegar salad dressing
2 tablespoons sugar
3/4 ounce fresh basil leaves
6 to 8 cups mixed salad greens
1 cup coarsely crumbled feta cheese

Teresa Saxon
Kroger
Suwanee, Georgia

Combine the beans, artichokes, tomatoes, cucumber, celery, red pepper and olives in a bowl and mix gently. Process the dressing, sugar and basil in a blender just until the basil is chopped.

Arrange the salad greens on a serving platter or on individual salad plates. Mound the bean mixture over the salad greens and sprinkle with the cheese. Drizzle with the dressing or serve on the side.

Serves 8

Cauliflower Salad

1 head cauliflower, trimmed and chopped
9 slices bacon, crisp-cooked and crumbled
1 large sweet onion, chopped (optional)
1 (2-ounce) can sliced black olives, drained
1 (10-ounce) package frozen green peas
2 cups dry-roasted peanuts

1 1/2 cups (6 ounces) shredded mild
   Colby cheese
3/4 cup (3 ounces) grated Parmesan cheese
2/3 cup sugar
1 large head iceberg lettuce, torn
1 3/4 cups mayonnaise-type salad dressing

Layer the cauliflower, bacon, onion, olives, peas, peanuts, Colby cheese, Parmesan cheese, sugar, lettuce and salad dressing in the order listed in a large bowl. Chill, tightly covered, for 8 to 10 hours. Toss to coat just before serving. Store any leftovers in the refrigerator.

Serves 8

This is always a big hit at picnics, potlucks, and holiday dinners.

Linda Hess
Kroger
Addison, Michigan

Blue Cheese and Bacon Coleslaw

1 head green cabbage, chopped
4 green onions, chopped
1 red bell pepper, julienned
1 green bell pepper, julienned
1 cup mayonnaise

4 ounces blue cheese, crumbled
2 tablespoons horseradish, or to taste
2 tablespoons lemon juice
Salt and pepper to taste
4 slices bacon, crisp-cooked and crumbled

Toss the cabbage, green onions and bell peppers in a bowl. Mix the mayonnaise, cheese, horseradish and lemon juice in a bowl until combined. Add to the cabbage mixture and mix to coat. Season with salt and pepper. Chill, covered, for 2 hours to 10 hours. Sprinkle with the bacon just before serving.

Serves 10

Stephanie Smithmyer
Kroger
Alpharetta, Georgia

Pea Salad

1 (14-ounce) can garbanzo beans, drained
1 (14-ounce) can white Shoe Peg corn, drained
1 (14-ounce) can French-style green beans, drained
1 (15-ounce) can green peas, drained
1 (14-ounce) can baby lima beans, drained
4 or 5 ribs celery, chopped
1 green bell pepper, chopped
1 (2-ounce) jar pimento, drained and chopped
1 cup sugar
1 cup white vinegar
1/4 cup canola oil or vegetable oil

Combine the garbanzo beans, corn, green beans, peas and lima beans in a bowl and mix well. Stir in the celery, bell pepper and pimento. Whisk the sugar, vinegar and canola oil in a bowl until blended. Add to the bean mixture and mix to coat. Chill, covered, until serving time. Store for 2 weeks or longer in the refrigerator.

Serves 20

A customer shared this recipe with me about five years ago. It's fast and tasty and is especially good for family gatherings, potluck dinners, and holidays.

Linda Lemon
Kroger
Roanoke, Virginia

Kathy Bartz
King Soopers
Firestone, Colorado

Shoe Peg Relish Salad

2 (17-ounce) cans Shoe Peg corn, drained
1 (17-ounce) can small peas, drained
1 (16-ounce) can French-style green beans, drained
1 (8-ounce) can water chestnuts, drained and chopped
3 green onions, chopped
1 green bell pepper, chopped
1/2 cup chopped celery
1 (2-ounce) jar pimento, drained and chopped
1 cup sugar
3/4 cup vinegar
1/2 cup vegetable oil
1 teaspoon salt
1/4 teaspoon pepper

Combine the corn, peas, beans, water chestnuts, green onions, bell pepper, celery and pimento in a bowl and mix well. Bring the sugar, vinegar, oil, salt and pepper to a boil in a saucepan. Pour over the corn mixture and stir to coat.

Serves 10

Roasted Sweet Potato Salad

2 tablespoons olive oil
1 teaspoon fresh thyme leaves
1 teaspoon finely chopped fresh basil
1 teaspoon salt
1 teaspoon pepper
2 sweet potatoes, chopped
3/4 cup mayonnaise
1/4 cup honey
2 tablespoons brown mustard
1 teaspoon salt
1 teaspoon pepper

Basil is a delicate herb, so use a very sharp knife when chopping. A dull knife will bruise the leaves and cause them to blacken.

Howard Warren
Kroger
Atlanta, Georgia

Combine the olive oil, thyme, basil, 1 teaspoon salt and 1 teaspoon pepper in a bowl and mix well. Add the sweet potatoes and toss to coat. Arrange in a single layer on a baking sheet. Roast at 350 degrees for 20 to 30 minutes or until tender and light brown. Let stand until cool.

Whisk the mayonnaise, honey, mustard, 1 teaspoon salt and 1 teaspoon pepper in a bowl until blended. Add the sweet potatoes and toss to coat. Chill, covered, for 2 hours or longer before serving.

Serves 4

Avocado Cheese Slices

This recipe was handed down to me from my mother.

Debra Puckett
Kroger
Manvel, Texas

2 large avocados, peeled
1 cup cottage cheese
1/4 cup chopped green olives
1/4 cup chopped onion
1/4 cup chopped nuts (optional)
Salt and pepper to taste
1/2 cup lemon juice
4 lettuce leaves

Cut the avocados into halves and remove the pits. Scoop 1 tablespoon of pulp from the center of each avocado half. Combine the pulp, cottage cheese, olives, onion, nuts, salt and pepper in a bowl and mix well.

Mound equal portions of the cottage cheese mixture in the center of each avocado half. Press the halves together and coat the surface with the lemon juice. Wrap each stuffed avocado in plastic wrap and chill until serving time. To serve, arrange each half on a lettuce-lined salad plate.

Serves 4

Banana Salad

1 cup milk
3/4 cup sugar
1 tablespoon butter
1 egg, lightly beaten
3 to 4 tablespoons peanut butter
5 or 6 bananas

Combine the milk, sugar and butter in a heavy saucepan. Cook until the sugar dissolves and the butter melts, stirring frequently. Stir a small amount of the hot mixture into the egg; stir the egg into the hot mixture.

Cook until the sauce begins to steam, stirring constantly. Add the peanut butter and cook until thickened, stirring frequently. Let stand until cool.

Slice the bananas lengthwise and arrange evenly on each of five or six salad plates. Pour the cooled sauce over the bananas and serve immediately. Serve as a salad or dessert.

Serves 5 or 6

We found this recipe when going through my great grandmother's recipe file. The recipe was given to her by her grandmother McMullin, which would be my great-great-great grandmother.

Rebecca Lane
Scott's
Poneto, Indiana

Cranberry Salad

1 (16-ounce) can whole cranberry sauce
1 cup tropical fruit trail mix
   without bananas
1 (2-ounce) package pecan halves or
   walnuts, chopped
12 ounces frozen whipped topping, thawed

Stir the cranberry sauce in a bowl with a fork. Add the trail mix and pecans and mix well. Fold in the whipped topping until combined. Chill, covered, until serving time. The flavor is better when prepared and served the same day.

Serves 4 to 6

This is recipe is great for any holiday.

Glenda Roberts
Kroger
Brookhaven,
*   Mississippi*

Cranberry Gelatin

1 (6-ounce) package cranberry gelatin or
   raspberry gelatin
1 cup boiling water
1 (16-ounce) can jellied cranberry sauce
1 teaspoon cinnamon
1 (15-ounce) can mandarin oranges, drained
1 cup frozen strawberries, thawed
1 banana, cut into 1/4-inch slices

Dissolve the gelatin in the boiling water in a heatproof bowl. Add the cranberry sauce and whisk until dissolved. Stir in the cinnamon. Fold in the mandarin oranges, strawberries and banana.

Pour into a mold sprayed with nonstick cooking spray. Chill for 2 to 10 hours or until set. Serve with turkey, chicken or ham.

Serves 12

Pete, my brother-in-law, asks for this salad every holiday. The children even like it as dessert. The cinnamon is a wonderful touch.

Janet Bater
Kroger
Brighton, Michigan

Tropical Salad

1/2 cup strawberry yogurt
2 tablespoons olive oil
1 1/2 teaspoons white balsamic vinegar
5 cups spring salad mix

1/2 cup shredded coconut
1/2 cup strawberries, thinly sliced
1/2 cup mandarin oranges slices

Whisk the yogurt, olive oil and vinegar in a bowl until blended. Toss the salad greens, coconut, strawberries and mandarin oranges in a bowl. Add the yogurt dressing and mix to coat. Serve immediately.

Serves 4

John Szymanski
Kroger
Atlanta, Georgia

Watermelon Salad

1 (6-ounce) package strawberry gelatin
2 cups boiling water
3 cups chopped watermelon
1 (8-ounce) can crushed pineapple
1 cup pecans, chopped

8 ounces cream cheese, softened
1/4 cup milk
2 tablespoons sugar
4 ounces whipped topping
1/4 cup chopped pecans

Dissolve the gelatin in the boiling water in a heatproof bowl. Pour into a 9x13-inch dish and chill for 20 minutes. Mix the watermelon, undrained pineapple and 1 cup pecans in a bowl. Add to the gelatin and mix well. Chill until set.

Beat the cream cheese in a mixing bowl until light and fluffy. Add the milk and sugar and beat until smooth. Beat in the whipped topping. Spread over the top of the prepared layer and sprinkle with 1/4 cup pecans. Chill until serving time.

Serves 8

Dan Johnson
Kroger
Cincinnati, Ohio

Beef & Pork

Beef & Pork

Sweet-and-Sour Brisket

1 (3- to 4-pound) beef brisket
1 (16-ounce) can sauerkraut
1 (16-ounce) jar thick tomato sauce
1 cup packed brown sugar

Rinse the brisket and pat dry. Arrange fat side up in a roasting pan. Cover the roast with the undrained sauerkraut and top with the tomato sauce. Spread with the brown sugar. Chill, tightly covered with foil, for 8 to 10 hours.

Roast, covered, at 325 degrees for 3 to 3 1/2 hours or until tender. Slice the brisket against the grain and serve with the sauerkraut and pan juices. You may add 1 drained can of small whole white potatoes approximately 40 minutes before the end of the roasting process. Even sauerkraut haters love this recipe.

Serves 6 to 8

I was interviewed by our local newspaper, the *Atlanta Journal Constitution*, in October 2006. The interview appeared in the paper along with this recipe and my photograph with the brisket on October 25, 2006. The recipe was tested in the newspaper kitchen by the food editor.

Marci Abrams
Kroger
Roswell, Georgia

Beef and Noodle Bowl aka "Fake Chinese"

1 (2-pound) beef roast, cut into bite-size pieces
1 onion, chopped
8 ounces mushrooms, sliced
Crushed garlic to taste
Salt and pepper to taste
1 cup teriyaki sauce
1 cup zesty Italian salad dressing
1 teaspoon ground ginger
16 ounces noodles

Cook the beef, onion, mushrooms, garlic, salt and pepper in a 5-quart stockpot or Dutch oven over medium heat for 20 minutes or until brown. Stir in the teriyaki sauce, salad dressing and ginger. Simmer for 20 to 30 minutes or until of the desired consistency. Cook the pasta using the package directions; drain. Add the hot pasta to the beef mixture and mix well.

You may substitute two (5-ounce) cans sliced mushrooms for the fresh mushrooms. Add the canned mushrooms when adding the teriyaki sauce, salad dressing and ginger.

Serves 6

You may add different vegetables as desired. Broccoli and carrots may be cooked with the pasta and then added to the beef mixture. Add snow peas to the boiling pasta just a few minutes before the pasta is tender, and then add to the beef mixture. Or, just add cans of Chinese vegetables such as bean sprouts, bamboo shoots, or water chestnuts with the cooked pasta. Also good served over chow mein noodles. This dish is quick, easy, and never lasts long at my house.

Patricia Wolff-Keaton
Kroger
Hilliard, Ohio

Rustic Sicilian Beef Ragù

If you skip the browning step, skip the recipe. If you won't drink the wine you've chosen from a glass, then do not cook with it.

Michael Crow
Kroger
Spring, Texas

1 (1 1/2- to 2-pound) Private Selection Angus
   chuck roast
Salt and freshly cracked black pepper
   to taste
3 to 4 tablespoons extra-virgin olive oil
1 onion, cut into halves and sliced
2 garlic cloves, chopped
1 (750-milliliter) bottle (about) dry
   red wine
1 (14-ounce) can crushed tomatoes
1 (14-ounce) can diced tomatoes

8 ounces button mushrooms, thickly sliced
2 to 3 tablespoons chopped fresh
   flat-leaf parsley
1 tablespoon dried oregano
1 teaspoon dried basil
1/2 teaspoon crushed red pepper flakes
Private Selection linguini, cooked
   and drained
Freshly grated Parmigiano-Reggiano cheese
Extra-virgin olive oil for drizzling

Cut the beef into 1 1/2-inch pieces and sprinkle with salt and black pepper. Heat 2 tablespoons of the olive oil in a deep stockpot just until the oil begins to smoke and then add the beef in batches; do not crowd. Cook until brown on all sides, adding olive oil as needed. Remove the beef to a bowl using a slotted spoon, reserving the pan drippings.

Add the onion to the reserved pan drippings and season with salt. Cook until tender and then stir in the garlic. Deglaze the stockpot with a small amount of the wine and then add the beef. Add enough of the remaining wine to barely cover the beef.

Simmer until the liquid is reduced by one-fourth. Add the tomatoes, mushrooms, parsley, oregano, basil and red pepper and mix well. Simmer, covered, until the beef is tender. Spoon over hot cooked linguini on a serving platter. Top with cheese and a drizzle of olive oil.

Serves 4

Slow-Cooker New England Pot Roast

1 (3-pound) chuck roast
1 teaspoon salt
1/4 teaspoon pepper
2 onions, cut into quarters
4 carrots, cut into quarters
3 ribs celery, cut into chunks
5 cups water
1 bay leaf

1 teaspoon vinegar
1 wedge cabbage
3 tablespoons butter
1 tablespoon freeze-dried minced onion
2 tablespoons all-purpose flour
1 tablespoon horseradish
1/2 teaspoon salt

Charisse Thill
Kroger
Westfield, Indiana

Sprinkle the roast with 1 teaspoon salt and the pepper. Place the onions, carrots and celery in a slow cooker and top with the roast. Add the water, bay leaf and vinegar. Cook, covered, on Low for 5 to 9 hours or until the roast is tender. Remove the roast to a platter and cover to keep warm, reserving the broth and vegetables in the slow cooker. Increase the heat to High. Add the cabbage to the slow cooker and cook, covered, for 20 minutes or until the cabbage is tender. Discard the bay leaf. Strain 1 1/2 cups of the broth into a heatproof measuring cup.

Melt the butter in a saucepan and stir in the onion and flour. Cook until bubbly and then stir in 1 1/2 cups strained broth, the horseradish and 1/2 teaspoon salt. Cook over low heat until thickened and of a sauce consistency, stirring constantly. Arrange the vegetables around the roast on a serving platter and spoon the sauce over the roast.

Serves 6

A very simple dish to prepare that is frequently requested by friends and family. The odds of leftovers are small.

Chris Hjelm
Kroger
Cincinnati, Ohio

Grilled Beef Tenderloin

1/2 cup sea salt or kosher salt
2 garlic cloves, minced
1 tablespoon sugar
1 teaspoon coarsely ground black pepper
1/2 teaspoon crushed red pepper flakes, or
   1/4 teaspoon cayenne pepper
1 (4- to 5-pound) beef tenderloin

Combine the salt, garlic, sugar, black pepper and red pepper in a bowl and mix well. Rub half the salt mixture on one side of the tenderloin. Let stand at room temperature for 30 minutes. Turn and rub the remaining surface of the tenderloin with the remaining salt mixture.

Grill the tenderloin over hot coals until a meat thermometer registers 145 degrees for medium-rare or to the desired degree of doneness, turning every 4 minutes to prevent overbrowning. At medium-rare the ends will be a higher internal temperature and thus satisfy those guests who prefer more well-done beef. You may substitute a tri-tip beef roast for the tenderloin. Adjust the amount of rub according to the size of the roast.

Serves 8

Marinated Flank Steak

1/2 cup vegetable oil
1/4 cup soy sauce
3 tablespoons honey
2 tablespoons vinegar
1 teaspoon garlic powder
1 teaspoon grated fresh ginger
1 cup chopped green onions
1 (2- to 2 1/2-pound) flank steak

Whisk the oil, soy sauce, honey, vinegar, garlic powder and ginger in a bowl. Stir in the green onions. Pour over the steak in a shallow dish, turning to coat. Marinate, covered, in the refrigerator for 12 hours, turning occasionally; drain, discarding the marinade.

Sear both sides of the steak in a skillet over medium heat for about 5 minutes, turning once. Grill indirectly over medium heat until a meat thermometer registers 145 degrees for medium-rare, turning once. Let stand for 5 minutes. Slice diagonally against the grain into thin strips. You may substitute a 1 1/2-inch-thick tri-tip beef roast for the flank steak.

Serves 6

Best steak marinade around.

Laurie Bahe
Smith's
Salt Lake City, Utah

Steaks with Sautéed Scallops and Shrimp

2 to 4 beef fillet steaks or strip steaks
1/4 cup (1/2 stick) butter
8 ounces fresh mushrooms, sliced
4 scallions, chopped
1/2 teaspoon celery salt
1/4 teaspoon salt
1/4 teaspoon pepper
Dash of garlic salt
8 ounces medium shrimp, peeled and deveined
8 ounces bay scallops

Grill the steaks to the desired degree of doneness. Remove to a platter and cover to keep warm. Melt the butter in a skillet and stir in the mushrooms, scallions, celery salt, salt, pepper and garlic salt.

Sauté over medium-high heat for about 5 minutes or until the mushrooms are tender. Add the shrimp and scallops. Cook for 3 to 4 minutes or until the shrimp turn pink and the scallops are opaque, stirring frequently. Spoon equal portions over the steaks. Serve immediately.

Serves 2 to 4

In 1986, working as a seafood clerk, I prepared this recipe for our customers to sample. As a result of receiving such good feedback, we passed this recipe on to our customers every time shrimp went on sale.

Rebecca Griffin
Kroger
Atlanta, Georgia

Southern T-Sauce Steaks

1/2 cup lemon juice

1/2 cup pineapple juice

1/2 cup barbecue sauce

1/2 cup soy sauce

1/2 cup packed brown sugar

1/4 cup Southern Comfort (optional)

2 to 4 tablespoons Worcestershire sauce

1 teaspoon garlic powder or minced garlic

1 teaspoon onion powder

1/2 teaspoon ginger

Salt and pepper to taste

6 pineapple rings

4 choice T-bone, rib-eye or New York
  strip steaks

Christopher Bingham
Fry's
Tucson, Arizona

Combine the lemon juice, pineapple juice, barbecue sauce, soy sauce, brown sugar, liqueur, Worcestershire sauce, garlic powder, onion powder, ginger, salt and pepper in a blender. Process until blended.

Pour half the marinade over the pineapple rings in a sealable freezer bag. Seal tightly and turn to coat. Pour the remaining marinade over the steaks in a large sealable freezer bag and seal tightly. Turn to coat. Marinate the pineapple and steaks in the refrigerator for 24 hours, turning occasionally.

Drain the steaks, reserving the marinade. Grill the steaks over hot coals until medium-well or to the desired degree of doneness, basting with the reserved marinade and turning as little as possible. Stop basting 5 minutes before the steaks are done. Drain the pineapple slices, reserving the marinade. Arrange the pineapple slices on the grill rack approximately 5 to 10 minutes before the steaks are done. Grill until the pineapple is slightly caramelized, a color change is evident and grill marks appear.

Heat the reserved pineapple marinade in a saucepan until hot. Drizzle over the pineapple and steaks on a serving platter before serving. Serve with potatoes or your choice of vegetables.

Serves 4

Round Steak

All-purpose flour for coating
Salt and pepper to taste
1 (2- to 3-pound) round steak
Vegetable oil for browning

3 tablespoons vegetable oil
1 cup ketchup
1 cup packed brown sugar
1 large onion, sliced

Mix flour, salt and pepper in a shallow dish. Cut the round steak into six equal portions. Coat each with the flour mixture. Brown the steak on both sides in a small amount of oil in a nonstick skillet. Arrange the steaks in a single layer on a baking sheet with sides and drizzle with 3 tablespoons oil.

Combine the ketchup and brown sugar in a bowl and mix well. Spread half over the steaks. Bake at 350 degrees for 30 minutes. Spread the remaining ketchup mixture over the steaks and top with the onion. Bake for 20 minutes longer.

Serves 6

Beef Stroganoff

1 (2-pound) round steak
3 tablespoons vegetable oil
1 large onion, chopped
8 ounces fresh mushrooms

1 cup dry red wine
2 tablespoons dry mustard
8 ounces egg noodles
1 cup sour cream

Cut the steak into thin strips. Cook in the oil in a skillet until brown on both sides. Remove the steak to a platter using a slotted spoon, reserving the pan drippings. Sauté the onion and mushrooms in the reserved pan drippings until golden brown. Stir in the steak, wine and dry mustard. Simmer until the steak is tender, stirring occasionally.

Cook the pasta using the package directions; drain. Arrange the hot pasta on a serving platter and top with the beef stroganoff. Spoon the sour cream over the top. Serve immediately.

Serves 2 to 4

Bierocks

2 (1-pound) loaves frozen bread dough
1 pound ground beef
1 onion, chopped
1 garlic clove, crushed
1 1/2 teaspoons salt
1 1/2 teaspoons lemon pepper
1 small head cabbage, chopped
2 tablespoons Worcestershire sauce
2 teaspoons caraway seeds (optional)
All-purpose flour

Place the bread dough in a microwave-safe bowl. Microwave, covered with plastic wrap, on Low for 6 to 8 minutes or until pliable. Or, thaw using the package directions.

Brown the ground beef with the onion, garlic, salt and lemon pepper in a skillet, stirring until the ground beef is crumbly and the onion is tender. Stir in the cabbage, Worcestershire sauce and caraway seeds and cook until the cabbage is limp; drain.

Roll each bread loaf into a 12-inch round on a lightly floured surface. Cut each round into six wedges. Place approximately 1/3 cup of the ground beef mixture in the center of each wedge. Pinch the points together to seal. Coat your fingers lightly with flour and pinch the edges to seal, making three seams in each bierock.

Arrange the bierocks on a lightly greased baking sheet. Bake at 350 degrees for 30 minutes or until golden brown. Serve hot with a salad or soup, or freeze for future use. Reheat the bierocks until warm.

Makes 1 dozen bierocks

Part of my heritage is German. My mother passed this recipe down to my sisters and me. Change the fillings to combinations like as chicken and broccoli or ham and Swiss cheese. These are great for a light supper on a warm night after a long day at work.

Lynnea Mitchell
King Soopers
Denver, Colorado

My husband came up with this recipe. The vegetables give added texture and provide hidden vitamins. My two boys don't notice the vegetables. Great for a large group or a few days of leftovers.

Melissa Crawford

Fred Meyer

Vancouver,
   Washington

Not-Your-Normal Burritos

1 pound ground beef
2 (30-ounce) cans vegetarian refried beans
2 (14-ounce) cans green beans
1 (16-ounce) package frozen broccoli, cauliflower
   and carrots, thawed
1 (15-ounce) can enchilada sauce
20 (10-inch) flour tortillas, heated
16 ounces Cheddar cheese, shredded

Brown the ground beef in a skillet, stirring until crumbly; drain. Combine the ground beef, refried beans, undrained green beans, broccoli mixture and enchilada sauce in a stockpot and mix well.

Cook over medium heat until warm, stirring occasionally. Spoon the ground beef mixture evenly on the warm tortillas. Sprinkle with the cheese and any of your favorite toppings. Fold the sides over the fillings and roll to enclose.

Makes 20 burritos

Gram's Cabbage Rolls

1 large head cabbage, cored
2¹/2 pounds ground chuck or ground round
1¹/2 cups cooked rice
1 tablespoon onion powder
1 teaspoon poultry seasoning
1 egg, beaten
Salt and pepper to taste
10 ounces smoked sausage without casings

Combine the cabbage with water to cover in a stockpot. Simmer, covered, for about 30 minutes or until the cabbage is tender, removing the outer leaves as they soften. Drain and pat the leaves dry.

Combine the ground chuck, rice, onion powder, poultry seasoning, egg, salt and pepper in a bowl and mix well. Spoon about ¹/3 cup of the ground beef mixture in the center of each of fifteen cabbage leaves. Fold the leaves around the filling and roll tightly. Arrange the cabbage rolls seam side down in a 9x13-inch baking pan.

Chop the remaining cabbage and sprinkle over the top of the rolls. Cut the sausage into 1-inch slices and arrange over the prepared layers. Bake, covered with foil, at 325 degrees for 2 hours. You may make a double batch of the cabbage rolls and freeze for future use.

Makes 15 cabbage rolls

My mother-in-law taught me how to prepare these rolls a long time ago, but she never gave me a handwritten recipe. When I tried making them, they never tasted like hers. I tried different spices until I found her secret ingredient— it was one teaspoon of poultry seasoning!

Barbara Pentrack
Kroger
Lancaster, Ohio

This recipe came from my sister's boyfriend. I tweaked the recipe and my sister tweaked the boyfriend and married him. They have been married for more than thirty-five years and are still going strong.

Darrel Grathwohl
Kroger
Sparta, Illinois

C.W. Special

16 ounces wide egg noodles
1 1/2 pounds ground beef or chopped chicken
16 ounces cream cheese, cut into cubes and softened
1/2 cup sour cream
1 (15-ounce) can whole kernel corn
1/2 to 1 cup milk
Salt and pepper to taste

Cook the pasta using the package directions; drain. Brown the ground beef in a skillet, stirring until crumbly; drain. Add the cream cheese and sour cream and mix until combined. Stir in the undrained corn and then add the pasta.

Add enough milk to the ground beef mixture to reach the desired consistency and mix well. Season with salt and pepper. Cook until heated through. Serve immediately.

Serves 6

Hungarian Goulash

2 pounds ground chuck
8 ounces elbow macaroni
4 cups water
1 (8-ounce) can Private Selection tomato sauce
1 (4-ounce) can Private Selection tomato paste
Dried crushed red pepper to taste
Tabasco sauce to taste
Salt and black pepper to taste

Brown the ground chuck in a large skillet, stirring until crumbly; drain. Combine the browned ground chuck, pasta, water, tomato sauce, tomato paste, red pepper, Tabasco sauce, salt and black pepper in an 8-quart stockpot. Bring to a boil and then reduce the heat to low. Simmer for 30 minutes, stirring occasionally.

Serves 8

This is a third-generation recipe in my family that I used to watch my grandmother prepare.

Don Becker
Kroger
Cincinnati, Ohio

Stuffed Meat Loaf Roll

This is an awesome meat loaf. When you slice the meat loaf it pops with swirls of color and flavor. Experiment with different vegetable and cheese combinations until you find the combination that suits your taste.

Denise Barnes
Food 4 Less Midwest
Hammond, Indiana

1 (16-ounce) package frozen chopped
    spinach or vegetable of choice, thawed
    and drained
1 pound ground beef
1 pound ground pork
1 pound ground chicken
1 pound ground turkey
1 yellow onion, chopped
3 garlic cloves, minced
1/4 cup chopped basil

2 or 3 eggs, lightly beaten
1 cup bread crumbs
1 (8-ounce) can tomato sauce
6 ounces Colby Jack cheese or cheese of
    choice, shredded
8 ounces Italian sausage, casings removed
1 (8-ounce) can tomato paste
1/4 cup packed brown sugar
2 ounces Colby Jack cheese or cheese
    of choice, shredded

Squeeze any excess moisture from the spinach. Combine the ground beef, ground pork, ground chicken, ground turkey, onion, garlic and basil in a bowl and mix well. Add the eggs and 1/2 cup of the bread crumbs and mix well.

Sprinkle the remaining 1/2 cup bread crumbs on a sheet of parchment paper. Pat the ground beef mixture into a square on the prepared parchment paper. Spread with the tomato sauce and spinach and sprinkle with 6 ounces cheese. Arrange the sausage link at the bottom of the square and roll the ground beef mixture to enclose the filling. Place the roll in a 9x13-inch baking pan.

Mix the tomato paste and brown sugar in a bowl and spread over the top of the roll. Bake at 325 degrees for 2 hours or until the juices run clear. Sprinkle with 2 ounces cheese just before the end of the baking process. Slice as desired.

Serves 8

Stuffed Meat Loaf

1 pound ground beef
6 ounces cream cheese, softened
4 ounces blue cheese, crumbled
1 tablespoon yellow mustard
1 pound ground beef

Pat 1 pound of the ground beef over the bottom of a round baking dish. Combine the cream cheese, blue cheese and mustard in a bowl and mix well. Spread over the prepared layer. Pat 1 pound ground beef over the top, pinching the edge to seal. Bake at 325 degrees for 45 to 50 minutes or until cooked through and brown.

Serves 6 to 8

My family loves all these ingredients and this recipe is a way to make one large burger instead of four.

Marti Kautz
Baker's
Omaha, Nebraska

Bubble Pizza

2 (10-count) cans refrigerator buttermilk biscuits
1 1/2 pounds ground beef
1 (15-ounce) can pizza sauce
1 1/2 cups (6 ounces) shredded mozzarella cheese
1 cup (4 ounces) shredded Cheddar cheese

Separate the biscuits and cut each into quarters. Arrange in a greased 9x13-inch baking dish. Brown the ground beef in a skillet, stirring until crumbly; drain. Stir in the pizza sauce. Spoon the ground beef mixture over the prepared layer. Bake at 350 degrees for 35 minutes or until the biscuits are cooked through. Sprinkle with the mozzarella cheese and Cheddar cheese. Bake for 5 to 10 minutes longer or until the cheese melts.

Serves 6 to 8

Also great with the addition of some of your favorite pizza toppings such as mushrooms, onions and/or bell peppers.

Jo Young
Kroger
Franklin, Indiana

Elise Gossett
Kroger
Hillsboro, Ohio

Taco Ring

1 pound ground chuck
1 cup (4 ounces) shredded Cheddar cheese
1 envelope taco seasoning mix
2 tablespoons water
2 (8-count) cans refrigerator crescent rolls
1 green bell pepper (optional)
1 cup salsa or taco sauce
3 cups shredded lettuce
1 tomato, chopped
1/4 cup chopped onion
1/4 cup sliced black olives, drained (optional)

Brown the ground chuck in a skillet, stirring until crumbly; drain. Combine the browned ground chuck, cheese, seasoning mix and water in a bowl and mix well.

Unroll the crescent roll dough and separate into triangles. Arrange the triangles in a circle with the wide ends overlapping in the center and the points facing outward on a 13-inch baking stone or a pizza pan lightly sprayed with nonstick cooking spray. There should be a 5-inch diameter opening in the center.

Spread the ground chuck mixture evenly on the widest end of each triangle. Bring the points of the triangles up over the filling and tuck under the wide ends at the center of the ring; the filling will not be completely covered. Bake at 375 degrees for 20 to 25 minutes or until golden brown.

Cut off the top of the bell pepper and discard. Remove the membranes and seeds. Fill with the salsa. Arrange in the center of the ring. Layer the lettuce, tomato, onion and olives around the bell pepper in the order listed. Garnish with sour cream. Cut into eight wedges.

Serves 8

Mom's Sloppy Joes

3/4 cup water
2 tablespoons Cream of Wheat
3/4 cup plus 2 tablespoons ketchup
1 tablespoon mustard
1 teaspoon chili powder
1/2 teaspoon salt
1/2 teaspoon sugar
1/2 teaspoon vinegar
Dash of pepper
1 1/2 pounds lean ground beef
6 to 8 hamburger buns

Bring the water to a boil in a small saucepan and then stir in the Cream of Wheat. Cook until slightly thickened. Stir in the ketchup, mustard, chili powder, salt, sugar, vinegar and pepper. Cook for 10 minutes, stirring constantly.

Brown the ground beef in a skillet, stirring until crumbly; drain. Add the sauce mixture and mix well. Cook for 10 minutes, stirring occasionally. Serve on hamburger buns.

Serves 6 to 8 generous servings

Dave Dillon
Kroger
Cincinnati, Ohio

Ella Green
Kroger
Clarksburg,
*   West Virginia*

Tiella

2 potatoes, sliced
2 pounds ground beef
1 (16-ounce) can tomatoes
1 (8-ounce) can tomato sauce
1 (8-ounce) can tomato paste
2 cups water
1 zucchini, sliced
1 green bell pepper, sliced
1 hot chile, chopped (optional)
4 slices bread, crumbled
2 teaspoons basil
1 teaspoon oregano
$1/2$ teaspoon garlic salt
Salt and pepper to taste
Grated Parmesan cheese

Cook the potatoes in boiling water in a saucepan until partially cooked; drain. Brown the ground beef in a skillet, stirring until crumbly; drain. Combine the tomatoes, tomato sauce, tomato paste and water in a bowl and mix well.

Layer the ground beef, zucchini, potatoes, bell pepper, hot chile, bread, basil, oregano, garlic salt, salt, pepper, cheese and tomato mixture half at a time in the order listed in a greased 3-quart baking dish. Sprinkle with additional cheese

Bake, covered, at 350 degrees for 50 minutes, placing a larger pan on the oven rack below the baking dish to catch any spills. Remove the cover and bake for 10 minutes or until most of the liquid has evaporated and the top is brown. You may stir during the baking process, but do so carefully so as not to disturb the layers.

Serves 8 to 10

Mustard and Herb–Crusted Rack of Lamb

2 racks of lamb
1 1/2 teaspoons salt
1/2 teaspoon coarsely ground pepper
1/4 cup whole grain mustard
1 teaspoon prepared horseradish
1/2 cup coarse fresh bread crumbs
1 tablespoon chopped fresh parsley

Season the lamb with the salt and pepper. Mix the mustard and horseradish in a small bowl. Combine the bread crumbs and parsley in a shallow dish and mix well. Spread the mustard mixture over the top of the lamb and then press the coated side in the bread crumb mixture.

Arrange the lamb on a baking rack in a shallow roasting pan. Roast at 400 degrees for 25 to 30 minutes or until a meat thermometer registers 145 degrees for medium-rare. Let stand for 5 to 10 minutes. Cut between the ribs into chops.

Serves 6

A very special recipe for Easter dinner or when entertaining guests for special occasions.

Nick Forrest
Kroger
Oxford, Ohio

Basil and Mushroom–Stuffed Pork Spirals

To roast red bell peppers, cut the bell peppers into quarters and discard the stems, seeds, and membranes. Arrange the quarters cut sides down on a baking sheet lined with foil. Roast at 425 degrees for 20 to 25 minutes or until the skins are blistered and charred. Wrap in foil and let stand for 15 minutes. Peel off the skin in strips using a sharp knife and discard. Chill the roasted bell peppers, covered, for up to twenty-four hours before using.

Chuck Walker
Smith's
Salt Lake City, Utah

1 (12-ounce) pork tenderloin
1 cup loosely packed spinach leaves, trimmed and julienned
1/3 cup finely chopped mushrooms
1/4 cup chopped fresh basil
2 tablespoons all-purpose flour
1 tablespoon finely shredded Parmesan cheese

1 egg white, lightly beaten
1 teaspoon olive oil
1 teaspoon pepper
2 red bell peppers, roasted
2 teaspoons olive oil
1 teaspoon red or white wine vinegar
2 small garlic cloves
Dash of salt

Butterfly the tenderloin and lay flat like a book. Place the tenderloin between two sheets of plastic wrap. Working from the center to the edges, pound lightly with the flat side of a meat mallet into an 11x17-inch rectangle. Fold in the narrow ends as necessary to even the sides.

Combine the spinach, mushrooms, basil, flour, cheese and egg white in a bowl and mix well. Spread over the surface of the tenderloin. Roll as for a jelly roll from the short side. Secure with kitchen twine at 11/2-inch intervals. Brush the surface with 1 teaspoon olive oil and sprinkle with the pepper.

Arrange medium-hot coals around a drip pan in a covered grill. Test for medium heat above the pan. Arrange the tenderloin on the grill rack directly over the pan, not over the coals. Grill, covered, for 25 to 30 minutes or until a meat thermometer registers 160 degrees or the juices run clear. Or, adjust the heat on a gas grill for indirect grilling. Test for medium heat where the pork will be placed. Arrange the tenderloin on the grill rack and grill, covered, over medium heat as directed above.

Combine the bell peppers, 2 teaspoons olive oil, the vinegar, garlic and salt in a food processor or blender. Pulse until puréed. Pour into a small saucepan and cook over medium heat until heated through. Remove the twine from the pork and slice as desired. Serve with the warm sauce. You may substitute half a 7-ounce jar roasted red peppers for the roasted fresh red bell peppers.

Serves 4

Southern Barbecued Pork Tenderloin with Mop Sauce

Pork Tenderloins

2 tablespoons brown sugar

1 tablespoon paprika

1 tablespoon chili powder

1 teaspoon cumin

1 teaspoon salt

1 teaspoon cayenne pepper

Freshly ground black pepper to taste

2 pork tenderloins

Mop Sauce

1/3 cup ketchup

1/4 cup cider vinegar

1/4 cup molasses

1 tablespoon Worcestershire sauce

To prepare the tenderloins, combine the brown sugar, paprika, chili powder, cumin, salt, cayenne pepper and black pepper in a bowl and mix well. Coat the surface of the tenderloins with half the brown sugar mixture. Let stand for 15 minutes. Coat with the remaining brown sugar mixture.

Arrange the tenderloins on a grill rack sprayed with nonstick cooking spray over indirect heat. Grill for 15 minutes and then turn. Continue grilling for 12 to 15 minutes longer or until a meat thermometer registers 160 degrees. Remove from the grill and cover loosely with foil. Let stand for 10 minutes before slicing.

To prepare the sauce, combine the ketchup, vinegar, molasses and Worcestershire sauce in a bowl and mix well. Serve with the tenderloins.

Serves 8

Use an outdoor grill for authentic flavor and taste. Serve with corn bread, green beans, and corn on the cob for a southern feast. Every time I serve this I receive requests for the recipe.

Ross Thomas
CB&S Advertising
Portland, Oregon

Orange-Sauced Tenderloin

Ken Certain
Kroger
Houston, Texas

2 (2-pound) pork tenderloins
2 tablespoons butter or margarine
3/4 cup chopped onion
1/4 teaspoon pepper
1/2 cup white wine
Juice of 2 oranges
3 tablespoons sugar
1 bay leaf
1 tablespoon chopped parsley
1/2 teaspoon salt
1 orange
1/4 cup water
2 1/2 teaspoons cornstarch
1 tablespoon water
4 cups hot cooked rice

Sauté the tenderloins in the butter in a Dutch oven until golden brown on all sides. Remove the tenderloins to a platter, reserving the pan drippings. Sauté the onion and pepper in the reserved pan drippings until the onion is tender. Return the tenderloins to the Dutch oven and add the wine, orange juice, sugar, bay leaf and parsley. Simmer, covered, for about 45 minutes or until a meat thermometer registers 160 degrees. Season with the salt.

Peel the orange and cut the peel into thin strips. Separate the orange into sections and set aside. Bring the orange peel and 1/4 cup water to a boil in a small saucepan. Boil until the peel is tender; drain.

Remove the tenderloins to a platter, reserving the pan drippings. Discard the bay leaf. Mix the cornstarch and 1 tablespoon water in a small bowl until blended and add to the reserved pan drippings. Cook until thickened and of a sauce consistency, stirring frequently.

Spoon the rice onto a serving platter. Cut the tenderloins into thick slices and arrange the slices over the rice. Drizzle with the sauce and top with the orange sections and orange peel.

Serves 6

Sun-Dried Tomato and Rosemary Pork Tenderloin

1 (1 1/2- to 2-pound) pork tenderloin
1 teaspoon dried rosemary
1 tablespoon olive oil
3 garlic cloves, finely chopped
2 cups red wine, such as merlot or cabernet sauvignon
1/4 cup light soy sauce
1/4 cup Worcestershire sauce
3 tablespoons sun-dried tomato pesto
1 (6-ounce) package sliced portobello mushrooms (optional)
1 teaspoon dried rosemary

Rub the surface of the tenderloin with 1 teaspoon rosemary. Heat the olive oil in a large skillet over medium-high heat and add the tenderloin. Sear on all sides. Remove the tenderloin to a platter, reserving the pan drippings.

Brown the garlic in the reserved pan drippings. Stir in the wine, soy sauce, Worcestershire sauce and pesto. Add the mushrooms and 1 teaspoon rosemary and mix well. Return the tenderloin to the skillet and reduce the heat to medium-low. Simmer, covered, for about 30 minutes or until a meat thermometer registers 160 degrees for medium.

Serves 3

Amanda Haenel
Kroger
Smyrna, Georgia

Susan Thomson
Smith's
Salt Lake City, Utah

Carnitas Tacos

1 (2 1/2- to 3-pound) boneless pork loin
　　roast, trimmed
3/4 teaspoon cumin
1/2 teaspoon chili powder
1 white onion, sliced
2 garlic cloves, minced
3/4 teaspoon cumin
1/2 teaspoon chili powder
1 lime, sliced
1 orange, sliced

2 cups (8 ounces) shredded
　　Colby Jack cheese
2 cups shredded carrots
2 cups shredded zucchini
2 tomatoes, chopped
2 avocados, chopped
1 bunch cilantro, trimmed and chopped
12 taco-size soft corn tortillas, or fajita-size
　　soft flour tortillas
Taco sauce

Sprinkle the roast with 3/4 teaspoon cumin and 1/2 teaspoon chili powder. Brown on all sides in a heavy skillet. Layer the onion, garlic, 3/4 teaspoon cumin, 1/2 teaspoon chili powder, the lime and orange in a slow cooker. Arrange the roast over the prepared layers. Cook on High for 1 hour. Reduce the heat to Low and cook for 5 to 6 hours or until the roast is cooked through and shreds easily. Do not add water, broth or any other liquid during the cooking process.

Remove the roast to a platter and shred. Discard the liquid and solids from the slow cooker. Return the shredded pork to the slow cooker to keep warm, adding a few drops of water for moisture if needed and any additional desired seasonings.

Layer the pork, cheese, carrots, zucchini, tomatoes, avocados and cilantro on the tortillas as desired. Drizzle with taco sauce.

Makes 20 tacos

Peppercorn Pork Loin with Apple Cider Gravy

Pork Loin

Olive oil for coating

1 (2-pound) pork loin roast

1/4 cup water

2 tablespoons all-purpose flour

2 tablespoons Dijon mustard

2 tablespoons cracked mixed peppercorns

2 tablespoons brown sugar

2 tablespoons fresh thyme, chopped

1 tablespoon margarine, softened

Apple Cider Gravy

1 1/2 cups apple cider

2 tablespoons all-purpose flour

1/3 cup low-sodium chicken broth

1 tablespoon cider vinegar

1 teaspoon Dijon mustard

Salt and freshly ground pepper to taste

Carrie Reinhard
Kroger
Franklin, Tennessee

To prepare the pork loin, heat a large skillet coated with olive oil until hot. Sear the roast in the hot oil until brown on all sides. Remove to a rack coated with nonstick cooking spray. Place the rack in a roasting pan and pour the water into the pan.

Combine the flour, Dijon mustard, peppercorns, brown sugar, thyme and margarine in a bowl and mix until of a paste consistency. Spread over the top and sides of the roast. Bake at 350 degrees for about 65 minutes or until a meat thermometer registers 160 degrees for medium. Remove the roast to a cutting board and tent with foil, reserving 2 tablespoons of the pan drippings.

To prepare the gravy, pour the reserved 2 tablespoons pan drippings into a heavy saucepan. Heat over medium heat until hot and then stir in the apple cider. Bring to a boil and boil until reduced to 3/4 cup. Blend in the flour and cook until the flour begins to brown, stirring constantly. Whisk in the broth.

Simmer for 2 minutes or until thickened, stirring frequently. Remove from the heat and stir in the vinegar and Dijon mustard. Season with salt and pepper. Serve with the roast.

Serves 6

Herbed Summer Pork Roast

1 (3- to 4-pound) boneless pork roast, trimmed
Salt and pepper to taste
2 cups chopped fresh herbs, such as parsley,
    sage, rosemary, oregano and thyme
2 garlic cloves, minced
2 tablespoons olive oil

Season the roast with salt and pepper. Combine the herbs, garlic and olive oil in a bowl and mix until a thick paste forms. Spread over the surface of the roast.

Grill, with the lid down, over indirect heat for about 1 hour or until a meat thermometer registers 160 degrees, turning once or twice. Remove to a platter and tent with foil. Let stand for 10 minutes before slicing. Or, bake at 375 degrees for 1 to 1 1/2 hours or until a meat thermometer registers 160 degrees.

Serves 4 to 6

My husband grows the herbs, and I cook with them. I get lots of compliments and requests for this recipe.

Donalu Evans
Kroger
Cincinnati, Ohio

Colorado-Style Southwestern Ribs

4 slices bacon
1 package St. Louis-style ribs, or 6 to 8 country-style ribs
Salt and pepper to taste
6 to 8 Roma tomatoes, cut into quarters
2 large yellow onions, sliced
6 to 8 jalapeño chiles, seeded and cut into thin strips
2 tablespoons all-purpose flour

Lay the bacon slices in a single layer over the bottom of a large roasting pan. Arrange a rack over the bacon. Season the ribs with salt and pepper and place on the rack. Top with the tomatoes, onions, jalapeño chiles, salt and pepper.

Bake at 225 degrees for 2 hours. Reduce the heat to 175 degrees if necessary and cover the pan with foil. Bake for 4 to 7 hours or until the ribs are tender. Remove the ribs and roasting rack, reserving the pan drippings and vegetables. Maintain the oven temperature.

Add the flour to the reserved pan drippings and vegetables and mix well. Cook over medium-high heat until the mixture comes to a boil or reaches the consistency of a thick salsa, stirring constantly. Remove from the heat and return the ribs to the pan. Keep warm in the oven until serving time. Serve with warm tortillas, sour cream and shredded Cheddar cheese.

Serves 6

The reserved pan drippings and vegetables may be processed using an immersion blender or in a blender to achieve the desired consistency.

Mark Zwisler
King Soopers
Kipling, Colorado

Spiral Ham with Honey Berry Glaze

This is a recipe
I found a few years
ago, and I have
added my own touch
for extra flavor.

Sharon Southwick
Kroger
Covington, Kentucky

1 (8- to 10-pound) sliced fully-cooked
   spiral ham
2 (16-ounce) cans whole cranberry sauce
2 cups packed dark brown sugar
1/2 cup honey

1/2 cup good-quality whiskey
6 tablespoons mustard
1 (6-ounce) can frozen orange juice
   concentrate, thawed

Line a large roasting pan with heavy-duty foil and spray with nonstick cooking spray. Arrange the ham in the prepared pan. Mix the cranberry sauce, brown sugar, honey, whiskey, mustard and orange juice concentrate in a bowl and pour over the ham.

Cover the pan with foil and make six small slits in the foil. Bake at 350 degrees for 2 hours, basting every 30 minutes with the pan drippings. Let stand for 15 to 20 minutes before serving.

Serves 6 to 10

Spaghetti Carbonara

This is a recipe that
my husband's family
brought from Aviano,
Italy, in the 1980s.
It came from a local
restaurant named
The Spaghetti House.

Joy Duncan
Kroger
Cincinnati, Ohio

8 ounces thin spaghetti
1/4 cup (1/2 stick) butter
1 cup whipping cream

1/2 cup chopped ham or prosciutto
Dash of pepper
1/3 cup grated Parmesan cheese

Cook the pasta using the package directions; do not drain. Melt the butter in a skillet and add the cream, ham and pepper.

Simmer over medium heat for 10 minutes, stirring occasionally; do not boil. Remove the pasta to serving plates using a pasta fork and top with the sauce. Sprinkle each serving lightly with the cheese. Serve immediately. You may substitute different types of spaghetti, angel hair pasta, fettuccini or your favorite pasta for the thin spaghetti. Add additional ingredients like parsley or pine nuts for more flavor.

Serves 4

Vegetable Medley Pasta

1 pound Italian sausage, casings removed and sausage sliced

1 to 2 tablespoons vegetable oil

2 cups (1/2-inch) slices yellow squash

2 cups (1/2-inch) slices zucchini

8 to 10 mushrooms, sliced

1 (2-ounce) jar pimentos

1 or 2 garlic cloves, minced

1 chicken bouillon cube

1/4 cup boiling water

1/4 cup cooking sherry

1/4 cup pine nuts

16 ounces pasta

Freshly grated Parmesan cheese

Brown the sausage in a skillet. Remove the sausage to a platter using a slotted spoon and discard the pan drippings; do not clean the skillet. Combine the oil, squash, zucchini, mushrooms, pimentos and garlic in the same skillet.

Sauté for 5 minutes or until the squash, zucchini and mushrooms are tender but not mushy. Dissolve the bouillon cube in the boiling water in a heatproof measuring cup. Add the bouillon, sherry and sausage to the squash mixture and mix well. Simmer over medium to medium-low heat for 15 minutes. Stir in the pine nuts and simmer for 5 minutes.

Cook the pasta using the package directions until al dente. Spoon onto a serving platter and top with the squash mixture. Sprinkle with cheese. Serve immediately.

Serves 4

If you are not watching calories, sauté the vegetables in the sausage drippings. You can add more or less of any vegetable depending on what you like. I tend to add more mushrooms as they cook down.

Rhonda Sheehan
Smith's
Salt Lake City, Utah

Poultry & Seafood

Poultry & Seafood

A quick-and-simple recipe for delicious baked chicken.

David Thomas

Kroger

Indianapolis, Indiana

Crunchy Baked Chicken

1 egg
1 tablespoon milk
1 (2-ounce) can French-fried onions, crushed
3/4 cup (3 ounces) grated Parmesan cheese
1/3 cup dry bread crumbs
1 teaspoon paprika
1/2 teaspoon salt
1/4 teaspoon ground pepper
1 (3- to 4-pound) chicken, cut up
2 tablespoons butter, melted

Combine the egg and milk in a shallow dish and whisk until blended. Combine the onions, cheese, bread crumbs, paprika, salt and pepper in a shallow dish and mix well. Dip the chicken in the egg mixture. Roll in the bread crumb mixture to coat.

Arrange the chicken in a 9×12-inch baking dish and drizzle with the butter. Bake at 350 degrees for 55 to 60 minutes or until cooked through.

Serves 4 to 6

Southern Chicken and Dumplings

Chicken

12 cups water
1 (3- to 4-pound) chicken, cut up
1 small onion, cut into wedges
2 ribs celery, chopped
1 1/2 teaspoons salt
1 garlic clove, cut into quarters
1 bay leaf
4 to 6 leaves parsley
1 tablespoon lemon juice

Dumplings

2 cups all-purpose flour
1 tablespoon baking powder
1 1/2 teaspoons salt
1 teaspoon poultry seasoning
1 cup plus 2 tablespoons milk

The secret to these dumplings is the poultry seasoning. I always double this recipe for my family, who can't get enough. These dumplings are the closest I have found to my Aunt Daisy's famous dumplings.

Juanita Barrett
Kroger
Alexandria, Kentucky

To prepare the chicken, bring the water to a boil in a large saucepan. Add the chicken, onion, celery, salt, garlic, bay leaf and parsley. Reduce the heat and simmer for 2 hours or until the chicken is cooked through. Remove the chicken to a platter, reserving the stock. Strain the stock, discarding the solids. Return 6 cups of the strained stock to the stockpot and stir in the lemon juice. Reheat over medium heat until simmering.

To prepare the dumplings, combine the flour, baking powder, salt and poultry seasoning in a bowl and mix well. Add the milk and stir until blended. Let stand for 10 minutes. Roll the dough 1/2 inch thick on a lightly floured surface and cut into 1- to 1 1/2-inch squares. Drop the dumplings into the simmering stock.

Simmer for 15 to 20 minutes or until tender. The dumplings will slowly shrink and partially dissolve, thickening the stock. Chop the chicken, discarding the skin and bones. Add the chicken to the dumplings and mix gently.

Serves 6 to 8

Jason Hardy
Kroger
Hardy, Virginia

Acapulco Chicken

2 cups unsalted chicken broth, skimmed

2 tablespoons pickling spices

1 pound boneless chicken breasts

1 onion, thinly sliced

3 garlic cloves, minced

1 tablespoon olive oil

1/3 cup rice wine vinegar

2 teaspoons cumin

1/2 red bell pepper, sliced

1/2 yellow bell pepper, sliced

2 tablespoons minced jalapeño chiles with seeds

1/4 cup fresh cilantro

Boil the broth and pickling spices in a large heavy saucepan for 10 minutes. Strain and return the liquid to the saucepan. Add the chicken, onion, garlic, olive oil, vinegar and cumin.

Simmer over very low heat for 10 minutes or just until the chicken is cooked through. Place the chicken and onion in a shallow dish using a slotted spoon, reserving the cooking liquid. Top with the bell peppers and jalapeño chile.

Boil the reserved cooking liquid for 10 minutes or until reduced to about 2/3 cup. Pour over the prepared layers and let stand for 30 minutes. Sprinkle with the cilantro. Marinate, covered, in the refrigerator for 4 to 24 hours, turning occasionally. Slice the chicken and serve with the vegetables and tortilla chips.

Serves 6

Almond Chicken

1 1/2 cups sliced mushrooms

4 ribs celery, chopped

3 green onions, chopped

1 small shallot, chopped

4 garlic cloves, minced

1/4 cup cornstarch

3 tablespoons water

4 cups low-sodium chicken broth

2 tablespoons chicken bouillon granules

2 tablespoons soy sauce

5 tablespoons cornstarch

5 tablespoons all-purpose flour

1 teaspoon baking powder

2 eggs, beaten

2 tablespoons water

1 (16-ounce) package panko

1 cup raw or salted almonds, finely ground

4 boneless chicken breasts

Canola oil or vegetable oil

This recipe leaves a lot of room for creativity. You may marinate the chicken, substitute or add your favorite spices, and add or omit vegetables from the sauce. For a thicker sauce, add additional cornstarch blended with cold water.

Michael Garrett
Fred Meyer
Renton, Washington

Sauté the mushrooms, celery, green onions and shallot in a nonstick skillet until tender. Add the garlic toward the end of the sauté process to prevent the garlic from burning. Sauté until the garlic is tender. Whisk 1/4 cup cornstarch and 3 tablespoons water in a saucepan until blended. Gradually mix in the broth, bouillon granules and soy sauce. Add the mushroom mixture and mix well. Bring to a boil, stirring constantly. Boil for 1 minute. Cover and keep warm over low heat.

Mix 5 tablespoons cornstarch, the flour and baking powder in a shallow dish. Whisk the eggs and 2 tablespoons water in a bowl until blended. Mix the bread crumbs and almonds in a shallow dish.

Cut the chicken breasts into halves and pound between sheets of waxed paper with a meat mallet until flattened. Coat the chicken with the flour mixture, dip in the egg mixture and then coat with the bread crumb mixture.

Pour enough canola oil into a skillet to measure 1/4 inch and heat over medium-high heat until hot. Cook the chicken in the oil for 5 to 7 minutes or until golden brown on both sides. Remove to a wire rack or paper towels to drain. Arrange the chicken on a serving platter and top with the mushroom sauce. Serve with steamed white rice and broccoli or your favorite vegetable.

Serves 4 to 6

Apricot Peanut Chicken

4 boneless skinless chicken breasts
1 onion, coarsely chopped
1 (16-ounce) jar apricot preserves
1 cup peanut butter
Salt, black pepper and red pepper flakes to taste

Combine the chicken, onion, preserves and peanut butter in a slow cooker. Season with salt, black pepper and red pepper flakes. Cook on High for 1 to 1 1/2 hours or until a meat thermometer registers 165 degrees.

Serves 4

I used this recipe and won a Dutch oven cook-off.

Scott Tippets
Kroger
Cincinnati, Ohio

Lemon Teriyaki-Glazed Chicken

1/2 cup lemon juice
1/2 cup soy sauce
1/4 cup granulated sugar
3 tablespoon brown sugar
2 tablespoons water
1 1/2 tablespoons minced garlic
3/4 teaspoon ground ginger
6 to 8 chicken thighs

Combine the lemon juice, soy sauce, granulated sugar, brown sugar, water, garlic and ginger in a large skillet. Cook over medium heat for 3 to 4 minutes or until the sugar dissolves, stirring frequently. Add the chicken and cook for 45 to 60 minutes or until cooked through, turning frequently.

Serves 3 to 4

This recipe may be time consuming, but it is worth the time for such wonderfully tender chicken.

Jennifer Bauler
Dillons
Winfield, Kansas

Chicken Asiago

6 ounces fresh spinach, thinly sliced
1 1/2 tablespoons chopped garlic
1 (3-ounce) jar oil-pack sun-dried tomatoes,
    drained and minced
6 ounces asiago cheese or
    Italian cheese blend, shredded
Salt and pepper to taste
4 to 6 boneless skinless chicken breasts

Combine the spinach, garlic, sun-dried tomatoes, cheese, salt and pepper in a large bowl and mix well using your hands. Butterfly the chicken breasts starting from the rounded lobe side, cutting to but not through the opposite side; lay flat. Spoon 1 to 2 tablespoons of the spinach mixture in the center of each breast. Spread the mixture evenly over the bottom side of the chicken breasts. Close the chicken breasts and secure with wooden picks.

Arrange the stuffed chicken breasts in a greased baking pan. Spoon any remaining spinach mixture over the chicken. Bake at 350 degrees for 45 to 60 minutes or until a meat thermometer registers 165 degrees. Remove the wooden picks before serving.

Serves 4 to 6

When I came to work at Fry's, I was in charge of developing a bistro program for their upscale Signature Stores. This recipe was the very first recipe that I included in the program. It is an old recipe that I used in a restaurant I owned prior to moving to the valley. It has turned out to be by far the most requested dish that our Bistros serve. I am proud to have brought it to Kroger and Fry's and love my Fry's family and customers!

Kathleen Morton
Fry's
Tolleson, Arizona

Chicken Cordon Bleu with Brandy Gravy

Tamela Moreno
Smith's
Rock Springs, Wyoming

6 large boneless skinless chicken breasts
6 slices Black Forest ham
6 slices baby Swiss cheese,
1 1/2 cups all-purpose flour
Salt and pepper to taste
2 to 3 tablespoons shortening or vegetable oil
2 to 3 tablespoons butter (optional)
1/4 cup (or more) all-purpose flour
1 to 2 cups milk
1/4 cup brandy

Pound the chicken breasts between sheets of waxed paper or plastic wrap with a meat mallet or rolling pin until flattened. Layer each with one slice of the ham and one slice of the cheese. Roll from the short side to enclose the filling and secure with two or three wooden picks. Mix 1 1/2 cups flour, salt and pepper in a shallow dish. Coat the chicken rolls with the flour mixture.

Heat the shortening in a skillet on high. Add the chicken rolls and then reduce the heat to medium-high. Cook for 15 minutes or until the chicken rolls are brown on all sides. Remove to a platter, reserving the pan drippings.

Scrape the browned bits from the bottom of the skillet using a spatula. Add the butter for additional drippings if needed. Add 1/4 cup flour to the pan drippings, stirring constantly until a paste forms. Gradually add the milk 1/4 cup at a time and cook until of the desired consistency, stirring constantly. Stir in the brandy and season with salt and pepper. Return the chicken rolls to the skillet and reduce the heat.

Simmer for 20 to 30 minutes or until the chicken is cooked through; do not overcook.

Serves 6

Chicken Over Pasta

4 boneless skinless chicken breasts
$^1/_2$ to I (16-ounce) bottle Private Selection
   Balsamic Basil Vinaigrette
16 ounces linguini
Sea salt to taste
$^1/_4$ cup olive oil
$^1/_2$ cup white wine
4 garlic cloves, chopped
I bunch green onions, chopped
4 tomatoes, finely chopped
$^1/_4$ teaspoon red pepper flakes
3 tablespoons chopped fresh flat-leaf parsley

Donna Giordano
QFC
Bellevue, Washington

Place the chicken in a nonreactive dish. Pour the vinaigrette over the chicken and marinate, covered, in the refrigerator for 45 minutes, turning occasionally. Remove the chicken from the dish and discard the marinade. Grill over medium heat until cooked through, turning once.

Cook the pasta using the package directions until al dente and adding a generous amount of sea salt to the water. Drain, reserving I cup of the cooking liquid. Do not rinse the pasta. Cover to keep warm.

Heat the olive oil in a skillet over medium heat. Add the wine, garlic, green onions, tomatoes and red pepper flakes and cook for about 8 minutes, stirring occasionally. Add the parsley, pasta and reserved cooking liquid and mix well. Cook just until heated through. Spoon on a platter and top with the chicken.

Serves 6 to 8

Grilled Chicken with Chipotle-Lime Butter

Chris Rodriguez
Kroger
Houston, Texas

4 chicken breasts
1/2 teaspoon salt
1/4 cup (1/2 stick) butter, softened
1/2 chipotle chile, minced
1 teaspoon fresh lime juice
1/2 teaspoon salt

Rinse the chicken and pat dry. Season the chicken with 1/2 teaspoon salt, tucking some under the skin. Place in a dish and chill, covered, for 2 to 10 hours.

Combine the butter, chipotle chile, lime juice and 1/2 teaspoon salt in a bowl and mix well. Rub the chicken with the butter mixture, tucking some under the skin. Let stand at room temperature for 30 minutes.

Place the chicken skin side up on an oiled grill rack and grill over indirect heat for 15 minutes. Turn the chicken and grill for 10 minutes longer. Grill over direct heat for 3 to 5 minutes or until the skin is brown and crisp and the juices run clear, turning once. Serve immediately.

Serves 4

Herb-Roasted Chicken Breasts with Mustard Marinade

1/2 cup minced shallots
1/4 cup red wine vinegar
1/2 cup olive oil
1/4 cup lemon juice
1/3 cup whole grain mustard
1 cup chopped fresh parsley
1 teaspoon crushed red pepper flakes
6 boneless chicken breasts
Salt and pepper to taste

Charles Harrelson
Gerbes
Columbia, Missouri

Combine the shallots, vinegar, olive oil, lemon juice, mustard, parsley and red pepper flakes in a bowl and mix well. Place the chicken in a large shallow dish. Pour the marinade over the chicken, turning to coat.

Marinate, covered, in the refrigerator for 1 hour or longer, turning occasionally. Drain the chicken, discarding the marinade. Place the chicken in a roasting pan and season with salt and pepper. Roast at 450 degrees for 45 minutes or until cooked through.

Serves 6

Lemon Butter Chicken

Michelle Speckman
Smith's
West Jordan, Utah

Lemon Butter Sauce

1/4 cup white wine

1/2 cup lemon juice

1/2 cup heavy cream

1 cup (2 sticks) butter, cut into pieces

Salt and pepper taste

Chicken

16 ounces angel hair pasta

6 boneless skinless chicken breasts

3/4 cup all-purpose flour

Dash of garlic powder

Salt and pepper to taste

2 tablespoons butter

Vegetable oil

12 to 16 ounces sliced bacon, crisp-cooked
  and crumbled

16 ounces mushrooms, sliced

2 (14-ounce) cans artichoke hearts, drained
  and chopped

2 tablespoons capers

To prepare the sauce, heat the wine in a saucepan over medium heat. Stir in the lemon juice and bring to a boil. Boil for 3 to 5 minutes. Mix in the cream and simmer for 3 to 4 minutes or until thickened, stirring frequently. Gradually add the butter and cook until melted, stirring frequently. Season with salt and pepper. If the sauce separates while preparing the chicken, pour the separated butter from the top into a measuring cup. Pour the remaining sauce into a blender. Add the butter to the blender gradually, processing constantly until incorporated.

To prepare the chicken, cook the pasta using the package directions. Pound the chicken between sheets of waxed paper with a meat mallet until flattened. Mix the flour, garlic powder, salt and pepper in a shallow dish. Coat the chicken with the flour mixture.

Heat the butter and vegetable oil in a skillet until the butter melts. Add the chicken and sauté until cooked through. Remove to a platter and cover to keep warm, reserving the pan drippings.

Add the bacon, mushrooms, artichokes and capers to the reserved pan drippings and cook until the mushrooms are tender. Combine the bacon mixture with half the sauce in a bowl and mix well. Spoon over the pasta on a serving platter. Arrange the chicken over the bacon mixture and drizzle with the remaining sauce. To prepare in advance, combine the pasta, chicken and bacon mixture in a bowl and place in a 9x13-inch baking pan. Pour the sauce over the top. (You may reserve some of the sauce to pour directly over each serving, if desired.) Store, covered, in the refrigerator. Bake at 350 degrees for 30 minutes.

Serves 6

Ham and Cheese-Stuffed Chicken Breasts

1/4 to 1/2 cup (1 to 2 ounces) shredded Swiss cheese,
    Monterey Jack cheese or part-skim mozzarella cheese
2 to 4 tablespoons chopped ham
1 to 2 teaspoons Dijon mustard
Freshly ground pepper to taste
4 (4- to 5-ounce) boneless skinless chicken breasts
1/2 cup plain or herb-seasoned bread crumbs
1 egg white, lightly beaten
2 teaspoons extra-virgin olive oil

Chelsey Halstad
Fred Meyer
Gresham, Oregon

Combine the cheese, ham, Dijon mustard and pepper in a bowl and mix well. Make a horizontal slit through the thickest portion of the chicken breasts, forming a pocket. Spoon an equal amount of the cheese mixture into each pocket. Close the pockets to completely enclose the filling, pressing the edges firmly to seal.

Place the bread crumbs in a shallow dish. Dip the chicken breasts in the egg white and then coat with the bread crumbs. Heat the olive oil in a large nonstick skillet over medium-high heat. Add the chicken breasts and cook for 2 minutes or until brown on one side. Arrange the chicken breasts browned side up on a baking sheet lightly sprayed with nonstick cooking spray. Bake at 400 degrees for 20 minutes or until cooked through and a meat thermometer registers 165 degrees.

Serves 4

Spinach and Portobello Mushroom–Stuffed Chicken Breasts

Michael Lanzezio
Ralphs
Compton, California

2 tablespoons chopped garlic
1/4 cup (1/2 stick) butter
1 pound portobello mushrooms, thinly sliced
32 ounces ricotta cheese
4 eggs, lightly beaten
1/2 cup (2 ounces) grated Parmesan cheese
8 ounces fresh baby spinach
1/2 cup fresh basil, chopped
2 teaspoons salt
2 teaspoons white pepper
16 boneless chicken breasts
Melted butter for brushing

Sauté the garlic in 1/4 cup butter in a skillet until golden brown. Add the mushrooms and sauté until the mushrooms are soft; drain. Let stand until cool. Combine the mushroom mixture with the ricotta cheese, eggs, Parmesan cheese, spinach, basil, salt and white pepper in a large bowl and mix well.

Spoon the mushroom mixture into a pastry bag. Lift the skin carefully from the chicken breast and pipe the mushroom mixture under the skin. Arrange the chicken in a baking dish and chill, covered, for 30 minutes. Brush the chicken with melted butter. Bake at 350 to 375 degrees for 35 minutes or until a meat thermometer registers 165 degrees. This recipe may be cut in half for a smaller crowd. This dish may be served hot or cold.

Serves 16

Pesto Chicken

4 boneless skinless chicken breasts

4 (14-ounce) cans garlic and herb chicken broth

3 tablespoons olive oil

1 red bell pepper, finely chopped

1 (10-ounce) package frozen broccoli florets, thawed

5 tablespoons olive oil

1 1/2 ounces fresh basil

1/2 cup fresh cilantro

1 tablespoon garlic powder

2 cups (8 ounces) shredded Parmesan cheese

16 ounces bow tie pasta, cooked and drained

Place the chicken in a slow cooker. Add the chicken broth and cook on High for 3 to 4 hours or until cooked through. Remove and chop the chicken. Reserve 1/2 cup of the broth.

Heat 3 tablespoons olive oil in a sauté pan over low heat. Add the bell pepper and broccoli and sauté for 15 minutes. Stir in the chicken. Combine the reserved broth, 5 tablespoons olive oil, the basil, cilantro and garlic powder in a blender and process until puréed. Add the cheese and pulse until combined and almost smooth.

Add the pasta to the chicken mixture and cook until heated through, stirring occasionally. Add the sauce and mix well. Cook for 10 minutes. Serve immediately.

Serves 6

I decided one weekend to throw a dinner party and wanted to impress my co-workers. I recalled a pesto pasta my mother made when I was a child. My mother's recipe called for powdered pesto. I decided I wanted to create my own recipe and it has been a hit ever since.

Dawna Cavinder
Kroger
LaPorte, Indiana

Angel Hair Pasta with Chicken

Katie Johnson
Fry's
Tempe, Arizona

1 tablespoon olive oil
2 boneless skinless chicken breasts,
    cut into 1-inch pieces
2 garlic cloves, minced
1 tablespoon olive oil
1 carrot, sliced diagonally into 1/4-inch pieces
1 (10-ounce) package frozen broccoli
    florets, thawed
2/3 cup chicken broth
1 teaspoon dried basil
1/4 cup (1 ounce) grated Parmesan cheese
12 ounces angel hair pasta, cooked and drained

Heat 1 tablespoon olive oil in a skillet over medium heat. Add the chicken and garlic and cook for 3 to 4 minutes or until the chicken is cooked through, stirring frequently. Remove to a paper towel-lined plate, reserving the pan drippings.

Heat 1 tablespoon olive oil with the reserved pan drippings and add the carrot. Cook for 3 to 4 minutes, stirring frequently. Add the broccoli and cook for 2 minutes or until the broccoli is tender-crisp, stirring frequently. Add the broth, basil, cheese and chicken and mix well. Reduce the heat and simmer for 4 minutes, stirring occasionally. Place the pasta in a large serving bowl. Top with the chicken mixture. Serve immediately.

Serves 4

Chicken Spaghetti

1 (3- to 4-pound) chicken
8 ounces thin spaghetti
1/4 cup (1/2 stick) butter
1/4 cup all-purpose flour
1 cup cream
1 cup mayonnaise
1 cup sour cream
1 cup (4 ounces) grated Parmesan cheese

1/3 cup white wine
2 tablespoons lemon juice
1 teaspoon dry mustard
1 teaspoon salt
1/2 teaspoon garlic powder
1/2 teaspoon cayenne pepper
8 ounces portobello mushrooms, sliced
1/4 cup (1/2 stick) butter

The recipe was given to me by Mr. and Mrs. Bob Zincke. Bob was an Executive Vice-President at The Kroger Co. for forty years before his retirement in 2004. Bob and Janet are well known throughout Krogerland and now reside in The Woodlands, Texas.

Brenda Bruns
Kroger
Cincinnati, Ohio

Combine the chicken with water to cover in a stockpot. Bring to a boil and boil for about 1 hour or until the chicken is tender. Remove the chicken to a platter, reserving the stock. Let cool slightly and then chop the chicken, discarding the skin and bones.

Bring the reserved stock to a boil. Break the pasta into thirds and add to the stock. Cook using the package directions. Drain, reserving 1 cup of the stock.

Melt 1/4 cup butter in a saucepan and stir in the flour. Cook until bubbly, stirring constantly. Stir in the cream and reserved 1 cup stock and cook until thickened and of a sauce consistency, stirring frequently. Add the mayonnaise, sour cream, cheese, wine, lemon juice, dry mustard, salt, garlic powder and cayenne pepper and mix well.

Sauté the mushrooms in 1/4 cup butter in a skillet. Combine the mushrooms, chicken and pasta in a bowl and mix well. Stir in the sauce.

Spoon the chicken mixture into a 9x13-inch baking dish. Bake at 350 degrees for 30 to 40 minutes or until heated through. You may prepare in advance and store, covered, in the refrigerator. Bake just before serving.

Serves 8

Chicken Mushroom Alfredo Puff Pastries

Cynthia Payne
Kroger
Conroe, Texas

6 to 8 boneless skinless chicken breasts, chopped
16 ounces mushrooms, chopped
1 tablespoon crushed fresh garlic
1 tablespoon kosher salt
1 tablespoon white pepper
2 tablespoons olive oil
2 eggs
1 1/2 cups milk
2 puff sheets pastry
1 (15-ounce) jar Alfredo sauce
1/2 cup (2 ounces) shredded Parmesan cheese

Sauté the chicken, mushrooms, garlic, salt and white pepper in the olive oil in a skillet until the chicken is cooked through. Whisk the eggs and milk together in a bowl. Brush over the pastry sheets. Cut thirty rounds of pastry using a 2 1/2-inch biscuit cutter. Score the middle of each pastry round using a small bottle cap. Arrange the pastry rounds on a baking sheet.

Bake at 350 degrees until light golden brown; let cool. Heat the Alfredo sauce in a saucepan over medium heat, stirring occasionally. Stir in the cheese. Cut off the top of each pastry circle and remove the filling, forming a shell. Spoon the chicken mixture into the pastry shells and top with the Alfredo sauce. Replace the pastry tops.

Serves 10

Green Chile Chicken Casserole

4 large chicken breasts, cooked and cut into bite-size pieces
1/2 cup cooked chopped onion
1 (10-ounce) can cream of mushroom soup
1 to 1 1/4 cups sour cream
1 or 2 (4-ounce) cans chopped green chiles
3 or 4 flour tortillas
3 cups (12 ounces) shredded mild Cheddar cheese

Combine the chicken, onion, soup, sour cream and green chiles in a bowl and mix well. Spray a deep 10- to 12-inch baking dish with cooking spray. Place a tortilla in the bottom of the baking dish.

Layer one-third of the chicken mixture and one-third of the cheese in the prepared baking dish. Repeat the layering process two more times with the remaining ingredients. Bake at 350 degrees for 30 minutes. Let stand for 15 minutes before serving. You may substitute cream of chicken soup for the cream of mushroom soup, if desired.

Serves 4

This dish is great baked ahead and reheated. It can also be doubled.

Paul Scutt
Kroger
Cincinnati, Ohio

I have never shared this with anyone who didn't love it. This recipe is perfect for tailgating, parties, or any large crowd.

Cezanne Weis

Dillons

Hutchinson, Kansas

Mama's Jambalaya

5 to 6 cups converted rice
I pound boneless skinless chicken breasts, chopped
I pound large shrimp, peeled and deveined
I pound kielbasa, sliced
3 (14-ounce) cans French onion soup
3 (14-ounce) cans beef broth
3 (8-ounce) cans tomato sauce
8 ounces mushrooms, sliced
I bunch green onions, sliced
I cup (2 sticks) margarine, softened
4 or 5 bay leaves
Thyme to taste
Tony Chachere's Cajun seasoning to taste

Combine the rice, chicken, shrimp, kielbasa, soup, broth, tomato sauce, mushrooms, green onions and margarine in a large roasting pan and mix well. Add the bay leaves and sprinkle with thyme and Cajun seasoning.

Bake, covered, at 350 degrees for I hour. Remove the lid and bake for 30 to 60 minutes longer or until the liquid is absorbed and the rice is fully cooked. Discard the bay leaves. Serve with hot French bread.

Serves 10 to 12

Jambalaya Rice

2 tablespoons margarine
1 cup chopped celery
1 cup chopped onion
1 cup chopped mixed bell peppers
3 ounces smoked sausage, sliced
3/4 cup uncooked rice
2 bay leaves
1 teaspoon minced fresh garlic
1 teaspoon thyme
1 teaspoon cayenne pepper
1 teaspoon chicken bouillon powder
1 teaspoon salt
1/2 teaspoon black pepper
4 ounces chopped cooked chicken
2 tomatoes, finely chopped
1 cup chicken broth
1/4 cup chopped fresh parsley

Fritz Herfarth
Kroger
Pearland, Texas

Melt the margarine in a large saucepan. Add the celery, onion, bell peppers, sausage and rice and mix well. Stir in the bay leaves, garlic, thyme, cayenne pepper, bouillon, salt and black pepper.

Cook over medium-high heat for 8 minutes or until the onion is tender. Stir in the chicken, tomatoes, broth and parsley. Bring to a boil and boil for 2 minutes. Reduce the heat to medium and simmer, covered, for 25 minutes. Discard the bay leaves and ladle into soup bowls.

Serves 8 to 10

Katie Wolfram
King Soopers
Denver, Colorado

Crescent Chicken

3 ounces cream cheese, softened
2 tablespoons butter, melted
2 cups chopped cooked chicken
2 teaspoons milk
2 teaspoons chopped onion
1/4 teaspoon salt
1/4 teaspoon pepper
1 (8-count) can crescent rolls
1 tablespoon butter, melted
3/4 cup herb-seasoned stuffing mix
2 tablespoons butter
2 tablespoons all-purpose flour
1 cup milk
1/4 to 1/2 teaspoon chopped basil

Combine the cream cheese and 2 tablespoons melted butter in a bowl and mix until smooth. Stir in the chicken, 2 teaspoons milk, the onion, salt and pepper.

Unroll the crescent roll dough and separate into four rectangles. Press the perforations to seal. Spoon about 1/2 cup of the chicken mixture in the center of each rectangle. Pull the four corners together and twist to seal. Brush with 1 tablespoon melted butter and arrange in an 8x8-inch baking pan. Sprinkle with the stuffing mix. Bake at 350 degrees for 20 to 25 minutes or until brown.

Melt 2 tablespoons butter in a saucepan and then stir in the flour. Cook until bubbly, stirring constantly. Gradually add 1 cup milk, stirring constantly. Mix in the basil. Cook over medium heat until thickened, stirring constantly. Serve with the crescent chicken.

Serves 4

Mexican Chicken

3 cups (or more) crushed tortilla chips

1 roasted chicken

1 (15-ounce) can garbanzo beans, drained

1 (15-ounce) can kidney beans, drained

1 (15-ounce) can corn, drained

1 (8-ounce) can tomato sauce

1 cup salsa

1 cup chopped red onion

1/2 cup chopped fresh cilantro

1 tablespoon minced garlic

Salt and pepper to taste

8 ounces sharp Cheddar cheese, shredded

8 ounces Monterey Jack cheese, shredded

This is a wonderful dish for large crowds. People who are not fans of Mexican food even tend to like it.

Denise Presley
Kroger
Huber Heights, Ohio

Spread the tortilla chips over the bottom of a greased 9x13-inch baking dish. Chop the chicken, discarding the skin and bones. Combine the chicken, garbanzo beans, kidney beans, corn, tomato sauce, salsa, onion, cilantro, garlic, salt and pepper in a bowl and mix well. Spoon half over the tortilla chips.

Combine the Cheddar cheese and Monterey Jack cheese in a bowl. Sprinkle half over the chicken mixture. Top with the remaining chicken mixture. Bake at 350 degrees for 25 minutes. Sprinkle with the remaining cheese and bake for 5 minutes or until the cheese is light golden brown. Garnish with chopped tomatoes, sour cream and additional chopped fresh cilantro.

Serves 10

Dave Savage
King Soopers
Aurora, Colorado

Quick-and-Easy Chicken Potpie

2 cups chopped cooked chicken
1 (26-ounce) jar Alfredo sauce
2 cups frozen peas and carrots, thawed
2 (8-count) cans crescent rolls

Combine the chicken, Alfredo sauce and vegetables in a bowl and mix well. Spoon into a 9x9-inch baking pan sprayed with nonstick cooking spray. Lay the crescent roll dough flat and press the perforations to seal. Arrange over the chicken mixture, pinching the dough to the edge of the pan to seal. Remove and discard any excess dough.

Pierce holes in the dough using a wooden pick. Bake at 375 degrees for 15 to 20 minutes or until the mixture is heated through and the crust is light brown.

Serves 4 to 6

Maple-Roasted Chicken with Root Vegetables

1 1/2 pounds chicken thighs and drumsticks
Poultry seasoning to taste
Salt and pepper to taste
2 cups (1-inch) pieces carrots
2 cups (1-inch) pieces sweet potatoes
1 cup (1-inch) pieces turnip
1/2 red onion, cut into 1-inch pieces
3/4 cup Private Selection Maple Syrup
2 tablespoons olive oil
2 tablespoons chopped fresh thyme, or to taste

Lee Garcia
Smith's
Los Lunas,
*   New Mexico*

Arrange the chicken in an 8x13-inch baking dish. Sprinkle with the poultry seasoning, salt and pepper. Place the carrots, sweet potatoes, turnip and onion in the dish. Drizzle with the maple syrup and olive oil. Sprinkle with the thyme and toss to coat.

Bake, covered with foil, at 375 degrees for 30 minutes, stirring every 10 minutes. Remove the foil and cook for about 15 minutes or until the chicken is golden brown and a meat thermometer registers 165 degrees. Let stand, covered with foil, for 5 to 8 minutes before serving.

Serves 4

Baked Turkey and Sausage Spaghetti

When my wife Michelle (also a Kroger pharmacist) makes this dish, the entire pharmacy staff says it's the best spaghetti dish they have ever had. The rest of our family agrees as well.

Blake Cook
Kroger
Garner, North Carolina

1 pound ground turkey

8 ounces 30%-less-fat ground sausage or pork

3 garlic cloves, minced

1/2 cup chopped onion

1/2 cup chopped green bell pepper

2 cups canned diced tomatoes with onion and peppers

2 cups tomato sauce

1 cup water

1 tablespoon seasoned salt

1 1/2 teaspoons Italian seasoning

1 1/2 teaspoons sugar

1/2 teaspoon garlic salt

1/4 teaspoon pepper

3 cups (12 ounces) shredded Italian cheese blend or other cheese blend

8 ounces spinach or whole wheat spaghetti, cooked and drained

Brown the ground turkey and ground sausage in a skillet over medium heat, stirring until crumbly; drain. Add the garlic, onion and bell pepper and sauté for 7 minutes. Add the tomatoes, tomato sauce, water, seasoned salt, Italian seasoning, sugar, garlic salt and pepper and bring to a boil, stirring occasionally. Reduce the heat and stir in 1 cup of the cheese.

Simmer for 30 minutes, stirring occasionally. Combine the sauce, pasta and 1 cup of the remaining cheese in a large bowl and mix well. Spoon into a greased 9x13-inch baking dish. Bake at 350 degrees for 30 minutes. Sprinkle the remaining 1 cup cheese over the top and bake for 15 to 20 minutes or until the cheese is light brown.

Serves 10

Flounder Rolatini

1 (16-ounce) package frozen spinach, thawed and drained
8 ounces cream cheese, softened
1 egg
2 teaspoons Worcestershire sauce
1 teaspoon garlic powder
Salt and pepper to taste
1 (8-ounce) can artichoke hearts, drained and
   coarsely chopped
4 flounder fillets
1 (16-ounce) jar pasta sauce
Grated Parmesan cheese

Joseph Lozano
Kroger
Houston, Texas

Squeeze any excess moisture from the spinach. Beat the cream cheese in a mixing bowl until creamy. Add the egg, Worcestershire sauce, garlic powder, salt and pepper and mix until blended. Fold in the spinach and artichokes.

Season the fillets lightly with salt and pepper. Spread the cream cheese mixture over one side of each fillet. Roll to enclose the filling and arrange in an 8x8-inch baking dish or small loaf pan. Spoon 1 1/2 cups of the sauce over the rolls.

Bake at 350 degrees for 25 to 30 minutes or until the fillets flake easily. Top with the remaining pasta sauce and grated Parmesan cheese. Serve with your favorite salad.

Serves 4

Halibut Steak with Olive Salad

Sonya Jizmejian
Ralphs
Dana Point, California

Olive Salad

2/3 cup green olives, coarsely chopped
2/3 cup brine-cured olives,
    coarsely chopped
2/3 cup niçoise olives, coarsely chopped
1/3 cup finely chopped red bell pepper
1/3 cup finely chopped red onion
3 tablespoons fresh lemon juice
2 tablespoons chopped fresh mint
1 tablespoon finely chopped garlic
1 teaspoon grated lemon zest
1 tablespoon olive oil
Salt and pepper to taste

Halibut and Assembly

5 tablespoons olive oil
1/4 cup fresh lemon juice
1 tablespoon finely chopped garlic
2 teaspoons dried oregano
Salt and pepper to taste
3 (6-ounce) halibut steaks

To prepare the salad, combine the olives, bell pepper, onion, lemon juice, mint, garlic, lemon zest, olive oil, salt and pepper in a bowl and mix well. Let stand at room temperature for 20 minutes.

To prepare the halibut, whisk the olive oil, lemon juice, garlic, oregano, salt and pepper in a 9x13-inch baking dish until combined. Add the halibut and turn to coat. Marinate, covered, in the refrigerator for 30 minutes or up to 4 hours, turning occasionally; drain. Grill the halibut over medium-high heat for 4 minutes per side or until opaque in the center. Arrange each halibut steak on a serving plate and top with equal portions of the salad. Serve immediately.

Serves 3

Beer-Battered Salmon

2/3 cup all-purpose flour
1 teaspoon salt
1/2 teaspoon baking powder
Cayenne pepper to taste
1 egg, beaten
2 teaspoons vegetable oil
2/3 to 1 cup beer, at room temperature
2 pounds salmon fillets, skin removed and fillets
    cut into 1-inch strips
Vegetable oil for cooking

Linda Griffith
King Soopers
Pueblo, Colorado

Combine the flour, salt, baking powder and cayenne pepper in a shallow dish and mix well. Add the egg and 2 teaspoons oil and mix well. Stir in enough of the beer until the mixture is thin and runny.

Dip the salmon in the batter until coated. Cook in hot oil in a skillet over medium-high heat for 1 to 2 minutes or until golden brown. Drain on paper towels.

Serves 4

Judith Williamson

Kroger

Cumming, Georgia

Fresh Salmon and Vegetables

1 pound salmon, skin removed

Lemon pepper to taste

8 ounces mushrooms, sliced

1 green bell pepper, cut into 1-inch strips

1 red bell pepper, cut into 1-inch strips

1 yellow bell pepper, cut into 1-inch strips

1 sweet onion, sliced and separated into rings

3 to 4 tablespoons olive oil

1 (3-ounce) jar capers

1/2 cup white wine, such as chardonnay or pinot grigio

Lightly season both sides of the salmon with lemon pepper. Place in an airtight container and marinate in the refrigerator for up to 24 hours. Sauté the mushrooms, bell peppers and onion in the olive oil in a skillet over medium-high heat for 3 to 5 minutes or just until tender-crisp. Remove to a bowl using a slotted spoon, reserving the pan drippings.

Sear the salmon in the reserved pan drippings for about 2 minutes on each side; reduce the heat to medium. Spoon the vegetables over the salmon and sprinkle with the capers. Pour the wine over the top. Simmer, covered, for 5 to 8 minutes or until the fish just begins to flake. Increase the heat and cook, uncovered, until the liquid is reduced by half. Serve with hot cooked rice and a mixed green salad.

Serves 4

Salmon Loaf

1/2 cup sour cream
1/2 cup chopped cucumber
1/2 teaspoon lemon juice
1/4 to 1/2 teaspoon dill weed
1 cup cracker crumbs
1 egg

2/3 cup milk
2 tablespoons finely chopped onion
2 tablespoons margarine, melted
1 tablespoon lemon juice
1 (15-ounce) can salmon, drained and flaked

Clara Tisdale
Kroger RASC
Nashville, Tennessee

Combine the sour cream, cucumber, 1/2 teaspoon lemon juice and the dill weed in a bowl and mix well. Chill, covered, for 2 hours to 24 hours. Combine the cracker crumbs, egg, milk, onion, margarine, 1 tablespoon lemon juice and the salmon in a bowl and mix well. Shape into a loaf in a greased loaf pan. Bake at 350 degrees for 1 hour. Serve with the cucumber sauce.

Serves 8

Tangy Salmon Fillets

2 pounds salmon fillets
1 cup yellow mustard
1 cup lemon juice
1 cup Italian salad dressing

This recipe was created by a friend who likes to experiment with different food combinations. She hit on a winner with this one.

Patricia Porter
Kroger
Durham,
* North Carolina*

Place the salmon in a shallow 8x11-inch baking dish. Combine the mustard, lemon juice and dressing in a bowl and whisk until blended. Pour over the salmon.

Bake, covered with foil, at 350 degrees for 40 minutes. You may cut the sauce ingredients in half, if desired.

Serves 6

Suzanne
  Magni-Waddell

Kroger
Atlanta, Georgia

Pistachio-Encrusted Salmon

1/2 cup unsalted pistachios
1/3 cup fresh whole wheat bread crumbs
2 tablespoons grated fresh Parmesan cheese
1/4 teaspoon kosher salt
Freshly ground pepper to taste
1 to 2 tablespoons olive oil
4 (4-ounce) wild salmon fillets (sockeye or coho)
2 tablespoons Dijon mustard

Combine the pistachios, bread crumbs, cheese, salt and pepper in a food processor and process until the mixture resembles fine crumbs. Pour into a shallow bowl. Drizzle with the olive oil and toss with a fork until moistened.

Fold under any narrow ends of the fillets to create fillets of uniform thickness. Spread the Dijon mustard over one side of each fillet. Press each fillet mustard side down in the bread crumb mixture to coat. Arrange coated side up on a baking sheet sprayed with nonstick cooking spray. Sprinkle with any remaining bread crumb mixture.

Bake at 425 degrees for 10 to 12 minutes or until the coating is crisp and brown and the fillets flake easily. You may substitute wild cod or chicken for the salmon, if desired.

Serves 4

Pan-Seared Salmon with Cannellini Beans and Arugula

4 (6-ounce) salmon fillets

1 tablespoon olive oil

Sea salt and freshly ground pepper to taste

2 tablespoons olive oil

2 tablespoons olive oil

1 tablespoon unsalted butter

1/2 yellow onion, finely chopped

1 garlic clove, minced

1 (19-ounce) can cannellini beans, rinsed and drained

1 ounce arugula

1/4 cup red wine vinegar

1/4 red onion, thinly sliced

1 tablespoon drained capers

2 tablespoons shelled pistachios

Kendra Carey
Kroger
Houston, Texas

Drizzle both sides of the salmon with 1 tablespoon olive oil and season with salt and pepper. Heat 2 tablespoons olive oil in a skillet over medium heat. Cook the salmon in the hot oil for 8 to 10 minutes or until the salmon begins to flake, turning once. Remove to a platter and keep warm.

Heat 2 tablespoons olive oil and the butter in a saucepan. Add the yellow onion and garlic and cook until translucent, stirring frequently. Add the beans and cook for 5 minutes or until heated through, stirring occasionally. Season with salt and pepper.

Combine the arugula, vinegar, red onion and capers in a bowl. Toss to coat. Divide the bean mixture among four plates. Arrange the salmon over the beans and top with the arugula mixture. Sprinkle with the pistachios.

Serves 4

Fiesta Tilapia with Saffron Rice

1 (10-ounce) package saffron rice
4 ounces garlic, chopped
1 green bell pepper, chopped, or
    5 to 7 jalapeño chiles, seeded and minced
2 ounces Roma tomatoes, chopped
2 ounces red onion or Spanish onion,
    chopped (1 or 2 onions)
1 ounce cilantro, chopped
1 teaspoon salt
1 teaspoon pepper
1/4 cup olive oil
4 (7-ounce) tilapia fillets
2 tablespoons pepper, or to taste
1 tablespoon kosher salt
6 tablespoons fresh lime juice or lemon juice

Prepare the rice using the package directions. Combine the garlic, bell pepper, tomatoes, onion, cilantro, 1 teaspoon salt, 1 teaspoon pepper and the olive oil in a bowl and mix well.

Rinse the fillets with cold water and arrange in a medium baking pan; do not allow the fillets to touch. Sprinkle with 2 tablespoons pepper and 1 tablespoon kosher salt.

Spoon the tomato mixture over the fillets and drizzle with the lime juice. Bake, covered with foil, for 18 to 25 minutes or until the fillets flake easily. Serve with the rice. You may substitute a mixture of 10 ounces long grain rice and 3 strands of fresh saffron for the packaged saffron rice.

Serves 4

Tuna with Mango Salsa

1 mango, chopped
1 cup chopped fresh cilantro
1/2 jalapeño chile, sliced
1 garlic clove, minced
Juice of 2 limes
2 tablespoons soy sauce
Pinch of sugar
Salt and pepper to taste
4 tuna steaks
2 tablespoons olive oil
8 ounces somen noodles
1 avocado, sliced

Phil Webb
King Soopers
Loveland, Colorado

Combine the mango, cilantro, jalapeño chile, garlic, lime juice, soy sauce, sugar, salt and pepper in a bowl and mix well. Let stand for 30 minutes or longer to allow the flavors to blend. Season the steaks with salt and pepper.

Heat the olive oil in a grill pan or skillet over medium-high heat. Add the tuna and sear for 1 minute per side for rare or for 2 to 3 minutes per side for medium-rare to medium, topping the steaks with half the salsa after turning. Do not overcook.

Cook the noodles in boiling water to cover in a large saucepan for 2 to 3 minutes; drain. Spoon the noodles onto serving plates. Top with the tuna. Garnish with the avocado and serve with the remaining salsa.

Serves 4

Diane Thompson
Kroger
Houston, Texas

Cajun Crawfish Pie

3/4 cup (1 1/2 sticks) butter

2 onions, chopped

4 ribs celery, chopped

1 bell pepper, chopped

1/4 cup chopped green onions

1/4 cup parsley, chopped

1 pound crawfish tails

4 garlic cloves, chopped

1 teaspoon salt

1/2 teaspoon black pepper

1/2 teaspoon white pepper

1/2 teaspoon red pepper

1 egg, lightly beaten

1/4 cup tomato sauce

1 (10-ounce) can cream of celery soup

2/3 cup Italian-style bread crumbs

4 (9- or 10-inch) refrigerator pie pastries

Melt the butter in a 10-inch skillet and add the onions, celery, bell pepper and green onions. Sauté until the onions are tender. Add the parsley, crawfish tails, garlic, salt, black pepper, white pepper and red pepper. Cook over medium heat for 1 minute.

Whisk the egg and tomato sauce in a bowl until blended. Stir in the soup. Add to the crawfish mixture. and mix well. Cook over medium heat for 1 to 2 minutes. Add the bread crumbs and mix well.

Fit two of the pastries in each of two 9- or 10-inch pie plates. Pour the crawfish mixture evenly into the pastries. Top with the remaining pastries, crimping the edges and cutting vents or piercing holes with a fork. Bake at 350 degrees for 40 minutes or until the crusts are golden brown and the filling is bubbly.

Makes 2 pies, or 16 servings

Aztec Gold Stuffed Lobster

1 (20-ounce or larger) lobster tail, or
   2 (9- to 10-ounce) lobster tails
1 cup crab meat
1 cup small shrimp or chopped shrimp
1 cup chopped sea scallops
1/4 cup minced scallions
1/4 cup cilantro, minced
1/4 cup minced red bell pepper
1 teaspoon cayenne pepper
Zest of 1 lemon
Zest of 1 orange
1 cup mayonnaise
2 cups panko
1/2 cup pine nuts, toasted and finely chopped
All-purpose flour
2 eggs, beaten

Patrick Valentine
City Market
Durango, Colorado

Cut the 20-ounce lobster tail lengthwise into four long slices, or cut each of the 9- or 10-ounce lobster tails lengthwise into two slices. Pound the slices 1/4 inch thick between sheets of waxed paper with a meat mallet. Be careful not to tear the slices.

Combine the crab meat, shrimp, sea scallops, scallions, cilantro, bell pepper, cayenne pepper, lemon zest and orange zest in a bowl and mix well. Add the mayonnaise and stir to coat. Divide the crab meat mixture into four equal portions. Shape each portion into a ball.

Wrap one lobster slice around each crab meat ball and secure with wooden picks. Press down lightly to firm the ball and distribute the stuffing. Mix the bread crumbs and pine nuts in a shallow dish. Coat the stuffed lobster with flour and then dip in the eggs. Gently roll in the bread crumb mixture.

Arrange the stuffed lobster rolls in a lightly oiled baking dish and spray each with nonstick cooking spray. Bake at 375 degrees for 30 to 45 minutes or until golden brown. Serve with pineapple salsa, sautéed corn and peppers and warm flour tortillas.

Serves 4

This dish has been a family tradition for many years. The aroma of the cooking brings back great holiday memories.

David Cole

Kroger

Auburn, Indiana

Grandma Kate's Oyster Dressing

8 ounces oysters

12 ounces butter crackers, crushed

1 cup milk

2/3 to 1 cup turkey broth or chicken broth

1 cup (2 sticks) butter, melted

Combine the oysters with liquor, cracker crumbs, milk, broth and butter in a large bowl and mix well. Spoon the dressing into an 8x10-inch glass baking dish. Bake at 350 degrees for 45 to 50 minutes or until light brown.

This dish is best served with homemade turkey gravy spooned over the top.

Serves 8

Scalloped Oysters

2 cups cracker crumbs
1/2 cup (1 stick) butter, melted
1/2 teaspoon salt
1/8 teaspoon pepper
3 (8-ounce) containers whole oysters, drained
1/4 teaspoon Worcestershire sauce
1 cup milk

Shelly Larsen
King Soopers
Arvada, Colorado

Combine the crackers crumbs, butter, salt and pepper in a bowl and mix well. Sprinkle one-third of the crumb mixture over the bottom of a buttered 9x9-inch baking dish. Arrange half the oysters over the prepared layer. Repeat the layering process with one-half of the remaining crumb mixture and the remaining oysters. Combine the Worcestershire sauce and milk in a bowl and pour over the top. Sprinkle with the remaining crumb mixture. Bake at 350 degrees for 30 minutes.

Serves 8 to 10

Scallops Provençale

Don McGeorge
Kroger
Cincinnati, Ohio

1 1/2 pounds scallops
2 tablespoons fresh lemon juice
1/4 cup (1/2 stick) butter
1 or 2 garlic cloves, crushed
2 shallots, minced
3 tomatoes, peeled, seeded and chopped, or
    1 (14-ounce) can fire-roasted diced tomatoes
1/2 cup dry white wine
1/4 teaspoon salt
1/4 teaspoon white pepper
Finely chopped fresh parsley

Combine the scallops and lemon juice in a bowl and let stand for 15 minutes. Drain, discarding the liquid. Pat the scallops dry using a paper towel and cut into halves or quarters. Heat the butter in a large skillet over medium-high heat until foamy. Add the scallops in batches and cook for 2 minutes or until brown, turning once. Do not crowd the scallops in the skillet as they will stew rather than brown. Remove the scallops to a plate using a slotted spoon, reserving the pan drippings.

Reduce the heat and add the garlic, shallots, tomatoes, wine, salt and white pepper to the reserved pan drippings. Cook for 15 minutes, stirring occasionally. Add the scallops and cook, covered, for 5 to 6 minutes or until the scallops are cooked through, shaking the pan frequently to prevent sticking. Adjust the seasonings to taste and spoon into a serving bowl. Sprinkle with parsley and serve immediately.

Serves 3 or 4

Santa Fe Scallops with Cilantro Lime Beurre Blanc

Scallops

12 thick slices bacon

12 large sea scallops

2 teaspoons ground cumin

Salt and pepper to taste

Cilantro Lime Beurre Blanc and Assembly

3 tablespoons light fruity white wine

3 tablespoons white wine vinegar

1 tablespoon fresh lime juice

2 tablespoons finely chopped shallots

1/2 cup (1 stick) butter, chilled and
   cut into pieces

2 tablespoons cilantro, finely chopped

Salt and pepper to taste

1 jalapeño chile, seeded and finely chopped

1 Roma tomato, seeded and cut into
   1/4-inch pieces

1 avocado, cut into 1/4-inch pieces

To prepare the scallops, arrange the bacon in a baking pan lined with baking parchment. Bake at 400 degrees for 10 to 12 minutes or until the bacon is cooked through but still flexible. Drain on paper towels, reserving 3 tablespoons of the bacon drippings.

Sprinkle the scallops with the cumin, salt and pepper. Wrap each scallop with one slice of the bacon and secure with a wooden pick. Add the reserved bacon drippings to a 14-inch sauté pan and heat over medium-high heat. Add six of the scallops to the hot drippings and cook for 3 to 4 minutes per side or until the scallops are opaque and slightly firm. Remove to a heated platter. Repeat the process with the remaining scallops. You may grill the scallops and omit cooking in the bacon drippings, if desired.

To prepare the beurre blanc, combine the wine, vinegar, lime juice and shallots in a small saucepan. Cook over medium-high heat until the mixture is reduced by half. Add the butter one piece at a time and cook until incorporated. Stir in the cilantro, salt and pepper. Arrange three scallops on each of four serving plates and drizzle each with some of the beurre blanc. Top with the jalapeño chile, tomato and avocado. Serve with steamed vegetables, hot cooked basmati rice and Oregon riesling or pinot gris.

Serves 4

Oregon riesling and pinot gris are perfect light, fruity wines to use in the sauce and of course to serve with the dish.

Timothy Phillipott
Fred Meyer
Corvallis, Oregon

Camarónes con Chile Verde

1 to 2 pounds medium-large shrimp,
   peeled and deveined
1/4 cup extra-virgin olive oil
1/4 cup (1/2 stick) butter
2 large tomatoes, blanched, peeled, seeded
   and finely chopped
1 onion, chopped
2 large garlic cloves, chopped
8 to 10 green chiles, roasted, peeled, seeded
   and finely chopped
1/2 cup fresh lemon juice
1/4 teaspoon oregano
Dash of salt
2 cups white rice, steamed
1 lime, thinly sliced

This is a filling meal that is delicious. I recommend using medium to medium-hot green chiles. Brave souls can certainly use hotter chiles. I like to serve this with frozen margaritas or mojitos.

Deirdra Rivera
Smith's
Albuquerque,
* New Mexico*

Sauté the shrimp in the olive oil in a heavy nonstick skillet over medium heat for 3 to 5 minutes or just until pink. Remove the shrimp to a bowl using a slotted spoon, reserving the pan drippings. Add the butter, tomatoes, onion, garlic, green chiles, lemon juice, oregano and salt to the reserved pan drippings and mix well.

Heat for 8 to 10 minutes or just until the mixture begins to bubble. Add the shrimp and heat for 2 to 3 minutes. Serve over the rice and top with the lime slices. You may substitute spaghetti, linguini or angel hair pasta for the rice and garnish with tortilla chips, if desired.

Serves 6 to 8

Linguini with Shrimp, Asparagus and Bell Peppers

1 pound asparagus, cut into 3-inch pieces
1 red bell pepper, coarsely chopped
1 yellow bell pepper, coarsely chopped
1/2 cup olive oil
1/3 cup lemon juice
2 tablespoons yellow mustard
2 tablespoons dill weed, chopped
1 teaspoon salt
1/2 teaspoon pepper
1 pound shrimp, peeled and deveined
16 ounces linguini, cooked and drained

Stir-fry the asparagus in a nonstick skillet over medium-high heat until tender-crisp. Add the bell peppers and stir-fry until the bell peppers are slightly charred.

Combine the olive oil, lemon juice, mustard, dill weed, salt and pepper in a bowl and whisk until combined. Add the asparagus mixture and toss to coat. Add the shrimp to the skillet and stir-fry until the shrimp turn pink and start to curl. Add the shrimp and linguini to the asparagus mixture and stir gently to mix. You may substitute peeled cooked shrimp for the fresh shrimp and stir-fry until brown.

Serves 4

Tony Cetta
Smith's
Dayton, Nevada

Rebecca Kane
Kroger
Carmel, Indiana

Twice-Cooked Coconut Shrimp

Shrimp

1/2 cup all-purpose flour

1/2 cup cornstarch

1 tablespoon salt

1 1/2 teaspoons white pepper

1 cup ice water

2 tablespoons vegetable oil

2 cups shredded coconut

4 cups vegetable oil

1 1/2 pounds large shrimp,
   peeled and deveined

Orange Dijon Dipping Sauce

1/2 cup orange marmalade

1/4 cup Dijon mustard

1/4 cup honey

1/4 teaspoon hot red pepper sauce

To prepare the shrimp, mix the flour, cornstarch, salt and white pepper in a bowl and mix well. Add the ice water and 2 tablespoons oil and mix well. Spread the coconut in a shallow dish.

Heat 4 cups oil in a deep skillet to 350 degrees. Dip the shrimp in the batter one at a time and coat with the coconut. Fry the shrimp in the hot oil for about 4 minutes or until light brown. Arrange in a single layer in a baking pan and bake at 300 degrees for 5 minutes.

To prepare the sauce, combine the marmalade, Dijon mustard, honey and hot sauce in a bowl and mix well. Serve with the shrimp.

Makes 4 entrée servings, or 6 appetizer servings

Easy O's Seafood Delight

2 tablespoons butter
2 tablespoons olive oil
1 red bell pepper, chopped
1/2 cup sliced mushrooms
2 green onions, chopped
1 teaspoon chopped garlic
8 ounces large shrimp, peeled and deveined
8 ounces small to medium scallops
1 (6-ounce) can crab meat
1 (2-ounce) can anchovies, chopped
1 cup whipping cream
1 tablespoon Dijon mustard
Hot red pepper sauce to taste
1 tablespoon chopped fresh parsley
Hot cooked rice or pasta

Orlando Hall
King Soopers
Brighton, Colorado

Heat the butter and olive oil in a skillet until the butter melts. Add the bell pepper, mushrooms, green onions and garlic and sauté over medium-high heat for 3 to 5 minutes or until tender. Add the shrimp, scallops, crab meat and anchovies and mix well.

Cook for 5 to 6 minutes or until the shrimp turn pink and the scallops are tender; do not overcook. Stir in the cream, Dijon mustard and pepper sauce. Cook for 3 to 5 minutes and stir in the parsley. Serve over hot cooked rice or pasta with your favorite wine.

Serves 4

Leonora Smith
Kroger
Dickinson, Texas

Seafood Primavera

16 ounces linguini
1/2 cup olive oil
1 onion, chopped
4 green onions, minced
3 garlic cloves, minced
3 carrots, julienned
1 zucchini, julienned
1 small red bell pepper, julienned
1 small yellow bell pepper, julienned
3 ounces snow peas
1/3 cup sliced mushrooms
8 ounces peeled deveined medium shrimp

8 ounces medium scallops
2/3 cup clam juice
1/3 cup dry white wine or dry sherry
1 cup heavy cream
1/2 cup (2 ounces) grated fresh
   Parmesan cheese
2/3 cup flaked crab meat
2 tablespoons lemon juice
2 tablespoons chopped parsley
1/4 teaspoon dried basil
1/4 teaspoon dried oregano leaves, crushed
Freshly ground pepper to taste

Cook the pasta using the package directions. Drain and cover to keep warm. Heat the olive oil in a large skillet over medium heat. Add the onion, green onions and garlic and cook until the onion is tender. Stir in the carrots, zucchini, bell peppers, snow peas and mushrooms and mix well.

Reduce the heat to medium-low and simmer, covered, until the vegetables are tender, stirring occasionally. Remove the vegetables to a bowl with a slotted spoon, reserving the pan drippings. Add the shrimp and scallops to the reserved pan drippings and cook until the scallops are opaque and the shrimp turn pink. Remove the shrimp mixture to a bowl, reserving the pan drippings.

Add the clam juice and wine to the reserved pan drippings and bring to a boil. Stir in the cream and cheese. Reduce the heat to low and simmer for 3 minutes or until slightly thickened, stirring constantly. Return the vegetables and shrimp mixture to the skillet and mix well. Cook until heated through, stirring occasionally. Stir in the lemon juice, parsley, basil, oregano and pepper. Spoon over the hot pasta in a large bowl and toss gently to coat. Serve immediately.

Serves 6 to 8

Seafood Stew

1 cup sliced mushrooms

1 cup chopped onion

1 cup chopped celery

1 cup chopped carrots

3 large garlic cloves, minced

4 teaspoons olive oil

1 bay leaf

1 (16-ounce) can vegetable juice cocktail or tomato juice

1 (10-ounce) can chicken broth

1 (14-ounce) can chopped Italian-style tomatoes

1 cup water

8 ounces halibut fillets or cod fillets

8 ounces scallops

8 ounces prawns

1 (10-ounce) can whole baby clams

1 (10-ounce) can clam juice

1 cup dry white wine or sherry

Chopped fresh basil to taste

Salt and pepper to taste

This recipe was put together by my mother-in-law Leona Baker, the queen of comfort food. You can add or omit whatever sounds good to you. This is a great recipe for large gatherings.

Dawn Baker

QFC

Bellevue, Washington

Sauté the mushrooms, onion, celery, carrots and garlic in the olive oil in a stockpot over medium heat until tender. Add the bay leaf, vegetable juice cocktail, broth, tomatoes and water and bring to a boil. Reduce the heat.

Simmer for 15 minutes, stirring occasionally. Add the halibut, scallops, prawns and clams and simmer for 10 minutes or until the halibut flakes easily. Add the clam juice, wine, basil, salt and pepper and cook until heated through. Discard the bay leaf. Ladle into soup bowls and serve with French bread. Add mussels, oysters and/or shrimp for variety.

Serves 8

Vegetables & Side Dishes

Vegetables & Side Dishes

Louis Buennagel
QFC
Bellevue, Washington

Roasted Asparagus with Sesame Vinaigrette

2 pounds asparagus
2 teaspoons sesame oil
2 teaspoons olive oil
1/2 teaspoon salt
1 tablespoon soy sauce
2 tablespoons rice vinegar
1 1/2 tablespoons sesame oil
1 teaspoon sugar
Black sesame seeds

Snap off the woody ends of the asparagus and arrange the spears in a medium rectangular baking dish. Mix 2 teaspoons sesame oil, the olive oil and salt in a small bowl. Pour over the asparagus, turning the spears to coat. Bake at 400 degrees for 10 to 12 minutes. Combine the soy sauce, rice vinegar, 1 1/2 tablespoons sesame oil and the sugar in a jar with a tight-fitting lid and seal tightly. Shake to mix. Pour over the hot asparagus. Sprinkle with black sesame seeds. If you are unable to find black sesame seeds, you may use toasted white sesame seeds.

Serves 6 to 8

Aunt Lill's Baked Beans from Scratch

2 cups dried navy beans, sorted and rinsed
1 onion, chopped
1/4 cup (or more) packed brown sugar
2 tablespoons molasses
2 tablespoons ketchup
1/2 teaspoon dry mustard
1 1/2 teaspoons salt
8 ounces bacon, crisp-cooked and crumbled

Cover the beans with water in a saucepan. Boil for 1 1/2 hours, adding boiling water as needed to keep the beans covered. Stir in the onion, brown sugar, molasses, ketchup, dry mustard and salt. Add additional water if needed to cover the beans. Simmer, covered, for 5 hours. Stir in the bacon. Simmer, covered, for 1 hour longer.

Serves 15

This dish is best when made one to two days ahead. It freezes beautifully and may be doubled. This is a great dish to serve at outdoor summer gatherings. It can also be made in a slow cooker. Combine all the ingredients and water to cover in the slow cooker and cook on Low for 8 to 10 hours.

Nancy Johnson
King Soopers
Greenwood Village,
  Colorado

215

This dish is a favorite holiday side dish served with Standing Rib Roast.

Tao Irtz

Kroger

Lexington, Kentucky

Herb Lima Beans

1/2 cup chopped onion

1/4 cup chopped celery

3 tablespoons butter

2 tablespoons all-purpose flour

1 1/2 cups milk

1/4 cup (1 ounce) shredded Cheddar cheese

2 teaspoons Worcestershire sauce

1 teaspoon dried basil

1 teaspoon dried marjoram

1/2 to 1 teaspoon dried rosemary

1/2 to 1 teaspoon dried thyme

1/4 teaspoon dry mustard

Dash of cayenne pepper

Dash of salt (optional)

2 (6-ounce) packages frozen Fordhook lima beans

Sauté the onion and celery in the butter in a saucepan until tender-crisp. Add the flour and milk gradually, stirring constantly until combined. Stir in the cheese, Worcestershire sauce, basil, marjoram, rosemary, thyme, dry mustard, cayenne pepper and salt.

Prepare the lima beans according to the package directions; drain. Fold into the sauce.

Serves 8 to 10

Broccoli Casserole

2 (1-pound) packages frozen chopped broccoli,
   thawed and drained
1 tablespoon all-purpose flour
16 ounces pasteurized processed cheese, cut into cubes
16 ounces cottage cheese
2 eggs, beaten
2 tablespoons butter

Toss the broccoli with the flour in a bowl. Stir in processed cheese and cottage cheese. Stir in the eggs. Spoon into a 3-quart or 9x13-inch baking dish and dot with the butter. Bake at 350 degrees for 55 to 65 minutes until the top is light golden brown. The casserole will thicken slightly as it cools. This casserole may be assembled 1 to 2 days ahead. Chill, covered, until ready to bake.

Serves 8

Emily Anderson
Kroger
Indianapolis, Indiana

Crispy Cabbage

2 slices bacon, chopped
1 small onion, chopped
1 teaspoon minced garlic
1 (16-ounce) package cole slaw mix
2 teaspoons balsamic vinegar, or to taste
1/2 teaspoon salt, or to taste
1/4 teaspoon pepper, or to taste

Cook the bacon in a skillet until brown and crisp. Add the onion and garlic and cook over medium heat until the onion is tender. Add the cole slaw mix, vinegar, salt and pepper. Cook until the cabbage is heated through and tender-crisp, stirring often. Serve warm immediately or chill, covered, until serving time.

Serves 6 to 8

Buck Boulden
Kroger
Hot Springs, Arkansas

Cajun Corn

1 (14-ounce) package frozen white Shoe Peg corn, thawed
1 (15-ounce) can yellow corn, drained
1 tablespoon garlic powder
1/2 to 1 (4-ounce) can chopped jalapeño chiles, drained
8 ounces cream cheese, chopped and softened

Combine the shoe peg corn, yellow corn, garlic powder, jalapeño chiles and cream cheese in a 9×9-inch baking dish. Bake at 375 degrees for 10 minutes or until the cream cheese gets very soft and begins to melt. Remove from the oven and stir until well blended. Bake for an additional 10 to 15 minutes or until the edges are light brown.

Serves 6

Melinda Creppel
Kroger RASC
Nashville, Tennessee

Southwest's Best Corn Pudding

1/3 cup sugar
3 tablespoons all-purpose flour
2 teaspoons baking powder
1 1/2 to 2 teaspoons salt
1 teaspoon cumin
2 cups whipping cream
1/2 cup (1 stick) butter, melted
6 extra-large eggs, beaten
6 cups drained canned Shoe Peg corn

Mix the sugar, flour, baking powder, salt and cumin together. Combine the cream and butter in a bowl and stir until blended. Stir in the eggs. Add the sugar mixture gradually, stirring constantly until combined. Stir in the corn. Pour into a buttered 9x13-inch baking dish. Bake at 350 degrees for 45 to 50 minutes or until the center is firm and the top is golden brown. Let stand for 15 minutes before serving.

Serves 8 to 10

This is the only recipe that I have ever prepared that I have never messed up and that is always a hit with my guests.

Kim Storch
Kroger
Cypress, Texas

Ronda Benning
Dillons
Topeka, Kansas

Greens

16 ounces collard greens
8 ounces mustard greens
8 ounces turnip greens
6 to 8 cups water
2 smoked turkey legs or ham hocks
1/2 cup chopped onion
1/2 teaspoon salt, or to taste
1/4 teaspoon pepper, or to taste

Rinse the collard greens, mustard greens and turnip greens in cold water repeatedly until free of grit. Remove the stems and center stalk of the leaves and discard. Place the leafy parts in a large saucepan or stockpot and cover with water. Add the turkey, onion, salt and pepper. Bring the liquid to a boil and boil for 15 minutes. Reduce the heat to a simmer and simmer for 2 hours. All collard greens may be used instead of the mixture of greens, if preferred.

Serves 6

This dish is such a family favorite that we usually triple the recipe.

Stephen Redman
Kroger
Kettering, Ohio

Balsamic Onion

1 large onion, thinly sliced
1 tablespoon canola oil
1 1/2 tablespoons sugar
1 teaspoon kosher salt
1/2 teaspoon pepper
2 tablespoons balsamic vinegar

Combine the onion, canola oil, sugar, salt and pepper in a bowl and toss to coat. Cook in a large skillet for 8 to 10 minutes or until deep golden brown. Remove to a bowl and add the vinegar. Toss to coat. This dish may be made in advance.

Serves 4

Crispy Barbecue Onions

4 cups all-purpose flour
3 tablespoons paprika
2 tablespoons kosher salt
1 tablespoon pepper
1 tablespoon chili powder
1 tablespoon cumin
1 tablespoon granulated sugar
1 tablespoon brown sugar
2 large Vidalia onions, sliced into $1/8$-inch-thick rings
2 cups milk
Vegetable oil for frying

David Fero
Kroger
Sugarland, Texas

Combine the flour, paprika, salt, pepper, chili powder, cumin, granulated sugar and brown sugar in a large sealable plastic bag. Mix well. Add the onions to the flour mixture, seal the bag and shake to coat. Dip the onions in the milk and then immediately back to the flour mixture. Seal the bag and shake to coat. Cook in 350-degree oil in a large deep skillet or deep fryer for 3 minutes or until crisp and golden brown; drain.

Serves 6 to 8

Chantilly Potatoes

2 pounds russet potatoes
16 ounces shredded cheddar cheese
2 cups sour cream
1 cup julienned ham

Peel the potatoes and cut them into quarters or bite-sized pieces. Place the potatoes in a saucepan or stockpot and cover with water. Bring the water to a boil and then boil for 5 to 7 minutes or just until the potatoes are tender; drain. Mix the cheese and sour cream in a bowl. Fold in the potatoes and ham. Spoon into a 2-quart baking dish sprayed with nonstick cooking spray. Bake at 350 degrees for 15 minutes or until heated through and bubbly.

Serves 6 to 8

Bill Eger
Kroger
Durham,
   North Carolina

Grilled Potatoes

8 potatoes, sliced
1 small white onion, sliced
1 small yellow onion, sliced
1/4 large red onion, sliced
1 green bell pepper, sliced
4 jalapeño chiles, sliced, or to taste
1 teaspoon celery salt
1 teaspoon seasoned salt
1/2 cup (1 stick) butter, sliced
16 ounces shredded cheddar cheese

Debbie Routh
Smith's
Rock Springs, Wyoming

Combine the potatoes, white onion, yellow onion, red onion, bell pepper and jalapeño chiles in a bowl. Toss to combine. Season with the celery salt and seasoned salt. Pour onto half of a large piece of heavy duty foil. Layer the butter and cheese on top. Fold the foil over and seal the edges. Place on a grill rack over medium hot coals and cook for 50 to 60 minutes or until the potatoes are tender.

Serves 8 to 10

Do-Ahead Mashed Potatoes

This dish has made our Thanksgiving dinners much easier to prepare with no last minute boiling and mashing. I can prepare this dish the weekend prior to the holiday. I always have to double the recipe so that the children can take home leftovers.

Charlotte Warner
Fred Meyer
Portland, Oregon

6 large baking potatoes
$^1/_2$ cup (1 stick) butter, softened
6 ounces cream cheese, softened
Pinch of baking soda
$^1/_2$ teaspoon celery salt
$^1/_8$ teaspoon pepper
$^1/_3$ to $^1/_2$ cup cream (optional)
2 to 3 tablespoons butter
1 teaspoon dried parsley

Bake the potatoes on a baking pan at 400 degrees for 75 minutes or until tender. Place $^1/_2$ cup butter and the cream cheese in a mixing bowl. Carefully slice the hot potatoes into halves and scoop the centers into the bowl. Discard the skins. Add the baking soda, celery salt and pepper. Beat until blended and smooth. If too thick, add the cream gradually, mixing constantly until of the desired consistency. Spoon into a buttered baking dish. Dot with the 2 to 3 tablespoons butter and sprinkle with the parsley. Chill, covered, for 1 to 5 days. Bake at 350 degrees for 30 to 45 minutes.

Serves 6

Romano Potatoes

2 pounds red potatoes
1/4 to 1/2 cup unsalted butter
2 teaspoons minced garlic
1/2 cup milk
3 tablespoons grated Romano cheese
1/2 cup (2 ounces) shredded Monterey Jack cheese
1/2 cup (2 ounces) shredded Cheddar cheese
2 tablespoons chopped green onions
2 teaspoons salt
1 teaspoon black pepper
1/2 teaspoon white pepper
1 tablespoon grated Romano cheese
1 teaspoon paprika

Place the potatoes in a large saucepan or stockpot and cover with cold water. Bring to a boil. Boil for 25 to 30 minutes or just until tender. Chill, covered, for 8 to 10 hours. Drain and then slice the potatoes into quarters. Melt the butter with the garlic in a saucepan. Combine the garlic butter, potatoes, milk, 3 tablespoons Romano cheese, the Monterey Jack cheese and green onions in a large bowl. Season with the salt, black pepper and white pepper. Mix with your hands, squeezing gently until combined. Do not overmix; some large chunks should remain. Spoon into a lightly greased baking dish. Sprinkle with 1 tablespoon Romano cheese and the paprika. Bake at 350 degrees for 35 minutes or until the top is golden brown.

Serves 8

Mary Bowman
Kroger
Sugarland, Texas

Pierogi

For anyone of Polish heritage, this is a dish that most of our grandmothers made. I spent many hours, starting at a very young age, in both of my grandmothers' kitchens making pierogi. Making pierogi is what Polish grandmothers do with their granddaughters while they tell them family stories.

Mary Beth Bowen
Smith's
Albuquerque,
  New Mexico

4 cups all-purpose flour
1 teaspoon salt
1 egg, lightly beaten
1 cup lukewarm water, or as needed
1 cup prepared cheese mashed potatoes
2 tablespoons melted butter, plus more for sautéing
3 quarts water
1/4 cup chopped onion
1/4 cup crumbled crisp-cooked bacon

Sift flour and salt together into a bowl. Stir in the egg. Add the water gradually, kneading constantly until the dough is smooth, elastic and does not stick to your hands. Roll the dough to 1/8-inch-thick and cut into circles with a 2-inch round cookie cutter or biscuit cutter. Turn each round of dough over. Place 1 teaspoon of the mashed potatoes in the center of each round of dough. Fold half of the dough over making a half circle pocket. Pinch and seal the edges.

Bring 3 quarts water to a boil in a large saucepan. Drop the dumplings six to eight at a time carefully into the water and cook for 2 minutes or until the dumplings rise to the surface, stirring only if the dumplings stick to the bottom of the saucepan. Remove with a slotted spoon and place in a glass baking dish. Brush the tops of the dumplings with melted butter. Repeat with the remaining dumplings. The dumplings may be layered in the baking dish. Melt butter in a skillet. Add the onion, bacon and dumplings. Cook until the dumplings are golden brown on each side.

You may use your favorite cheese in the prepared mashed potatoes. Polish pierogi are most commonly made using farmer's cheese.

Makes 36

Mashed Potato Pancakes

2 cups cold prepared mashed potatoes
3 tablespoons all-purpose flour
1 egg, lightly beaten
1/2 small white onion, chopped
2 teaspoons salt, or to taste
1/2 teaspoon pepper
1/2 cup milk
Sour cream

Mix the mashed potatoes, flour and egg in a bowl. Stir in the onion, salt and pepper. Add the milk gradually, stirring constantly until of a batter consistency. The batter will be lumpy. Pour 3 to 4 tablespoons of batter per pancake onto a hot skillet sprayed with nonstick cooking spray. Cook for 5 minutes or until the center is firm and the edge is golden brown, flipping once. Serve three pancakes per serving with a dollop of sour cream. Season with additional salt to taste.

Serves 4

My Father was the cook in our family. He'd sit in a chair in the corner of the kitchen peeling potatoes into a brown paper bag. We all loved mashed potatoes, but we really loved potato pancakes made from leftover mashed potatoes. They were part of "breakfast" for dinner. Dad served them with sausages and scrambled eggs.

Karen Pierce
Fred Meyer
Issaquah, Washington

Squash Casserole

Judy Polach
Kroger
Houston, Texas

Salt to taste
2 pounds yellow squash, sliced
1 onion, finely chopped
1 carrot, grated
1 (10-ounce) can cream of chicken soup
1 cup sour cream
1 (2-ounce) jar diced pimento
1 (8-ounce) package cornbread stuffing mix
$1/2$ cup (1 stick) butter or margarine, melted
1 teaspoon salt
$1 1/2$ teaspoon white pepper
$1/4$ cup ($1/2$ stick) butter, melted

Bring enough lightly salted water to cover the squash to a boil. Add the squash and boil for 7 to 10 minutes; drain. Combine the squash, onion, carrot, soup, sour cream, pimento and half of the stuffing mix in a large bowl. Mix well. Stir in $1/2$ cup butter, 1 teaspoon salt and the pepper. Spoon into a large baking dish or two small baking dishes. Mix the remaining stuffing mix and $1/4$ cup butter in a bowl. Spread on top of the casserole. Bake at 350 degrees for 30 to 40 minutes. This dish freezes well.

Serves 8 to 10

Spinach Dumplings

1 (16-ounce) package frozen spinach, thawed
2 tablespoons butter
1 cup (4 ounces) shredded Swiss cheese
1 cup (4 ounces) shredded provolone cheese
1 cup (4 ounces) shredded mozzarella cheese
1 cup all-purpose flour
8 cups water
1/2 cup (2 ounces) grated Parmesan cheese

Squeeze any excess moisture from the spinach. Sauté the spinach in the butter for 3 to 5 minutes. Add the Swiss cheese, provolone cheese and mozzarella cheese one at a time, stirring well after each addition just until melted. Remove from the heat. Shape the mixture into six balls and roll each in the flour, coating well. Bring the water to a rolling boil. Drop the dumplings gently into the water one or two at a time. Cook for 1 minute or until the dumplings begin to float to the surface. Remove with a slotted spoon to a buttered baking dish. Repeat with the remaining dumplings. Sprinkle with the Parmesan cheese. Bake at 350 degrees for 20 minutes.

Serves 6

This is a Greek recipe that my mother made for holiday dinners. I have loved them ever since.

Nicole Floyd
Scott's
Bluffton, Indiana

Pacific Island Sweet Potatoes with Coconut Sauce

1 1/2 pounds sweet potatoes or yams
6 cups water
6 to 8 tablespoons unsalted butter
1/4 cup packed light brown sugar
1/4 cup unsweetened coconut milk
1 cup miniature marshmallows

Combine the sweet potatoes with the water in a 3 quart saucepan. Bring the water to a boil and boil until a fork inserted into the center of the sweet potatoes comes out easily. Drain and let stand for 5 minutes. Peel the warm sweet potatoes and slice them into 1/4-inch-thick slices. Arrange them in a baking dish; set aside.

Melt the butter in a skillet. Add the brown sugar and cook over medium heat for 5 to 7 minutes or until blended, stirring constantly. Add the coconut milk and cook until heated through and the sauce is a light caramel color, stirring constantly. Pour over the sweet potatoes. Sprinkle with the marshmallows. Bake at 350 degrees for 8 to 10 minutes or until the marshmallows are light brown. Let stand for 5 minutes. Serve warm.

Serves 4

My beloved mother taught me this Pacific Island recipe and I am willing to share it with you. It is great for the holidays, special occasions, impressing your friends or just a great side dish anytime. I hope you enjoy.

Jenillee Ngiralulk
Kroger
Knoxville, Tennessee

Mashed Sweet Potatoes with Goat Cheese

3 pounds sweet potatoes, peeled and roughly chopped

8 ounces goat cheese, softened

6 tablespoons (3/4 stick) butter

1/2 cup sour cream

3 green onions, chopped

1 teaspoon salt, or to taste

1/2 teaspoon pepper, or to taste

1/3 cup cream or milk (optional)

Combine the sweet potatoes with water to cover in a large saucepan. Bring to a boil over high heat. Reduce the heat and simmer for 15 to 20 minutes or until the sweet potatoes are tender. Remove from the heat. Drain and place the sweet potatoes back in the saucepan or in a mixing bowl. Add the goat cheese, butter, sour cream and green onions. Mash with a potato masher or beat with a hand mixer until of the desired consistency. Season with the salt and pepper. Add the cream gradually, beating constantly until of the desired consistency.

Serves 8

This is the first savory sweet potato dish my wife ever tasted. To this day, this is her favorite way to eat sweet potatoes.

Troy Deutschendorf
Dillons
Newton, Kansas

Baked Sweet Potato Casserole

Slow-roasted sweet potatoes are the important component in this recipe. They impart a very sweet flavor. It's worth the extra effort, and this recipe is a nice change from the marshmallow-topped casserole.

James McArthur
Michigan Dairy
Livonia, Michigan

3 to 4 pounds large sweet potatoes
1/4 cup (1/2 stick) salted butter, softened
1/3 cup packed light brown sugar
1/4 cup maple syrup
2 tablespoons frozen orange juice concentrate, thawed
1 tablespoon finely grated orange zest
1/2 teaspoon cinnamon
1 teaspoon onion powder
1/4 teaspoon garlic powder
1/4 teaspoon pepper
1/4 teaspoon nutmeg
2 cups chunky applesauce
Butter

Prick the sweet potatoes with a fork a few times. Wrap each sweet potato tightly with foil and place on a baking sheet. Bake at 275 degrees for 3 hours or until very tender when gently squeezed. Let stand until cool enough to handle. Remove and discard the skins. Combine the sweet potatoes, 1/4 cup butter, the brown sugar, maple syrup, orange juice concentrate, orange zest, cinnamon, onion powder, garlic powder, pepper and nutmeg in a mixing bowl. Beat until blended. Fold in the applesauce. Spoon into a 9x13-inch baking dish. Dot with additional butter. Bake at 350 degrees for 30 to 45 minutes or until golden brown and bubbly.

Serves 6 to 8

Zucchini Boats

3 zucchini
1 tablespoon olive oil
3 cups (8 ounces) mushrooms, chopped
1 tablespoon butter or olive oil
1 tablespoon butter
1 tablespoon all-purpose flour
Dash of salt
Dash of white pepper
2/3 cup milk
1 tablespoon grated Parmesan cheese
1/2 cup (2 ounces) grated Parmesan cheese or
　　shredded mozzarella cheese

Becky Casey
Fred Meyer
Marysville, Washington

Slice the zucchini into halves lengthwise. Scrape out the center of five of the halves with a spoon, leaving a shell; discard the pulp. Rub the outside of the shells with the olive oil and place on a baking sheet. Bake at 350 degrees for 20 minutes. Chop the reserved zucchini half. Sauté the chopped zucchini and the mushrooms in 1 tablespoon butter in a skillet until tender; set aside.

Melt 1 tablespoon butter in a saucepan over medium-low heat. Add the flour and cook until blended, stirring constantly. Season with salt and pepper. Add the milk and 1 tablespoon cheese gradually, stirring constantly until blended. Cook until slightly thickened. Keep warm.

Spoon the mushroom mixture into the zucchini shells. Sprinkle evenly with 1/2 cup cheese. Broil for 40 seconds. Spoon 1 tablespoon of the warm sauce on top of each zucchini boat.

Serves 5

Cappy Luce
Kroger
Houston, Texas

Vegetable Burritos

Avocado Dressing

1 large or 2 small avocados
2 small tomatillos, minced
1 small jalapeño chile, seeded and minced
1 teaspoon minced onion
1 garlic clove, mashed (optional)
1 cup sour cream
2 tablespoons lemon juice

Burritos

1 onion, thinly sliced
1 garlic clove, minced
1/2 green bell pepper, cut into strips
1 zucchini, cut into thin strips
1 carrot, thinly sliced
1 tomato, chopped
1 sweet potato, thinly sliced
1 1/2 tablespoons fresh cilantro, finely chopped
1/4 teaspoon black pepper
1/4 teaspoon red pepper
1/8 teaspoon cumin
2 tablespoons olive oil
1 (14-ounce) can black beans, drained and rinsed
1 jalapeño chile, minced
6 to 8 (8-inch) flour tortillas

To prepare the dressing, mash the avocado in a bowl. Stir in the tomatillos, jalapeño chile, onion, garlic, sour cream and lemon juice. Or, roughly chop all of the ingredients and process in a food processor or blender until blended. Chill, covered, until serving time. Make in advance so that flavors meld.

To prepare the burritos, combine the onion, garlic, bell pepper, zucchini, carrot, tomato and sweet potato. Sauté the vegetables with the cilantro, black pepper, red pepper and cumin in the olive oil in a large skillet until the vegetables are tender crisp. Fold in the beans and cook until the beans are heated through, stirring occasionally. Spoon onto the tortillas and roll to enclose the filling, tucking the ends inside. Slice into halves and serve with the dressing.

Serves 6 to 8

Hominy Casserole

2 (15-ounce) cans white hominy, drained
1 (4-ounce) can chopped green chiles
1 1/2 cups sour cream
1 1/2 cups (6 ounces) shredded Monterey Jack cheese
1/4 cup minced onion
Salt and pepper to taste
1/4 cup dry bread crumbs
1/4 cup (1/2 stick) butter
1 (4-ounce) can whole green chiles, sliced into strips

Katherine Clingman
King Soopers
Highlands Ranch,
Colorado

Mix the hominy, chopped green chiles, sour cream, cheese and onion in a bowl. Season with salt and pepper. Spoon into a lightly greased 9x9-inch baking dish. Sprinkle with the bread crumbs and dot with the butter. Arrange the strips of green chiles on top. Bake at 350 degrees for 30 to 45 minutes.

Serves 4 to 6

Old-Fashioned Dressing

Maradith Dondlinger
Kroger
Monticello, Indiana

3 1/2 cups bread crumbs
3 1/2 cups corn bread crumbs
1 cup chopped onion
2 cups chopped celery
2 eggs, lightly beaten
1 1/3 cups milk
1 1/4 cups turkey broth
2/3 cup (1 1/2 sticks) margarine, melted
2 teaspoons salt
1 1/2 teaspoons sage
1/2 teaspoon pepper
1/2 teaspoon poultry seasoning

Combine the bread crumbs, corn bread crumbs, onion and celery in a bowl and mix well. Stir in the eggs, milk, broth and margarine. Add the salt, sage, pepper and poultry seasoning and mix well. Spoon into a greased 9x12-inch baking dish. Bake at 325 degrees for 1 hour.

Serves 12

Burgundy Risotto

1 beet, peeled and chopped
1/2 cup chopped red onion
1 teaspoon minced garlic
1 teaspoon olive oil
1 cup burgundy
1 cup chicken broth
1 cup jasmine rice
3/4 cup heavy whipping cream
1/2 cup (2 ounces) grated Parmesan cheese
Salt and pepper to taste

Sauté the beet, onion and garlic in the olive oil in a 2-quart saucepan until the beet and onion are tender. Add the wine and broth. Bring to a boil and stir in the rice. Simmer for 15 to 20 minutes or until the liquid is absorbed, stirring frequently. Spread the rice on a baking sheet. Chill, covered, for 30 minutes or until cool.

Combine the cooked rice and the cream in a saucepan. Bring to a boil. Boil for 1 minute, stirring gently. Reduce the heat and then fold in the cheese. Cook for 1 minute. Season with salt and pepper. Serve immediately.

Serves 6

This recipe was discovered by accident when I added diced beets instead of red onions. The result is a tasty and colorful side dish.

Christopher Johnson
Kroger
Lebanon, Ohio

This is a great side dish that I serve when my vegetarian daughter and son-in-law come to dinner. It has enough protein to serve to her as an entrée, and it pairs well as a side dish with the meat I am serving for the rest of us.

Linda Langlitz
Kroger
Cincinnati, Ohio

Festive Pasta

1 (13-ounce) package whole wheat penne
1 green bell pepper, chopped
1 red bell pepper, chopped
2 garlic cloves, minced
2 tablespoons olive oil
1 (16-ounce) can red kidney beans, rinsed and drained
1 teaspoon dried basil
1 teaspoon dried chives
1 teaspoon salt
1/4 teaspoon pepper
1/4 cup (1 ounce) grated Parmesan cheese
1 1/2 cups (3 ounces) fresh spinach, torn

Prepare the pasta according to the package directions. Drain and set aside. Sauté the bell peppers and garlic in the olive oil in a large skillet. Stir in the beans and cooked pasta. Add the basil, chives, salt and pepper and mix well. Stir in the cheese and remove from the heat. Add the spinach and toss to coat.

Serves 8

Angel Hair with Tomatoes, Basil and Garlic

16 ounces angel hair pasta
1 tablespoon minced garlic
1/4 cup vegetable oil
5 cups chopped tomatoes
1/2 teaspoon dried basil
Salt and pepper to taste
3/4 cup chicken broth
5 tablespoons grated Parmesan cheese

Prepare the pasta according to the package directions. Drain and set aside. Sauté the garlic in the oil for 1 minute. Add the tomatoes and basil. Season with salt and pepper. Sauté for 3 minutes. Add the pasta and toss to coat. Add the broth and mix well. Add the cheese and toss to coat. Serve immediately. This dish may be served as an entrée with garlic bread.

Serves 6 to 8

Laurine Rogers
King Soopers
Colorado Springs,
Colorado

Macaroni and Cheese

We took several ideas
and ingredients from
our favorite recipes
and kept modifying
them until we created
this recipe. We think
this is the best!

Rodney McMullen
Kroger
Cincinnati, Ohio

1 cup elbow macaroni
1 1/2 tablespoons butter
1 tablespoon all-purpose flour
1 cup milk
1/8 teaspoon ground red pepper, or to taste
3 to 4 slices Private Selection mild
    Cheddar cheese, chopped
3 to 4 slices Private Selection Monterey Jack
    cheese, chopped

Prepare the pasta according to the package directions. Drain and set aside. Melt the butter in a saucepan. Stir in the flour and cook until combined, stirring constantly. Add the milk and cook until thick and bubbly, stirring constantly. Cook for 1 to 2 minutes longer. Season with red pepper. Stir in the cheeses and cook until melted. Fold in the pasta. Pour into an 1 1/2-quart baking dish. Bake at 350 degrees for 15 to 30 minutes or until heated through.

Serves 4 to 6

Cheryl's Cheesy Macaroni

2 cups (about) uncooked elbow macaroni
2 cups (8 ounces) shredded Cheddar cheese
3 eggs, beaten
6 ounces lemon-flavored yogurt
1/2 cup milk
2 to 4 tablespoons butter, softened
1/2 teaspoon salt
Additional shredded Cheddar cheese

Prepare the pasta according to the package directions. Drain and return to the saucepan.
Gently stir in 2 cups cheese. Mix the eggs, yogurt, milk, butter and salt in a bowl. Stir into
the pasta mixture. Pour into a lightly greased baking dish. Bake at 350 degrees for 30 to 35 minutes
or until light golden brown and bubbly. Top with additional cheese, if desired.

Serves 6 to 8

This is an old family
recipe. The original
used sour cream.
One day when I was
preparing this dish,
I realized that I was
out of sour cream, but
I did have a 6-ounce
container of Lemon
Burst Yoplait Yogurt,
so I used that instead.
My family complimented
me on how light, fluffy
and yummy it was.
They ate every bit and
asked me to make it
that way every time.
It is now my family's
favorite dish.

Cheryl Steele
QFC
Edmonds, Washington

Sue Gibbs
Fred Meyer
Clackamas, Oregon

Dan's Ultimate Macaroni and Cheese

1 (22-ounce) package large elbow macaroni
1 1/2 cups finely chopped onion
2 tablespoons seeded deveined and
    minced jalapeño chile
1/2 cup (1 stick) butter
1/2 cup all-purpose flour
2 1/2 cups milk
1 (12-ounce) can evaporated milk
2 cups (8 ounces) grated Gruyère cheese
3 cups (12 ounces) Tillamook cheese or
    extra-sharp Cheddar cheese
4 to 6 ounces grated pecorino Romano cheese
6 slices American cheese, chopped
1/4 teaspoon cayenne pepper
3 tablespoons dry mustard
3 tablespoons yellow mustard
1/2 cup plain bread crumbs

Prepare the pasta according to the package directions until al dente. Drain and set aside. Sauté the onion and the jalapeño chile in the butter in a saucepan for 7 minutes or until the onion is translucent. Add the flour and cook for 4 minutes, stirring constantly. Gradually add the milk and evaporated milk, stirring constantly until blended. Bring the mixture just below a simmer. Stir in the Gruyère cheese, Tillamook cheese, pecorino Romano cheese and American cheese. Cook just below a simmer for 25 to 30 minutes or until the cheeses are melted, stirring constantly. Stir in the cayenne pepper, dry mustard and yellow mustard. Remove from the heat and fold in the pasta. Spoon into a 5-quart baking dish sprayed with nonstick cooking spray. Sprinkle with the bread crumbs. Bake at 350 degrees for 25 to 30 minutes.

Serves 12 to 15

Slow-Cooker Macaroni and Cheese

8 ounces elbow macaroni
3 cups (12 ounces) shredded sharp Cheddar cheese
1 (12-ounce) can evaporated milk
1 1/2 cups milk
2 eggs, lightly beaten
1 teaspoon salt
1/4 teaspoon pepper
1 cups (4 ounces) shredded sharp Cheddar cheese
4 slices American cheese

Prepare the pasta according to the package directions; drain. Mix the cooked pasta, 3 cups Cheddar cheese, the evaporated milk, milk, eggs, salt and pepper in a greased slow cooker. Sprinkle with 1 cup Cheddar cheese and arrange the American cheese on top. Cook, covered, on Low for 3 to 4 hours. Do not remove the lid or stir while cooking.

Serves 8 to 10

An elderly neighbor shared this recipe with me. When I made the dish I would always share it with her. I no longer live near her, but I think of her whenever I make this.

Sandy McIntosh
Kroger
Cincinnati, Ohio

Cakes & Pies

SERVING CUSTOMERS
for 125 Years
1883 Kroger 2008

Cakes & Pies

Kristin Goldstein
Kroger
Plano, Texas

Angel Food Cake

1 cup cake flour

3/4 cup plus 2 tablespoons sugar

12 egg whites, at room temperature
   (1 1/2 cups)

1 1/2 teaspoons cream of tartar

1/4 teaspoon salt

3/4 cup sugar

1 1/2 teaspoons vanilla extract

1/2 teaspoon almond extract

Mix the cake flour and 3/4 cup plus 2 tablespoons sugar together in a bowl. Beat the egg whites, cream of tartar and salt in a large mixing bowl until foamy. Add 3/4 cup sugar 2 tablespoons at a time, beating at high speed until stiff peaks form. Fold in the vanilla and almond extract. Fold in the flour mixture 1/4 cup at a time. Spoon into an ungreased tube pan. Cut through the batter 1 inch from the center of the pan with a knife. Bake at 375 degrees for 25 to 30 minutes or until the top springs back when lightly touched. Invert the pan onto a funnel. Let stand until the cake is completely cool. Loosen the cake from the side of the pan. Invert onto a cake plate.

Serves 16

Linda Stephens
Scott's
Fort Wayne, Indiana

Apple Cake

3 eggs

1 3/4 cups sugar

3/4 cup vegetable oil

1 teaspoon vanilla extract

2 cups all-purpose flour

1 teaspoon salt

1 teaspoon baking soda

2 tablespoons cinnamon

3 cups Granny Smith or Gala apple
   slice halves

1/2 cup chopped walnuts (optional)

Cream the eggs, sugar, oil and vanilla in a mixing bowl. Stir in the flour, salt, baking soda and cinnamon. Fold in the apples and walnuts. Spoon into a greased 9x13-inch cake pan. Bake at 350 degrees for 30 to 40 minutes or until a wooden pick inserted in the center comes out clean.

Serves 12 to 15

Grandmother's Applesauce Cake

Cake

All-purpose flour for coating

1 cup raisins

1 cup nuts

2 cups all-purpose flour

1 cup sugar

1/2 teaspoon salt

1 teaspoon cinnamon

1/2 teaspoon nutmeg

1/2 teaspoon ground cloves

2 teaspoons baking soda

1 1/2 cups unsweetened applesauce, warmed

2/3 cup vegetable oil

Caramel Icing

1/2 cup (1 stick) butter

2 cups packed light brown sugar

1/2 cup milk

1 teaspoon vanilla extract

This is a very old recipe.

Paula Richerson
Kroger
East Peoria, Illinois

To prepare the cake, coat the raisins and nuts with a small amount of flour. Sift 2 cups flour, the sugar, salt, cinnamon, nutmeg and cloves into a large mixing bowl. Stir the baking soda into the warm applesauce. Add the applesauce mixture and oil to the flour mixture and mix well. Fold in the flour-coated raisins and nuts. Spoon into a greased and floured tube pan. Bake at 350 degrees for 40 to 50 minutes or until the cake tests done. Cool in the pan for 10 minutes. Invert onto a wire rack to cool completely.

To prepare the icing, melt the butter in a medium saucepan. Stir in the brown sugar and milk. Cook to 234 to 240 degrees on a candy thermometer, soft-ball stage. Remove from the heat. Add the vanilla and beat until the icing holds its shape; do not overbeat. Spread over the cooled cake.

Serves 18 to 20

This recipe makes a very moist cake and stores well.

Helen Bruenn

Dillons

Pittsburg, Kansas

Banana Nut Cake

Cake

3 cups all-purpose flour

1 1/2 teaspoons baking powder

1 1/4 teaspoons baking soda

1 teaspoon salt

2 1/4 cups sugar

3/4 cup shortening

1 1/2 cups mashed ripe bananas (3 bananas)

3 eggs

1 1/2 teaspoons vanilla extract

1 cup buttermilk

1 1/2 cups chopped pecans

Banana Frosting

1 cup mashed ripe bananas (2 bananas)

3 tablespoons butter, softened

2 1/2 to 3 cups confectioners' sugar

1 1/2 cups chopped pecans

To prepare the cake, mix the flour, baking powder, baking soda and salt together. Cream the sugar and shortening in a mixing bowl. Add the bananas, eggs and vanilla and mix well. Add the flour mixture alternately with the buttermilk, beating well after each addition. Beat at medium speed for 3 minutes. Stir in the pecans. Spoon into three 9-inch cake pans sprayed with nonstick cooking spray. Bake at 350 degrees for 30 minutes or until the cake tests done. Cool in the pans for 10 minutes. Remove to wire racks to cool completely.

To prepare the frosting, beat the bananas, butter and 2 1/2 cups of the confectioners' sugar in a mixing bowl. Add enough of the remaining confectioners' sugar to make of a spreading consistency. Stir in the pecans. Spread between the layers and over the top and side of the cake.

Serves 12

Blackberry Jam Cake

Cake

2 cups all-purpose flour

1 tablespoon baking cocoa

1 teaspoon baking soda

1 teaspoon cinnamon

3/4 teaspoon ground cloves

3/4 teaspoon nutmeg

3/4 teaspoon allspice

1 cup shortening

1 1/2 cups sugar

3 eggs

1 cup buttermilk

1 cup blackberry jam

Dark Caramel Icing

1/2 cup (1 stick) butter

1 cup packed dark brown sugar

1/4 cup milk

3 to 3 1/4 cups confectioners' sugar

This cake is even better the second day.

Evelyn McClanahan

Kroger

Maysville, Kentucky

To prepare the cake, sift the flour, baking cocoa, baking soda, cinnamon, cloves, nutmeg and allspice together. Cream the shortening and sugar in a large mixing bowl. Beat in the eggs one at a time. Add the flour mixture alternately with the buttermilk, mixing well after each addition. Add the jam and beat for 2 minutes. Spoon into two greased 9-inch cake pans. Bake at 350 degrees for 30 to 35 minutes or until the layers test done. Cool in the pans for 10 minutes. Remove to wire racks to cool completely.

To prepare the icing, melt the butter in a saucepan. Add the brown sugar. Bring to a boil, stirring constantly. Boil for 1 minute or until slightly thickened, stirring constantly. Remove from the heat to cool slightly. Add the milk and beat until smooth. Add enough of the confectioners' sugar to make of a spreading consistency. Spread between the layers and over the top and side of the cake.

Serves 12

Kentucky Butter Cake

Great for a family or church gathering. They will love the rich flavor and moist texture.

Mary Jane Harris
Kroger
Steubenville, Ohio

Cake

3 cups all-purpose flour
1 teaspoon salt
1 teaspoon baking powder
1/2 teaspoon baking soda
2 cups sugar
4 eggs
1 cup (2 sticks) butter, softened
2 teaspoons rum
1 cup buttermilk

Butter Sauce

3/4 cup sugar
1/3 cup butter
2 tablespoons water
2 teaspoons rum

Assembly

Confectioners' sugar

To prepare the cake, mix the flour, salt, baking powder and baking soda in a large bowl. Combine the sugar, eggs, butter, rum and buttermilk in a bowl and mix well. Add to the flour mixture and beat for 3 minutes. Spoon into a greased and lightly floured 12-cup bundt pan. Bake at 350 degrees for 55 to 70 minutes or until the cake tests done. Remove from the oven and pierce the cake with a long-tined fork. Let stand in the pan until cool.

To prepare the sauce, combine the sugar, butter, water and rum in a saucepan and mix well. Heat over low heat until the sugar is dissolved, stirring constantly; do not boil.

To assemble, pour the hot sauce over the cake and let stand for 5 to 10 minutes. Invert the cake onto a cake plate. Sprinkle lightly with confectioners' sugar.

Serves 18 to 20

Apple Carrot Cake

Cake

3 cups all-purpose flour

2 cups sugar

2 teaspoons baking soda

1/2 teaspoon salt

1 1/2 teaspoons cinnamon

1/2 teaspoon nutmeg

1/2 teaspoon cloves

1 cup mayonnaise

2 eggs

1/3 cup milk

1 1/2 cups coarsely chopped apples

1 1/2 cups finely shredded carrots

1 cup raisins

1 cup coarsely chopped walnuts

Cream Cheese Frosting

16 ounces cream cheese, softened

3 tablespoons unsalted butter, softened

1 (1-pound) package confectioners' sugar

1 teaspoon milk

1 teaspoon vanilla extract

This is almost a carrot cake but the apples make it even more moist. This cake can be topped with 8 ounces whipped topping instead of the frosting to give it a less sweet taste as well as fewer calories.

Judy Dovidio
Fry's
Phoenix, Arizona

To prepare the cake, mix the flour, sugar, baking soda, salt, cinnamon, nutmeg and cloves in a large mixing bowl. Add the mayonnaise, eggs and milk. Beat at medium speed until blended, scraping the side of the bowl frequently. The batter will be thick. Stir in the apples, carrots, raisins and walnuts. Spoon into a greased and floured 9x13-inch cake pan. Bake at 350 degrees for 35 to 40 minutes or until a wooden pick inserted in the center comes out clean. Remove from the oven and cool completely on a wire rack.

To prepare the frosting, beat the cream cheese and butter in a medium mixing bowl until smooth and creamy. Add the confectioners' sugar gradually, beating constantly until smooth. Add the milk and vanilla and beat for 2 minutes or until fluffy. Spread over the top of the cooled cake.

Serves 12 to 15

Carrot Cake

This is the cake my Mother would make for all birthdays and holidays for our family. When she passed away the holidays and birthdays did not seem the same without the carrot cake. I found her recipe and started making it for our family.

Robert Porter
Kroger
Garner, North Carolina

Cake

4 eggs
1/2 cup applesauce
3/4 cup vegetable oil
2 cups sugar
2 teaspoons vanilla extract
2 cups self-rising flour
1 tablespoon cinnamon
1 (8-ounce) can crushed pineapple
3 cups grated carrots
1 cup chopped pecans

Pecan Cream Cheese Frosting

1/2 cup (1 stick) butter, softened
8 ounces cream cheese, softened
4 cups confectioners' sugar
1 1/2 teaspoons vanilla extract
1 cup chopped pecans

To prepare the cake, combine the eggs, applesauce, oil, sugar and vanilla in a mixing bowl and beat well. Add the flour and cinnamon and mix well. Stir in the pineapple and carrots. Stir in the pecans. Pour into a greased and floured 9x13-inch cake pan. Bake at 350 degrees for 50 to 55 minutes or until a wooden pick inserted in the center comes out clean. Remove to a wire rack to cool.

To prepare the frosting, combine the butter, cream cheese, confectioners' sugar and vanilla in a mixing bowl and beat until smooth and creamy. Stir in the pecans. Spread over the top of the cooled cake.

Serves 16

Chocolate "Coffee" Cake

2 cups all-purpose flour
2 cups sugar
Dash of salt
1 teaspoon baking powder
2 teaspoons baking soda
3/4 cup baking cocoa
1 cup hot black coffee
2 eggs
1 cup milk
1 teaspoon vanilla extract

Sift the flour, sugar, salt, baking powder, baking soda and baking cocoa into a mixing bowl. Add the coffee, eggs, milk and vanilla and beat until well blended. The batter will be very thin. Pour into a greased 9x13-inch cake pan. Bake at 350 degrees for 30 to 35 minutes or until the cake tests done. Do not overbake. Remove to a wire rack to cool.

Frost with vanilla frosting, if desired. You may bake in a bundt pan for 35 to 45 minutes, or for cupcakes, bake in paper-lined muffin cups for 18 to 20 minutes.

Serves 8 to 10

This recipe was given to me in 1964 by my high school friend's mom, Sue Wideker. I have made it for every family birthday since.

Judith Benham
Dillons
Topeka, Kansas

Laura Bennett

Peyton

Bluffton, Indiana

Chocolate Cake with Peanut Butter Frosting

Cake

2 cups all-purpose flour

2 cups sugar

2/3 cup baking cocoa

2 teaspoons baking soda

1 teaspoon baking powder

1/2 teaspoon salt

2 eggs

1 cup milk

2/3 cup vegetable oil

1 teaspoon vanilla extract

1 cup brewed coffee, at room temperature

Peanut Butter Frosting

3 ounces cream cheese, softened

1/4 cup creamy peanut butter

2 cups confectioners' sugar

2 tablespoons milk

1/2 teaspoon vanilla extract

To prepare the cake, mix the flour, sugar, baking cocoa, baking soda, baking powder and salt in a large mixing bowl. Add the eggs, milk, oil and vanilla and beat for 2 minutes. Stir in the coffee. The batter will be very thin. Pour into a greased 9x13-inch cake pan. Bake at 350 degrees for 45 to 50 minutes or until a wooden pick inserted in the center comes out clean. Remove to a wire rack to cool completely.

To prepare the frosting, beat the cream cheese and peanut butter in a mixing bowl until smooth. Add the confectioners' sugar, milk and vanilla and beat well. Spread over the top of the cooled cake.

Serves 16

Chocolate Oatmeal Cake

1 3/4 cups boiling water
1 cup rolled oats
1 cup packed brown sugar
1 cup granulated sugar
1/2 cup (1 stick) butter or margarine
2 eggs
1 3/4 cups all-purpose flour
1 teaspoon baking soda
1/2 teaspoon salt
2 tablespoons baking cocoa
2 cups (12 ounces) milk chocolate chips
3/4 cup chopped walnuts

Dianna MacMasters
City Market
Northglen, Colorado

Pour the boiling water over the oats in a large bowl. Let stand for 10 minutes. Add the brown sugar, granulated sugar and butter and stir until the butter melts. Add the eggs and mix well. Add the flour, baking soda, salt and baking cocoa and mix well. Stir in 1 cup of the chocolate chips. Pour into a greased and floured 9x13-inch cake pan. Sprinkle with the remaining chocolate chips and walnuts. Bake at 350 degrees for 35 to 40 minutes or until the cake tests done.

Serves 16 to 24

Bob's Coconut Cake

This recipe was originally made by former employee Bob Wedemeyer. This recipe freezes well. Bring to room temperature before serving. You may also bake in smaller cake pans or paper-lined muffin cups for cupcakes.

Craig Ledbetter
Fred Meyer
Everett, Washington

Cake

3 1/3 cups sifted cake flour

1 3/4 cups ultra-fine pure cane sugar

3/4 teaspoon baking soda

1/2 teaspoon salt

3/4 cup water

3/4 cup vegetable oil

11 egg yolks

1 teaspoon vanilla extract

14 egg whites, at room temperature

Pinch of salt

1/2 cup ultra-fine pure cane sugar

Coconut Syrup

1 cup water

3/4 cup ultra-fine pure cane sugar

Pinch of salt

1/4 cup cream of coconut

To prepare the cake, coat three 9-inch cake pans with cooking spray and line with baking parchment. Sift the flour, 1 3/4 cups sugar, the baking soda and 1/2 teaspoon salt into the bowl of an electric mixer fitted with the paddle attachment. Whisk the water, oil, egg yolks and vanilla in a bowl. Add to the flour mixture and beat at medium-high speed for 2 minutes or until smooth. Spoon into a large bowl. Place the egg whites and a pinch of salt in the bowl of an electric mixer fitted with the whisk attachment. Beat at medium speed until foamy. Increase the speed to medium-high and beat until soft peaks form. Add 1/2 cup sugar gradually, beating until stiff glossy peaks form. Fold one-quarter of the egg white mixture into the batter with a rubber spatula. Fold in the remaining egg white mixture in two batches. Divide the batter evenly among the prepared pans. Bake at 325 degrees for 30 to 35 minutes or until the layers are golden brown and spring back when lightly pressed. Remove from the oven and invert onto wire racks to cool. Remove the baking parchment.

To prepare the coconut syrup, bring the water, sugar, salt and cream of coconut to a boil in a small saucepan, stirring occasionally. Boil for 1 minute. Remove from the heat and set aside.

Coconut Swiss Meringue Buttercream

10 egg whites

2 1/4 cups ultra-fine pure cane sugar

1/4 teaspoon salt

4 cups (8 sticks) unsalted butter, softened

1/2 cup cream of coconut

1/2 teaspoon coconut extract

Assembly

1 1/3 cups sweetened coconut

To prepare the buttercream, whisk the egg whites, sugar and salt in a heatproof bowl of an electric mixer set over a pan of simmering water for 3 minutes or until the sugar dissolves and the mixture registers 160 degrees on a candy thermometer. Attach the bowl to the electric mixer fitted with a whisk attachment. Beat at medium-high speed for 10 minutes or until cool. Reduce the speed to medium. Add the butter and beat until pale and fluffy. Beat in the cream of coconut and coconut extract. The buttercream can be stored in an airtight container in the refrigerator for up to 3 days. Beat before using.

To assemble, trim the cake layers level. Place one cake layer on a cake plate and brush with 1/3 cup of the coconut syrup. Spread with 1 cup of the buttercream and sprinkle with 1/3 cup of the coconut. Top with another cake layer. Brush with 1/3 cup of the remaining coconut syrup and spread with 1 cup of the remaining buttercream. Sprinkle with 1/3 cup of the remaining coconut. Top with the remaining cake layer. Brush with the remaining coconut syrup. Chill in the refrigerator until firm. Spread 1 1/4 cups of the remaining buttercream over the top and sides of the cake. Chill in the refrigerator for 30 minutes or until firm. Spread 1 1/2 cups of the remaining buttercream over the top and side of the cake. Chill in the refrigerator for 1 hour or until very firm. Fill a pastry bag fitted with a 1-inch basketweave tip (such as Ateco #898) with some of the remaining buttercream. Holding the bag perpendicular to the cake, pipe the sides in a back-and-forth motion, starting at the bottom. Refill the bag as needed with the remaining buttercream. Sprinkle the top with the remaining 2/3 cup coconut. The cake can be chilled in the refrigerator for 2 to 4 days. Let stand at room temperature for 20 minutes before serving.

Serves 15

Old-Fashioned Oatmeal Cake

Cake

1 1/4 cups boiling water

1 cup rolled oats

1 cup packed brown sugar

1 cup granulated sugar

1/2 cup (1 stick) butter, melted

2 eggs

1 1/3 cups all-purpose flour

1 teaspoon baking soda

1/2 teaspoon salt

1/2 teaspoon cinnamon

1/2 teaspoon nutmeg

1 teaspoon vanilla extract

Coconut Peanut Icing

1 cup packed brown sugar

1/4 cup (1/2 stick) butter, melted

1 cup shredded coconut

1/2 cup evaporated milk

1/2 cup crushed peanuts

This recipe has been in my family for over fifty-five years. My great-aunt made them for our family get-togethers and family reunions. It was passed down to me when I got married in 1971. My family loves this recipe. My aunt would make extra cakes and store them in the freezer to use on special occasions. I make four or five a year. The cake tastes fresh after thawing from the freezer.

Patty Hanshaw
Kroger
Maysville, Kentucky

To prepare the cake, pour the boiling water over the oats in a bowl. Cover and set aside. Cream the brown sugar, granulated sugar and butter in a mixing bowl until light and fluffy. Add the eggs and beat well. Whip the oat mixture and add to the creamed mixture. Add the flour, baking soda, salt, cinnamon, nutmeg and vanilla and beat well. Spoon into a greased and floured 9x13-inch cake pan. Bake at 350 degrees for 45 to 50 minutes or until a wooden pick inserted in the center comes out clean. Remove to a wire rack to cool.

To prepare the icing, combine the brown sugar, butter, coconut, evaporated milk and peanuts in a saucepan and mix well. Bring to a boil over medium heat. Boil for 1 minute, stirring constantly. Pour over the top of the cooled cake.

Serves 16 to 24

Snazzy Peach Cake

1 (15-ounce) can sliced peaches in light syrup
1 cup granulated sugar
1/2 cup peach schnapps or orange juice
1/4 cup orange juice
1 (2-layer) package yellow cake mix
1 (4-ounce) package vanilla instant pudding mix
4 eggs, beaten
1 cup chopped pecans
2/3 cup vegetable oil
1 1/2 cups sifted confectioners' sugar

Carolyn Lees
Kroger
Houston, Texas

Combine the undrained peaches, granulated sugar, peach schnapps and orange juice in a glass jar or bowl and mix well. Let stand, covered, at room temperature for 24 hours.

Drain the peaches, reserving the liquid. Chop the peaches. Combine the cake mix, pudding mix, eggs, pecans, oil, chopped peaches and 1/3 cup of the reserved liquid in a large bowl and stir until well combined. Pour into a greased and floured 10-cup bundt pan. Bake at 350 degrees for 40 to 45 minutes or until a wooden pick inserted in the cake comes out clean. Cool in the pan on a wire rack for 10 minutes. Remove from the pan.

Combine the confectioners' sugar and 1/4 cup of the remaining reserved liquid in a small bowl and mix until smooth. Drizzle over the warm cake. Cool completely before serving.

Serves 12 to 18

Chocolate-Marbled Pistachio Cake

My mother gave me this recipe about thirty years ago and I have been making it ever since. My family loves it.

Marilyn Fistler

Kroger

Richmond, Michigan

Cake

1 (2-layer) package white cake mix
1 (4-ounce) package pistachio instant
  pudding mix
4 eggs, lightly beaten
1/2 cup vegetable oil
1/2 cup water
1/4 cup orange juice
3/4 cup chocolate syrup

Buttercream Frosting

1 cup confectioners' sugar
2 1/2 tablespoons butter, softened
2 tablespoons cream
1/2 teaspoon vanilla extract

To prepare the cake, combine the cake mix, pudding mix, eggs, oil, water and orange juice in a mixing bowl and beat at medium-high speed for 5 minutes. Pour two-thirds of the batter into a greased 10-inch tube pan. Stir the chocolate syrup into the remaining batter. Pour the chocolate batter evenly over the pistachio batter and swirl with a knife to marbleize. Bake at 350 degrees for 45 to 50 minutes or until the cake tests done. Cool in the pan on a wire rack for 15 minutes. Remove to a wire rack to cool completely.

To prepare the frosting, combine the confectioners' sugar, butter, cream and vanilla in a microwave-safe bowl and mix until smooth. Microwave on High for 10 seconds. Drizzle over the cooled cake.

Serves 12

Camper Pineapple Cake

Cake
2 cups all-purpose flour
1 1/2 teaspoons baking soda
1/2 teaspoon baking powder
2 cups sugar
2 teaspoons vanilla extract
2 eggs
1 (20-ounce) can crushed pineapple

Cream Cheese Frosting
1/2 cup (1 stick) butter, softened
8 ounces cream cheese, softened
2 cups confectioners' sugar
1 teaspoon vanilla extract

Assembly
12 to 15 English walnut halves

To prepare the cake, combine the flour, baking soda, baking powder, sugar, vanilla, eggs and pineapple in a bowl and mix well with a fork. Pour into a greased and floured 9x13-inch cake pan. Bake at 325 degrees for 40 to 45 minutes or until the cake tests done. Remove from the pan to a wire rack.

To prepare the frosting, beat the butter and cream cheese in a mixing bowl until creamy. Add the confectioners' sugar and vanilla and mix until smooth.

To assemble, spread some of the frosting over the warm cake. Let stand until the frosting melts and soaks into the cake. Spread with the remaining frosting. Arrange the walnuts over the top.

Serves 12 to 15

Having a motor home, I met and joined a club in California. We would find some place to go and explore the Alcan Highway. One night after supper we all wanted something sweet, so we got together and made the first Camper Pineapple Cake.

Robert Fox
Kroger
Lexington, Kentucky

Pound Cake

3 cups cake flour
3 cups sugar
1 cup (2 sticks) unsalted butter, softened
6 eggs
2 teaspoons vanilla extract
1 cup whipping cream

Combine the flour, sugar, butter, eggs, vanilla and cream in a mixing bowl and beat until smooth. Pour into a greased bundt pan. Bake at 300 degrees for 1 1/2 hours or until a wooden pick inserted in the center comes out clean. Cool in the pan for 10 minutes. Invert onto a wire rack to cool completely.

Serves 12

All ingredients need to be at room temperature before preparation begins.

Pete Williams
Kroger
Cincinnati, Ohio

Brown Sugar Pound Cake

3 cups all-purpose flour
1/2 teaspoon baking powder
1/2 teaspoon salt
1/2 cup (1 stick) butter, softened
1/2 cup (1 stick) margarine, softened
1/2 cup shortening

1 (1-pound) package light brown sugar
1/2 cup granulated sugar
5 eggs
1 cup milk
1 teaspoon vanilla extract

Sift the flour, baking powder and salt together. Cream the butter, margarine and shortening in a mixing bowl. Add the brown sugar and granulated sugar and beat until light and fluffy. Add the eggs one at a time, beating well after each addition. Add the flour mixture and milk alternately, beating well after each addition. Stir in the vanilla. Pour into a greased and floured 10-inch tube or bundt pan. Bake at 325 degrees for 75 to 90 minutes or until the cake tests done. Cool in the pan for 10 to 15 minutes. Invert onto a wire rack to cool completely. Serve with Private Selection Vanilla Bean Ice Cream.

Serves 16 to 20

This was my maternal Grandmother Christian's recipe, circa 1920s.

Robin Kidd
Kroger
Roanoke, Virginia

Aunt Willora's Wonderful Crunchy Pound Cake

2 cups all-purpose flour
2 cups sugar
I cup shortening
6 eggs
I teaspoon vanilla extract
I teaspoon almond extract
I teaspoon lemon extract
¹/2 teaspoon salt

Combine the flour, sugar, shortening, eggs, vanilla, almond extract, lemon extract and salt in a mixing bowl and beat for 10 minutes, scraping the side of bowl frequently. Spoon into a well-greased and floured bundt pan. Bake at 325 degrees for 65 to 70 minutes or until the top is a beautiful golden brown. Cool in the pan for 10 minutes. Invert onto a wire rack. When cool enough to handle, turn the cake upright so the top can get its nice crunchy texture.

Serves 12 to 16

This is my family's favorite cake. My Aunt Willora passed away a few years ago at the age of ninety-two and I never found out where she got the recipe—it's just hers. The batter is so good that one time my sister and my grandmother were making the cake, and when it was time to spoon it into the pan there was only about half the batter left. My sister had nibbled half the batter away, while waiting for the long ten minute mixing time to be done.

Kathy Cooper
Smith's
Pleasant Grove, Utah

This recipe was purchased by my grandmother for ten cents at the Sunday school fund-raiser for the First Methodist Church in Compton, Kentucky, over seventy-five years ago. It is supposed to be the only cake the Queen herself would make.

Loveina Taylor
Kroger
Cincinnati, Ohio

Queen Elizabeth II Cake

Cake

1 cup boiling water
1 cup chopped dates
1 teaspoon baking soda
1/4 cup (1/2 stick) butter, softened
1 cup sugar
1 egg, beaten
1 1/2 cups sifted all-purpose flour
1 teaspoon baking powder
1/3 teaspoon salt
1 teaspoon vanilla extract
1/3 cup chopped nuts

Caramel Icing

5 tablespoons brown sugar
5 tablespoons evaporated milk
2 tablespoons butter

Assembly

1/4 cup shredded coconut
1/4 cup chopped nuts

To prepare the cake, pour the boiling water over the dates and baking soda in a large bowl. Cream the butter and sugar in a mixing bowl. Add the egg and beat well. Stir in the flour, baking powder, salt, vanilla and nuts. Add to the date mixture and mix well. Pour into a greased 8x8-inch cake pan. Bake at 350 degrees for 35 to 40 minutes or until the cake tests done.

To prepare the icing, combine the brown sugar, evaporated milk and butter in a saucepan. Bring to a boil and boil for 3 minutes, stirring constantly. Spread over the cake. Sprinkle with the coconut and nuts.

Serves 6

Sour Cream Cake

3 cups all-purpose flour
1/4 teaspoon baking soda
1 cup (2 sticks) butter, softened
3 cups sugar
6 eggs
1 cup sour cream
1 teaspoon almond extract

Mix the flour and baking soda together. Cream the butter and sugar in a mixing bowl until light and fluffy. Add the eggs one at a time, beating well after each addition. Add the flour mixture and sour cream alternately one-third at a time, beating well after each addition. Stir in the almond extract. The batter will be very thick. Spoon into a greased and floured bundt pan. Bake at 325 degrees for 1 1/4 hours. Cool in the pan for 10 minutes. Invert onto a wire rack to cool completely.

Serves 12

You can also fill three greased and floured 5x8-inch loaf pans halfway with the batter and bake for 45 to 60 minutes or until the loaves test done.

Deb Harrison
Fry's
Phoenix, Arizona

My mother always made this cake for ice cream socials while I grew up. This cake was consistently always purchased whole. It has been a family recipe for over seventy years.

Tamara Parry
Fry's
Globe, Arizona

Spice Cake

2 cups all-purpose flour
1 teaspoon baking soda
1 1/2 to 2 teaspoons cinnamon
1/2 to 1 teaspoon nutmeg
Pinch of salt
1/2 cup (1 stick) butter, cut into slices
1 cup sugar
2 eggs
1 cup buttermilk

Mix the flour, baking soda, cinnamon, nutmeg and salt in a bowl. Add the butter and mix well. Add the sugar and mix well. Reserve 1/2 cup of the flour mixture. Beat the eggs in a mixing bowl. Add the buttermilk and mix well. Add to the remaining flour mixture and beat until smooth. Pour into a greased and floured 8x8-inch cake pan. Sprinkle with the reserved 1/2 cup flour mixture. Bake at 350 degrees for 40 to 45 minutes or until the top is golden brown. Remove from the oven to cool.

Serves 9

Tres Leches Cake

1 1/4 cups cake flour
1 teaspoon baking powder
Pinch of salt
1 cup sugar
1/3 cup vegetable oil
1 teaspoon vanilla extract
5 eggs

1 cup milk
1 cup sweetened condensed milk
1 cup heavy cream
1 tablespoon rum (optional)
3/4 cup heavy whipping cream
1 tablespoon sugar
1 teaspoon vanilla extract

This recipe is from a long-time Kroger associate who is now a retiree, Phyllis Jackson. Phyllis made this cake and brought it to work a few years ago. It was delicious!

Della Wall
Kroger
Cincinnati, Ohio

Mix the flour, baking powder and salt together. Combine 1 cup sugar, the oil and 1 teaspoon vanilla in a mixing bowl and mix well. Add the eggs one at time, mixing well after each addition. Stir in 1/2 cup of the milk. Fold in the flour mixture a small amount at a time. Pour into a lightly greased 9x13-inch cake pan. Bake at 325 degrees for 20 to 25 minutes or until firm and a wooden pick inserted in the center comes out clean. Remove from the oven and cool in the pan to room temperature. Pierce the cake with a fork twenty to thirty times. Chill in the refrigerator for 30 minutes.

Whisk the remaining 1/2 cup milk, the condensed milk, 1 cup heavy cream and the rum in a bowl. Pour gradually over the chilled cake letting the mixture absorb into the cake. Chill in the refrigerator for 2 hours.

Beat 3/4 cup heavy whipping cream, 1 tablespoon sugar and 1 teaspoon vanilla in a mixing bowl until soft peaks form. Spread a thin layer over the cake. Garnish the cake with a sprinkle of cinnamon or with fresh berries.

Serves 12 to 15

Apple Streusel Pie

$1/2$ cup granulated sugar

$1/8$ teaspoon salt

2 tablespoons cornstarch

5 cups thinly sliced peeled Granny Smith apples

$1/2$ cup raisins

$1/2$ cup walnuts, chopped

$1 1/2$ tablespoons fresh orange juice

1 (9-inch) frozen deep-dish pie shell

$1/4$ cup packed brown sugar

$1/4$ cup granulated sugar

$1/3$ cup all-purpose flour

$1/2$ teaspoon cinnamon

$1/4$ cup ($1/2$ stick) butter, softened

$1/4$ cup walnuts, chopped

Mix $1/2$ cup granulated sugar, the salt and cornstarch together. Combine the apples, raisins and $1/2$ cup walnuts in a large bowl and mix well. Add the sugar mixture and orange juice and mix well. Spoon into the pie shell.

Mix the brown sugar, $1/4$ cup granulated sugar, the flour and cinnamon in a bowl. Cut in the butter until crumbly. Stir in $1/4$ cup walnuts. Sprinkle over the top of the pie. Loosely tent the pie with foil to prevent overbrowning. Bake at 350 degrees for 40 minutes. Remove the foil and bake for 15 minutes longer.

Serves 6 to 8

Creamy Banana Pecan Pie

1 cup all-purpose flour
1/2 cup (1 stick) butter, softened
1 cup finely chopped pecans
8 ounces cream cheese, softened
1 cup confectioners' sugar
8 ounces whipped topping
3 large bananas, sliced
1 (4-ounce) package vanilla instant pudding mix
1 1/3 cups cold milk

Randall Bare
Kroger
Cincinnati, Ohio

Combine the flour, butter and 1 cup pecans in a bowl and mix well. Press over the bottom and up the side of a greased 9-inch pie plate. Bake at 350 degrees for 20 to 25 minutes or until golden brown. Remove from the oven and cool completely.

Beat the cream cheese and confectioners' sugar in a mixing bowl until smooth. Fold in 1 cup of the whipped topping. Spread over the cooled crust. Arrange the bananas over the cream cheese mixture. Whisk the pudding mix and milk in a bowl until thickened. Pour over the bananas. Top with the remaining whipped topping. Garnish with additional pecans, if desired. Chill until serving time.

Serves 6 to 8

My grandmother gave me this recipe when I was a teenager. It was passed down to her from her mother. In all my years of making this dessert, it has never failed in baking or pleasing anyone who tried it. Anyone who likes chess pie will love this pie. Anyone who likes dessert will love this pie.

Cathy Hackney
Kroger RASC
Nashville, Tennessee

Buttermilk Pie

1 1/2 cups sugar
1 tablespoon all-purpose flour
1/2 cup (1 stick) butter or margarine, softened
1/2 cup buttermilk
3 eggs
1 tablespoon vanilla extract
1 unbaked (9-inch) deep-dish pie shell

Mix the sugar and flour in a large mixing bowl. Add the butter and buttermilk and beat well. Add the eggs one at a time, beating well after each addition. Stir in the vanilla. Pour into the pie shell. Bake at 325 degrees for 45 to 60 minutes or until set.

Serves 8

Hot Chocolate Pies

4 cups sugar

1/2 cup all-purpose flour

1 teaspoon salt

2 envelopes hot chocolate mix
   with marshmallows

1 tablespoon (heaping) baking cocoa

6 egg yolks, beaten

3 cups 2% milk

1 cup water

1/2 cup (1 stick) butter, softened

2 teaspoons vanilla extract

2 baked (9-inch) pie shells

6 egg whites, at room temperature

1/2 cup sugar

1 teaspoon vanilla extract

6 drops of water

Combine 4 cups sugar, the flour, salt, hot chocolate mix, baking cocoa, egg yolks, milk and 1 cup water in a microwave-safe bowl and mix well. Microwave on High for 12 to 14 minutes or until thickened, stirring three times. Add the butter and 2 teaspoons vanilla and beat until smooth. Pour into the baked pie shells.

Beat the egg whites in a mixing bowl until frothy. Add 1/2 cup sugar gradually, beating until stiff peaks form. Fold in 1 teaspoon vanilla and 6 drops of water. Top each pie with the meringue, sealing to the edge. Bake at 350 degrees for 8 to 10 minutes or until golden brown. Serve warm.

Serves 16

Preparing to make Grandma's Chocolate Pies one morning at 4:00 A.M. for a store dinner, I realized I was short of baking cocoa. I substituted 2 envelopes of hot chocolate mix and it was better than the original recipe. Hence the name Hot Chocolate Pies. Serve warm— it's wonderful.

Carole Swindle

Kroger

Plano, Texas

Ma's Lemon Sponge Pie

1 cup sugar
2 tablespoons butter, softened
1/4 cup all-purpose flour
1/4 cup lemon juice
2 teaspoons lemon zest

2 egg yolks, beaten
1 cup milk
2 egg whites, stiffly beaten
1 unbaked (9-inch) pie shell

Beat the sugar, butter and flour in a mixing bowl until smooth and creamy. Add the lemon juice, lemon zest, egg yolks and milk and mix well. Fold in the egg whites gently. Pour into the pie shell. Bake at 400 degrees for 5 minutes. Reduce the oven temperature to 350 degrees and bake for 25 minutes. Cover the edge with foil to prevent overbrowning. Bake for 15 minutes longer.

Serves 8

My "Ma" would make this pie for all special occasions, but it was our favorite at family picnics on Sundays when the whole family was together.

Roxanna Reiber
Kroger
Dayton, Ohio

Margarita Pie

1 1/4 cups finely crushed pretzels
1/2 cup (1 stick) butter or margarine, melted
1/4 cup sugar
1 (14-ounce) can sweetened
   condensed milk

Zest and juice from 2 limes
1/4 cup orange juice
8 ounces whipped topping

Reserve a small amount of the crushed pretzels for garnish. Combine the remaining pretzels, butter and sugar in a bowl and mix well. Press over the bottom and up the side of a 9-inch pie plate. Combine the condensed milk, lime zest, lime juice and orange juice in a bowl and mix well. Fold in the whipped topping. Spoon into the prepared pie plate. Sprinkle with the reserved crushed pretzels. Chill for 25 to 30 minutes or until set.

Serves 8

I'm not sure where I found this recipe, but it was a party favorite.

Danielle Scheumann
Scott's
Fort Wayne, Indiana

Isn't That Just Peachy Pie?!

2 refrigerator pie pastries
4 cups sliced peeled peaches
1/4 cup quick-cooking tapioca
1 1/4 cups sugar
2 teaspoons lemon juice
1/8 teaspoon almond extract
2 tablespoons unsalted butter, sliced
1 egg white
1 tablespoon cinnamon-sugar

Unroll one of the pie pastries and fit into a 9-inch pie plate. Combine the peaches, tapioca, sugar, lemon juice and almond extract in a large bowl and mix well. Pour into the prepared pie plate. Place the butter over the peaches. Unroll the remaining pie pastry and cut into strips. Arrange lattice-fashion over the pie, fluting the edge. Beat the egg white in a bowl until frothy. Brush over the pastry and sprinkle with cinnamon-sugar. Bake at 350 degrees for 30 to 35 minutes. Cover the edge with foil to prevent overbrowning and bake for 20 to 25 minutes longer.

You may also top with the remaining pastry, fluting the edge and cutting vents.

Serves 6 to 8

Every summer when peaches are in season, I bake and deliver my famous peach pies to friends on my exclusive Pie List. My number one fans include G. G. and Betty Rutherford, dad and grandmother of Skip Rutherford, Dean of the University of Arkansas Clinton School. Betty is 109 years old and tells everyone my peach pies are the best she has tasted in her life. It is an honor to have her praise; therefore, I would like to dedicate this recipe to her.

Jean Taylor
Kroger
Batesville, Arkansas

Turtle Tart

Karen Powers
Kroger
The Woodlands,
  Texas

1 (16-ounce) package oatmeal cookie mix
1/2 cup (1 stick) butter or margarine, softened
1 tablespoon water
1 egg
1 cup chopped pecans
40 caramels
1/3 cup whipping cream
3/4 cup chopped pecans
2 cups (12 ounces) milk chocolate chips
1/3 cup whipping cream
1/4 cup chopped pecans

Combine the cookie mix, butter, water and egg in a large bowl and stir to form a soft dough. Stir in 1 cup pecans. Press over the bottom and up the side of an ungreased 12-inch tart pan or 9x13-inch baking pan. Bake at 350 degrees for 18 to 21 minutes or until light golden brown. Cool for 10 minutes.

Place the caramels and 1/3 cup whipping cream in a medium microwave-safe bowl. Microwave on High for 2 to 4 minutes or until the caramels melt, stirring twice. Stir in 3/4 cup pecans. Spread over the cooled crust. Chill for 15 minutes.

Place the chocolate chips and 1/3 cup whipping cream in a medium microwave-safe bowl. Microwave on High for 1 to 2 minutes, stirring at 30-second intervals until smooth. Pour over the caramel layer. Sprinkle with 1/4 cup pecans. Chill for 2 hours or until set. Let stand at room temperature for 10 minutes before serving. Store, covered, in the refrigerator.

Serves 8

White Chocolate Fruit Tart

3/4 cup (1 1/2 sticks) butter, softened
1/2 cup confectioners' sugar
1 1/2 cups all-purpose flour
2 cups (12 ounces) white chocolate
   chips, melted
1/4 cup whipping cream
8 ounces cream cheese, softened
1 teaspoon vanilla extract

1 (20-ounce) can pineapple chunks
1 pint fresh strawberries, sliced
1 (11-ounce) can mandarin oranges, drained
2 kiwifruit, peeled and sliced
3/4 cup fresh blueberries
3 tablespoons granulated sugar
2 teaspoons cornstarch
1/2 teaspoon lemon juice

Robin Kaufhold
Fred Meyer
Kennewick,
   Washington

Cream the butter and confectioners' sugar in a mixing bowl until light and fluffy. Add the flour gradually, beating constantly. Press in an 11-inch tart pan or 12-inch pizza pan with sides. Bake at 300 degrees for 25 to 30 minutes or until light brown. Remove from the oven to cool.

Beat the melted white chocolate chips and whipping cream in a mixing bowl. Add the cream cheese and vanilla and beat until smooth. Spread over the cooled crust. Chill for 30 minutes.

Drain the pineapple, reserving 1/2 cup of the juice. Arrange the strawberries, pineapple, mandarin oranges and kiwifruit in concentric circles over the filling beginning at the outer edge. Sprinkle the blueberries over the fruit.

Combine the granulated sugar, cornstarch, lemon juice and reserved pineapple juice in a saucepan. Bring to a boil over medium heat. Boil for 2 minutes or until thickened, stirring constantly. Remove from the heat to cool. Brush over the fruit layers. Chill for 1 hour before serving. Store in the refrigerator.

Serves 12

Cookies Candies & Desserts

SERVING CUSTOMERS for 125 Years
1883 Kroger 2008

Cookies, Candies & Desserts

Holiday Almond Cookies

I started making this cookie thirty years ago when I first married. I have made them at every store I have worked at for Christmas. Some employees remember the cookies more than me.

Teri Sanders
Kroger
Beavercreek, Ohio

Cookies
1 cup (2 sticks) butter, softened
2/3 cup sugar
1 egg
2 1/2 cups all-purpose flour
1/2 teaspoon salt
1/2 teaspoon almond extract
2 egg whites, lightly beaten
1 1/4 cups finely chopped almonds

Almond Filling
2 tablespoons butter
1/4 cup shortening
2 cups confectioners' sugar
1 egg white
1/2 teaspoon almond extract

Assembly
1 (10-ounce) jar maraschino cherries, drained and cut into halves

To prepare the cookies, cream the butter and sugar in a mixing bowl until light and fluffy. Add the egg and beat well. Stir in the flour, salt and almond extract. Chill in the refrigerator. Shape the dough into small balls. Dip each ball into the egg white and roll in the almonds. Arrange on a greased cookie sheet and press the center of each with your finger to form an indentation. Bake at 350 degrees for 5 minutes. Press down the centers again. Bake for 3 to 5 minutes longer. Remove from the cookie sheet to cool.

To prepare the filling, heat the butter in a saucepan over medium heat until brown. Remove from the heat to cool. Beat the shortening, confectioners' sugar, egg white and almond extract in a small mixing bowl until fluffy. Beat in the butter, adding a few drops of water if the mixture needs to be thinner or adding additional confectioners' sugar if the mixture needs to be thicker.

To assemble, fill the center of each cookie with the almond filling and top with a maraschino cherry half.

For a wonderful chocolate almond cookie, substitute 1/3 cup of the all-purpose flour with baking cocoa.

Makes 4 1/2 dozen

Cappuccino Biscotti

3/4 cup hazelnuts

2 cups unbleached all-purpose flour

1 cup sugar

1/2 teaspoon baking soda

1/2 teaspoon baking powder

1/2 teaspoon salt

1/2 teaspoon cinnamon

1/4 teaspoon ground cloves

5 tablespoons cool strong-brewed espresso

4 teaspoons milk

1 egg yolk

1 teaspoon vanilla extract

1/2 cup (3 ounces) semisweet
   chocolate chips

Christina Ferrelli
Ralphs
Torrance, California

Place the hazelnuts in a single layer in a baking pan. Bake at 300 degrees for 5 to 10 minutes or until the skins begin to crack. Remove from the oven. Wrap the hazelnuts in a clean towel and let stand to steam. Rub the hazelnuts inside the towel to remove the skins. Chop the hazelnuts coarsely. Increase the oven temperature to 350 degrees.

Mix the flour, sugar, baking soda, baking powder, salt, cinnamon and cloves in the bowl of an electric mixer fitted with the paddle attachment. Whisk the espresso, milk, egg yolk and vanilla in a small bowl. Add to the flour mixture and beat until a soft dough forms. Stir in the hazelnuts and chocolate chips.

Place the dough on a lightly floured surface and knead several times. Cut the dough into two equal portions. Shape each portion with floured hands into a flat log 12 inches long and 2 inches wide on a large buttered and floured cookie sheet and place each log 3 inches apart. Bake on the middle oven rack for 35 minutes. Cool on the cookie sheet on a wire rack for 10 minutes. Reduce the oven temperature to 300 degrees.

Place the logs on a cutting board and cut crosswise on the diagonal into slices 3/4 inch thick. Arrange cut side down on the cookie sheet. Bake for 4 to 5 minutes on each side or until pale golden brown. Remove to a wire rack to cool. Store in airtight containers.

Makes 28 to 30

Grandma Woolary's Butterscotch Brownies

This is my grandmother's recipe. Everyone loved her Butterscotch Brownies.

Vicky Shrader
Kroger
Kokomo, Indiana

^{1}/2 cup (1 stick) butter, softened
2 cups packed light brown sugar
2 eggs
1 ^{1}/4 cups all-purpose flour
1 teaspoon baking powder
^{1}/4 teaspoon salt
1 teaspoon vanilla extract
^{1}/2 cup nuts (optional)
2 tablespoons confectioners' sugar

Cream the butter and brown sugar in a mixing bowl. Add the eggs and beat well. Add the flour, baking powder, salt and vanilla and mix well. Stir in the nuts. Pour into a greased and floured 9×9-inch baking pan. Bake at 350 degrees for 20 to 25 minutes or until the brownies rise to the top and then fall. Remove from the oven to cool. Sprinkle with the confectioners' sugar and cut into squares.

Serves 16

Brownies

Brownies

1 cup (2 sticks) butter

4 ounces unsweetened chocolate

2 cups sugar

1/2 teaspoon salt

4 eggs

1 cup all-purpose flour

2 teaspoons vanilla extract

1 cup nuts (optional)

Chocolate Frosting

1/2 cup (1 stick) butter

2 ounces unsweetened chocolate

1 egg

1 (1-pound) package confectioners' sugar

1 teaspoon vanilla extract

2 tablespoons cream

Steve Wood
Kroger
New Palestine, Indiana

To prepare the brownies, melt the butter and chocolate in a saucepan. Combine the sugar, salt and eggs in a bowl and mix well. Add the chocolate mixture and mix well. Stir in the flour. Add the vanilla and nuts and mix well. Pour into a well-greased shallow 9x13-inch baking pan. Bake at 325 degrees for 30 to 35 minutes or until the edges pull away from the sides of the pan.

To prepare the frosting, melt the butter and chocolate in a saucepan. Beat the egg well in a mixing bowl. Add the confectioners' sugar and beat well. Add the chocolate mixture and mix well. Stir in the vanilla and cream. Spread over the brownies.

If you are concerned about using raw eggs, use eggs pasteurized in their shells, or use equivalent amounts of pasteurized egg substitute.

Serves 20

Mom Mac's Mocha Fudge Brownies

Greg Fox
Kroger
Indianapolis, Indiana

Brownies
1 cup (2 sticks) butter, softened
3 ounces chocolate, melted
2 cups sugar
3 eggs
2 teaspoons vanilla extract
1 cup all-purpose flour
1 cup black walnuts, chopped (optional)
1/2 (10-ounce) package miniature marshmallows

Mocha Chocolate Icing
1/2 cup (1 stick) butter, melted
3 1/4 cups confectioners' sugar
6 tablespoons baking cocoa
1 teaspoon vanilla extract
6 tablespoons hot brewed coffee

To prepare the brownies, beat the butter, chocolate, sugar, eggs, vanilla and flour in a mixing bowl until smooth. Stir in the walnuts. Spoon into a greased 9x13-inch baking pan. Bake at 325 degrees for 30 to 35 minutes or until the brownies pull away from the sides of the pan. Remove from the oven. Place the marshmallows on top and press into the brownies. Let stand until cool.

To prepare the icing, combine the melted butter, confectioners' sugar, baking cocoa, vanilla and hot coffee in a mixing bowl and beat for 15 minutes. Spread over the top of the cooled brownies.

Serves 24

Italian Brides' Cookies

1/4 cup (1/2 stick) butter, softened
4 ounces cream cheese, softened
1 egg
1/2 teaspoon anise flavoring
2 teaspoons fresh lemon zest
3 tablespoons fresh lemon juice
1 (2-layer) package moist white cake mix
1/2 cup chopped almonds
1 cup confectioners' sugar
1 egg white
1/2 teaspoon anise flavoring

Cream the butter and cream cheese in a large mixing bowl. Add the egg, 1/2 teaspoon anise flavoring, the lemon zest and lemon juice and mix well. Add the cake mix and almonds and mix well. Drop by small ice cream scoopfuls onto baking parchment-lined cookie sheets. Bake at 350 degrees for 10 to 12 minutes or until light brown on the bottom. Cool on a wire rack.

Combine the confectioners' sugar, egg white and 1/2 teaspoon anise flavoring in a small bowl and mix well with a fork. Dip the top of each cookie into the frosting. Let stand until the frosting dries before serving.

Variation: For Italian Grooms' Cookies, substitute vanilla extract for the anise flavoring, orange zest for the lemon zest, orange juice for the lemon juice, chocolate cake mix for the white cake mix and pecans for the almonds and add 1/4 teaspoon ground cloves and 1/2 teaspoon cinnamon.

Makes 62

These cookies are based on a very old Italian recipe passed down through many generations. The flavor was always very good but the cookies were hard and dry, as many Italian cookies are. Over the years I have played with this recipe until my family thinks it's just right. I love to bake and take treats to work at least once a week. My coworkers encouraged me to submit this recipe.

Cheryl Juliano
Hilander
Rockford, Illinois

This recipe has been a family tradition for about twenty years and a must-have at Christmastime.

Joe Dandrea
Kroger
Cincinnati, Ohio

Cashew Cookies

Cookies

2 cups all-purpose flour

3/4 teaspoon baking soda

3/4 teaspoon baking powder

3/4 teaspoon salt

1/4 to 1/2 teaspoon nutmeg

1/2 to 1 teaspoon cinnamon

1/2 cup (1 stick) butter, softened

1 cup packed brown sugar

1 egg

1/2 teaspoon vanilla extract

1/3 cup sour cream

1 cup chopped cashews

Vanilla Frosting

3 tablespoons butter, softened

2 tablespoons milk

2 cups confectioners' sugar

1 teaspoon vanilla extract

To prepare the cookies, mix the flour, baking soda, baking powder, salt, nutmeg and cinnamon together. Cream the butter and brown sugar in a mixing bowl. Add the egg and vanilla and mix well. Add the flour mixture alternately with the sour cream, beating well after each addition. Stir in the cashews. Drop by tablespoonfuls onto a baking parchment-lined or greased cookie sheet. Bake at 350 degrees for 12 minutes or until light golden brown. Cool on a wire rack.

To prepare the frosting, beat the butter, milk, confectioners' sugar and vanilla in a mixing bowl until smooth and creamy. Spread over the cooled cookies.

Makes 3 dozen

Agnes's Chocolate Chip Cookies

1 cup shortening
2 eggs
1 cup granulated sugar
1/2 cup packed light brown sugar
2 teaspoons vanilla extract
2 cups all-purpose flour
1 teaspoon baking soda
1 teaspoon salt
2 cups (12 ounces) semisweet chocolate chips

Agnes Kessen
Kroger
Cincinnati, Ohio

Beat the shortening, eggs, granulated sugar, brown sugar and vanilla in a mixing bowl until light and fluffy. Add the flour, baking soda and salt and mix well. Stir in the chocolate chips. Drop by teaspoonfuls 2 inches apart onto a lightly greased cookie sheet. Bake at 375 degrees for 8 to 9 minutes or until golden brown. Cool on a wire rack.

Makes 7 1/2 dozen

More Than Just Chocolate Chip Cookies

2²/3 cups all-purpose flour

1/2 teaspoon baking soda
   (1 teaspoon below 5,000 feet elevation)

1 1/2 cups packed dark brown sugar

1 cup (2 sticks) butter, softened

2 teaspoons vanilla extract

1/4 teaspoon salt

2 eggs

1 cup shredded coconut

1 cup rolled oats

1 cup chopped walnuts or pecans

1 cup (6 ounces) semisweet chocolate chips

1 cup (6 ounces) milk chocolate chips

Sift the flour and baking soda together. Cream the brown sugar and butter in a mixing bowl. Add the vanilla and salt and mix well. Beat in the eggs. Add the flour mixture and mix well. Add the coconut and oats and mix well. Stir in the walnuts, semisweet chocolate chips and milk chocolate chips. Chill the dough for 2 hours. Shape the dough into rounded 2-tablespoon portions and place on a baking parchment-lined cookie sheet. Bake at 350 degrees for 12 to 15 minutes or until light brown. Cool on a wire rack. Store in an airtight container.

Tip: The baking time will depend on the altitude and the size of the cookie. The cookie dough may be portioned and frozen for baking later. Increase the baking time if the dough is frozen. This could easily become a breakfast cookie by substituting chopped dried apricots, dried cranberries, dried cherries or raisins or for the chocolate chips.

Makes 35

The Breckenridge City Market at an elevation of over 9,600 feet is the highest Kroger store. Baking at this altitude can be tricky, but I've had good results with this recipe at high and low elevations.

Denise Helmick
City Market
Breckenridge,
Colorado

Gobbs (Chocolate Sandwich Cookies)

Cookies

4 cups all-purpose flour

2 teaspoons baking powder

2 teaspoons baking soda

1/2 teaspoon salt

1/2 cup baking cocoa

1 tablespoon vinegar

1 cup milk

2 eggs

2 cups sugar

1/2 cup shortening

1/2 teaspoon vanilla extract

1/2 cup boiling water

Vanilla Cream Filling

2 tablespoons cornstarch

1 1/3 cups milk

1 cup shortening

1 2/3 cups confectioners' sugar

1 teaspoon vanilla extract

To prepare the cookies, sift the flour, baking powder, baking soda, salt and baking cocoa together. Stir the vinegar into the milk in a small bowl. Beat the eggs, sugar and shortening in a mixing bowl until creamy. Add the flour mixture and mix well. Beat in the milk mixture and vanilla. Add the boiling water and mix well. Drop by rounded tablespoonfuls onto ungreased cookie sheets, making sure they are uniform in shape. Bake at 350 degrees for 12 minutes. Cool on a wire rack.

To prepare the filling, dissolve the cornstarch in the milk in a saucepan. Cook over medium heat until thickened to a paste consistency, stirring constantly. Remove from the heat and cool completely. Cream the shortening, confectioners' sugar and vanilla in a mixing bowl until light and fluffy. Add the cooled milk mixture and mix well.

To assemble, spread the filling over one-half of the cookies. Top with the remaining cookies to form a sandwich cookie. Wrap each in waxed paper and freeze until firm.

Makes 2 1/2 dozen

These tasty frozen treats always bring back happy memories in the kitchen with my Grandma and Aunt laughing and having fun—sticking your finger in the cream filling and Grandma laughing.

Lindy Eversole
Scott's
New Haven, Indiana

This recipe was one my mom made when I was growing up. My wife has continued the tradition—it is one of our family's favorite cookies. I am not sure what her source for the recipe was originally.

Bruce Macaulay
Kroger
Westerville, Ohio

Merry Mallow Fudgies

15 marshmallows
3 cups sifted all-purpose flour
2/3 cup baking cocoa
1 teaspoon baking soda
1 teaspoon salt
1 cup shortening
1 cup granulated sugar
1/2 cup packed brown sugar
2 eggs
1 teaspoon vanilla extract
Granulated sugar for rolling

Cut the marshmallows into quarters and freeze. Sift the flour, baking cocoa, baking soda and salt together. Cream the shortening, 1 cup granulated sugar and brown sugar in a mixing bowl until light and fluffy. Add the eggs and vanilla and beat well. Stir in the flour mixture. Shape a heaping rounded teaspoonful of dough around each marshmallow quarter, sealing well. Roll in granulated sugar to coat and place on greased cookie sheets. Bake at 400 degrees for 6 to 8 minutes or just until the cookies begin to crack. Cool on the cookie sheets for 2 minutes. Remove to a wire rack to cool completely.

Makes 6 dozen

Coconut Crisps

1 cup (2 sticks) butter, softened
1 cup sugar
1 egg
1 teaspoon vanilla extract
1 teaspoon almond extract
2 cups all-purpose flour
$1/2$ teaspoon baking soda
$1/2$ teaspoon salt
2 cups flaked coconut
Sugar for sprinkling

Beat the butter lightly in a mixing bowl. Add 1 cup sugar gradually, beating constantly. Add the egg, vanilla extract and almond extract and beat well. Whisk the flour, baking soda and salt in a large bowl. Add the egg mixture and mix well. Stir in the coconut. Drop by rounded teaspoonfuls onto greased cookie sheets. Sprinkle each with sugar and press lightly with the bottom of a sugar-dipped glass. Bake at 325 degrees for 12 to 15 minutes; do not brown. Cool on a wire rack.

Makes 2 dozen

I fell in love with these cookies when a friend made them for my bridal shower. Every time I make them, others come to love them, too.

Lindsay Holmson
Fred Meyer
Portland, Oregon

Macadamia Macaroons

I made these for my family and they fell in love with them. They could not believe they were made with crackers.

Sheila Carroll
Kroger
Nokomis, Illinois

1 (7-ounce) package flaked coconut
1 cup macadamia nuts, chopped
1 (14-ounce) can sweetened condensed milk
1 teaspoon vanilla extract
30 saltine crackers, finely crushed
3 egg whites, at room temperature
2 ounces semisweet baking chocolate

Spread the coconut and macadamia nuts in a 10x15-inch baking pan. Bake at 350 degrees for 10 minutes or until lightly toasted, stirring frequently. Remove from the oven to cool. Maintain the oven temperature.

Combine the condensed milk and vanilla in a large bowl and mix well. Add the coconut mixture and cracker crumbs and mix well. Beat the egg whites at high speed in a small mixing bowl until stiff peaks form. Fold in the coconut mixture gently. Drop by rounded tablespoonfuls 2 inches apart onto a lightly greased cookie sheet. Bake for 10 to 12 minutes or until the edges of the cookies are light brown. Remove to a wire rack to cool completely.

Melt the chocolate using the package directions. Drizzle over the cookies. Place the cookies in a waxed paper-lined shallow pan. Chill until the chocolate is set.

Makes 3 dozen

Date Roly Poly

1 (16-ounce) package chopped pitted dates
1 cup water
^{1}/2 cup sugar
4 cups (or more) all-purpose flour
1 teaspoon baking soda
^{1}/2 teaspoon cream of tartar
^{1}/2 teaspoon salt
^{3}/4 cup (1 ^{1}/2 sticks) butter or shortening, softened
2 cups packed brown sugar
2 eggs
^{1}/2 teaspoon vanilla extract

Combine the dates, water and sugar in a saucepan and mix well. Cook until slightly thickened, stirring constantly. Remove from the heat to cool.

Mix the flour, baking soda, cream of tartar and salt together. Cream the butter and brown sugar in a mixing bowl until light and fluffy. Add the eggs and vanilla and mix well. Add the flour mixture and mix well. Roll the dough carefully into a 14x16-inch rectangle on a well-floured work surface. Spread with the date mixture and roll up as for a jelly roll with floured hands. Wrap tightly in waxed paper. Chill for 8 to 10 hours.

Unwrap and cut into slices ^{1}/4 inch thick. Place on a cookie sheet. Bake at 350 degrees for 18 to 20 minutes or until light brown. Cool on a wire rack.

For easier handling, you may divide the dough into two equal portions and roll each into a 7x8-inch rectangle.

Makes 3 ^{1}/2 dozen

This is a holiday tradition with our family. This recipe was given to me from my great-great-grandmother thirty years ago. I now share making it with my granddaughter. It's a fun, wonderful experience talking about how women so long ago made so many wonderful things from what they had on hand, and how strong they must have been to mix the dough.

Debbie Waybourn
Kroger
Katy, Texas

This is a good recipe to use up the end of the season green tomatoes.

Sheila Fritts Campbell
Kroger
Olympia, Kentucky

Green Tomato Bars

4 cups finely chopped green tomatoes
1 cup packed brown sugar
2 tablespoons lemon juice
1 teaspoon lemon extract
3/4 cup (1 1/2 sticks) butter, softened
1 cup packed brown sugar
1 1/2 cups all-purpose flour
1/2 teaspoon baking soda
1/2 teaspoon salt
2 cups rolled oats
1/2 cup nuts

Drain the green tomatoes on paper towels to remove the excess moisture. Combine the green tomatoes, 1 cup brown sugar and lemon juice in a saucepan and bring to a simmer. Simmer for 20 to 25 minutes or until thickened, stirring constantly. Remove from the heat and stir in the lemon extract.

Cream the butter and 1 cup brown sugar in a mixing bowl. Add the flour, baking soda and salt and mix well. Stir in the oats and nuts. Press 2 1/2 cups of the oat mixture over the bottom of a greased 9x13-inch baking pan and spread with the green tomato mixture. Crumble the remaining oat mixture over the top. Bake at 375 degrees for 30 to 35 minutes or until golden brown. Cool and cut into squares.

Makes 32 squares

Oat Cranberry Bars

1 cup fresh cranberries
2 teaspoons granulated sugar
2 cups all-purpose flour
2 cups rolled oats
1/2 cup packed brown sugar
1/2 teaspoon baking soda
1 cup (2 sticks) butter, melted
1 1/2 cups chopped dates
3/4 cup chopped walnuts
1 cup caramel topping
1/3 cup all-purpose flour

Heather Burley
Kroger
Cincinnati, Ohio

Mix the cranberries and granulated sugar in a bowl and set aside. Mix the flour, oats, brown sugar and baking soda in a bowl. Add the butter and mix well. Reserve 1/2 cup of the oat mixture for the topping. Press the remaining oat mixture over the bottom of a 9x13-inch baking pan. Bake at 350 degrees for 15 minutes. Sprinkle with a mixture of the dates and walnuts. Mix the caramel topping and flour in a bowl. Pour over the date mixture. Sprinkle with the cranberry mixture. Top with the reserved oat mixture. Bake for 20 minutes longer. Cool and cut into bars.

Makes 2 dozen

Hillbilly Turnovers

1 cup milk
1 envelope dry yeast
1 teaspoon vanilla extract
1/2 teaspoon salt
3 egg yolks, lightly beaten
2 cups shortening
4 cups all-purpose flour
Confectioners' sugar for rolling
1 (21-ounce) can favorite pie filling
2 tablespoons granulated sugar

Scald the milk in a saucepan and let cool to lukewarm. Add the yeast and stir until dissolved.
Let stand for 10 minutes. Add the vanilla, salt and egg yolks and mix well. Cut the shortening
into the flour in a bowl until crumbly. Add the yeast mixture and mix well. Roll into two
9x12-inch rectangles on a work surface sprinkled with confectioners' sugar. Cut each rectangle
into 3-inch squares. Place a spoonful of the pie filling into the center of each square. Fold the
dough over the filling to form a triangle, pressing the edges to seal. Sprinkle with the granulated
sugar. Bake at 350 degrees for 25 to 30 minutes or until the edges begin to turn light brown.
Cool on a wire rack.

Makes 2 dozen

Mother Lexia's Caramels

2 cups sugar
1 1/2 cups light corn syrup
1/2 cup evaporated milk
1 cup (2 sticks) butter or margarine, chopped
1/2 cup evaporated milk
2 teaspoons vanilla extract
1/2 cup chopped nuts (optional)

Combine the sugar, corn syrup and 1/2 cup evaporated milk in a saucepan and mix well. Cook over medium-low heat until the sugar is dissolved, stirring constantly. Add the butter a small amount at a time, stirring constantly. Cook until the mixture comes to a rolling boil. Stir in 1/2 cup evaporated milk gradually so the mixture does not stop boiling. Cook until the mixture turns in color and is thickened, stirring constantly. Cook to 240 degrees on a candy thermometer, soft-ball stage, stirring constantly. Remove from the heat and stir in the vanilla and nuts. Pour into a buttered 9x13-inch pan. Let stand until almost cool. Invert onto a cutting board and cut with a hot knife or scissors into 40 to 48 squares. Wrap each square in waxed paper.

Makes 40 to 48 pieces

My oldest daughter, Chrystal, carries on Mom's tradition by cooking her grandmother's recipe and sends a Christmas goodies package to the family.

Janice Tyrrell
Fry's
Tucson, Arizona

Wonderful Caramels

2 cups light corn syrup
1 (14-ounce) can sweetened condensed milk
1 1/2 cups milk
1 cup whipping cream
1 cup plus 1 tablespoon butter
4 cups sugar
2 teaspoons vanilla extract
2 cups nuts
Melted Belgian chocolate for dipping (optional)

Combine the corn syrup, condensed milk, milk, cream, butter and sugar in a 6-quart heavy Dutch oven. Cook over medium heat until the mixture comes to a boil, stirring occasionally with a wooden spoon. Cook for 25 minutes or to 240 degrees on a candy thermometer, soft-ball stage, stirring constantly. Remove from the heat. Stir in the vanilla and nuts. Pour into a buttered 9x13-inch pan; do not scrape the pan. Let stand at room temperature for 8 to 10 hours. Invert the candy onto a cutting board. Cut into 1-inch squares or rectangles with a heavy sharp knife. Dip in the chocolate and let stand until firm. Wrap in waxed paper.

If the caramels are undercooked, you can reheat by adding 1 1/2 cups hot water and cooking to the proper temperature.

Makes 117

The first weekend after Thanksgiving my daughters and granddaughters come to my kitchen to bake and make candies for the holiday season. This is one of our favorite candy recipes we make every year.

Phyllis Norris
City Market
Denver, Colorado

By Guess and By Golly Cracker Jacks

1 1/2 to 1 3/4 cups granulated sugar
3 to 4 heaping tablespoons brown sugar
1/2 to 3/4 cup light corn syrup
3/4 to 1 cup dark maple syrup
1 to 1 1/2 cups (2 to 3 sticks) margarine
1/4 teaspoon baking soda
5 to 6 quarts popped popcorn

Bring the granulated sugar, brown sugar, corn syrup and maple syrup to a boil in a saucepan. Cook to 240 degrees on a candy thermometer, soft-ball stage. Add the margarine. Cook to 260 degrees on a candy thermometer, hard-ball stage, being careful not to burn. Stir in the baking soda. Pour carefully over the popcorn and stir to coat. The syrup is very hot.

For a variation, you may add peanuts or any other nuts to the popcorn.

Makes 5 to 6 quarts

My father-in-law used to make this recipe with his maple syrup every year and give it to friends and family with love. Everyone loved it. This recipe is shared in the memory and love of James Smith.

Deloris Smith
Kroger
Huntington, Indiana

I make these at Christmastime and my family loves them. Be creative and try other flavorings such as chopped up candied cherries, lemon gelatin or maple flavoring. They will disappear fast.

Carolyn Hanley
Kroger
Plymouth, Indiana

Dipped Chocolate Creams

1/2 cup (1 stick) butter, softened
4 ounces cream cheese, softened
6 cups confectioners' sugar
1/3 cup chopped pecans
3 tablespoons dry orange gelatin
3 tablespoons dry raspberry gelatin
24 ounces chocolate bark

Cream the butter and cream cheese in a mixing bowl. Add the confectioners' sugar 1 cup at a time, beating well after each addition. The mixture will be the consistency of pie pastry dough. Divide the mixture into three equal portions. Knead the pecans into one portion. Knead the orange gelatin into one of the remaining portions. Knead the raspberry gelatin into the remaining portion. Shape the dough into 1-inch balls and place on a tray lined with waxed paper. Chill in the refrigerator.

Melt the chocolate bark using the package directions. Dip each ball into the chocolate and return to the tray. Chill until firm.

Makes 5 dozen

Dream Fudge

18 ounces special dark chocolate bars and
   regular chocolate bars
3 cups (18 ounces) chocolate chips
1 (12-ounce) can evaporated milk
3 1/2 cups sugar
1 teaspoon salt
1/4 cup (1/2 stick) butter
1 teaspoon vanilla extract
1 (7-ounce) jar marshmallow creme
1 1/2 cups chopped nuts (optional)

Break the chocolate bars into pieces and place in a large mixing bowl. Add the chocolate chips and set aside. Mix the evaporated milk, sugar, salt and butter in a heavy saucepan. Heat over medium-low heat until the butter and sugar melts. Increase the heat to medium and bring to a boil, stirring constantly. Boil for 4 1/2 minutes, stirring constantly. Pour over the chocolate and stir with a heavy spoon until melted and blended together. Add the vanilla and marshmallow creme and stir until blended. Cool for a couple of minutes. Beat with a heavy spoon until glossy and smooth but still soft enough to pour. Stir in the nuts. Pour into a buttered 9x13-inch pan. Let stand until cool. Cut and store, chilled, in airtight containers for up to 2 months.

Makes about 6 pounds

Many batches of this fudge were shipped overseas to our troops. This recipe has been used during the holiday season by my family since the 1940s. I can remember as a young child "helping" break the chocolate bars and holding the bowl as my Dad stirred. My children now take their turns with the stirring. I do believe some of this fudge has found its way into the break rooms of my QFC stores these past nineteen years.

Marcia Cline
QFC
Stanwood, Washington

Eggnog Fudge

2 cups sugar
1/2 cup (1 stick) butter
1 1/2 cups eggnog (12 ounces)
1 teaspoon rum flavoring
1 (13-ounce) jar marshmallow creme
2 cups (12 ounces) white chocolate chips

Bring the sugar, butter and eggnog to a rolling boil in a large saucepan over medium heat, stirring constantly with a wooden spoon to prevent scorching. Cook for 10 minutes or to 137 degrees on a candy thermometer, medium soft-ball stage or until a small amount of the hot mixture dropped into cold water can be picked up and shaped like soft clay. Remove from the heat. Stir in the rum flavoring. Add the marshmallow creme and stir until melted. Add the white chocolate chips and stir until melted and smooth. Pour into a 9x13-inch pan sprayed with nonstick cooking spray and spread evenly. Cool at room temperature or in the refrigerator for 8 to 10 hours. Cut into bite-size pieces.

Serves 40

You may use a candy thermometer but I have never had any luck with one of those. Also, if your fudge does not set, you did not cook it long enough. If it is hard or dry you cooked it too long. To make great fudge takes lots of practice. Wooden spoons work best and remember—weather, stoves, pans and altitude may make a big difference.

Sharli Kaltenbach
Smith's
Evanston, Wyoming

Lime in de Coconut Fudge

1/4 cup sliced almonds
3/4 cup flaked coconut
3 cups (18 ounces) white chocolate chips
1 (14-ounce) can sweetened condensed milk
1/8 teaspoon kosher salt
1/2 teaspoon coconut extract
1 teaspoon vanilla extract
1 teaspoon lime zest

Spread the almonds and coconut on a baking sheet. Bake at 325 degrees for 10 minutes or until toasted and fragrant. Remove from the oven to cool.

Combine the white chocolate chips, condensed milk and kosher salt in a 2-quart saucepan and mix well. Heat over low heat until the white chocolate chips melt and the mixture has a smooth consistency, stirring occasionally. Remove from the heat. Stir in the coconut extract and vanilla extract. Stir in the lime zest. Add the toasted coconut mixture and mix well. Shape the warm mixture into small mounds using a small spoon or 1-ounce scoop. Place the mounds into miniature muffin cup liners or bonbon papers. Chill in an airtight container; do not freeze.

Serves 20

A few years ago a good friend of mine gave me a Key Lime Almond Joy candy bar to try. It tasted really good, but unfortunately, it was a limited edition flavor and I haven't seen it available in the grocery stores since 2005. I wanted to enjoy those flavors again. So, I was inspired to make a white fudge that mimicked the candy bar. My friend told me that the fudge tastes just as good as the Key Lime Almond Joy bars. Enjoy!

Sandy La Gasse
Fred Meyer
Brookings, Oregon

White Chocolate Peppermint Bark

This candy is delicious.

Dody Upton
Kroger Wesco
Vero Beach, Florida

2 pounds white chocolate
1 cup crushed peppermint hard candies
1 tablespoon vegetable oil
1 1/2 teaspoons peppermint extract

Place the white chocolate in a microwave-safe bowl. Microwave on High for 1 1/2 to 2 minutes or until melted, stirring at 20-second intervals after 1 minute. Be careful not to burn. Stir in the crushed candies. Add the oil and peppermint extract and mix well. Pour onto a foil-lined 12x16-inch baking sheet. Chill for 1 hour or until firm. Break into pieces or cut into squares.

Makes 75 pieces

Baklava

1 1/2 pounds walnuts, finely chopped
3/4 cup granulated sugar
3 tablespoons cinnamon
1 (16-ounce) package frozen phyllo
    dough, thawed
2 cups (4 sticks) salted butter, melted

2 cups granulated sugar
1 cup water
2 cinnamon sticks
1/4 cup honey
1 cup confectioners' sugar
1 tablespoon milk

Leslee Ruppenthal
Kroger
Cincinnati, Ohio

Mix the walnuts, 3/4 cup granulated sugar and 3 tablespoons cinnamon in a bowl and set aside. Unroll the phyllo dough and cover with waxed paper topped with a damp towel. Keep the unused portion covered until needed. Layer ten to twelve sheets of phyllo dough in a buttered 9x13-inch baking pan, brushing each sheet with some of the butter. Spread one-half of the walnut mixture over the top. Cover with two to four more sheets of phyllo dough, brushing each sheet with some of the remaining butter. Spread the remaining walnut mixture evenly over the layers. Cover with the remaining phyllo dough, brushing each sheet with some of the remaining butter. Brush the top with the remaining butter. Cut the baklava into diamond shapes using a very sharp knife, cutting through all the layers. Bake at 350 degrees for 30 minutes. Reduce the oven temperature to 300 degrees. Bake for 30 minutes longer or until golden brown on top.

Combine 2 cups granulated sugar, the water and cinnamon sticks in a medium saucepan. Cook over high heat until the granulated sugar is dissolved and the liquid is clear, stirring constantly. Reduce the heat to low. Simmer until the mixture is the consistency of thin syrup, stirring occasionally. Discard the cinnamon sticks. Stir the honey into the hot syrup.

Remove the baklava from the oven. Pour the hot syrup over the baklava, covering the entire surface. Let stand until cool.

Mix the confectioners' sugar with enough of the milk in a bowl to make a thin glaze that can be drizzled and still hold its shape. Drizzle over the cooled baklava. Let stand for 1 to 2 hours or until the glaze is set. Recut the pieces to separate and place in paper liners. Store in an airtight container.

Makes 40 to 48

Cranberry Bread Pudding with Warm Lemon Sauce

I love bread pudding but never really cared for the raisins in it. So, when Dillons started baking fresh craisin bread, I decided to create my own version of bread pudding. It's so good, and it makes a wonderful holiday dessert!

Mitzi Russell
Dillons
Joplin, Missouri

Bread Pudding

Granulated sugar for sprinkling

1 1/2 loaves craisin bread, or 1 1/2 loaves
    cinnamon bread plus 1/2 cup
    dried cranberries

4 eggs

3 cups milk

1/2 cup granulated sugar

1 tablespoon vanilla extract

1 tablespoon Grand Marnier

1 1/2 teaspoons cinnamon

1 tablespoon fresh lemon juice

1/2 teaspoon fresh lemon zest

1/4 cup (1/2 stick) unsalted butter

1/2 cup packed brown sugar

Lemon Sauce

1/2 cup sugar

2 tablespoons cornstarch

1/2 teaspoon fresh lemon zest

1 cup water

1 tablespoon fresh lemon juice

2 tablespoons unsalted butter

To prepare the bread pudding, butter a 7x11-inch baking pan and sprinkle with granulated sugar. Trim the crusts from the bread and reserve. Cut the bread into cubes and set aside. Beat the eggs well in a large bowl. Whisk in the milk, 1/2 cup granulated sugar, the vanilla, Grand Marnier, cinnamon, lemon juice and 1/2 teaspoon lemon zest. Add the bread cubes and mix gently with a spoon until well coated. Let stand for 15 minutes. Spoon into the prepared pan. Pulse the reserved bread crusts, butter and the brown sugar in a food processor until the mixture is crumbly. Spread over the pudding layer. Set the pan into a 9x13-inch baking pan. Fill the larger pan with enough water to come halfway up the sides of the smaller pan. Preheat the oven to 350 degrees. Reduce the oven temperature to 325 degrees. Bake the bread pudding for 45 minutes.

To prepare the sauce, mix the sugar, the cornstarch and lemon zest in a small saucepan. Add the water and lemon juice. Cook until the mixture is bubbly, stirring constantly. Cook for 2 minutes longer. Remove from the heat. Stir in the butter until melted. Serve warm over the bread pudding.

Serves 12

Grandapa Porras's Capirotada

4 cups (1 quart) water
1 (1-pound) package brown sugar
3 cinnamon sticks
1 whole clove
6 to 8 slices toasted sweet French bread, cut into cubes
1 Granny Smith apple, thinly sliced
1 banana, sliced (optional)
1 cup raisins
3/4 to 1 cup chopped peanuts
1/2 cup blanched almonds
8 ounces Monterey Jack cheese, shredded

Bring the water to a boil in a saucepan. Add the brown sugar, cinnamon sticks and clove. Cook until the mixture forms a syrup, stirring constantly. Discard the cinnamon sticks and clove.

Layer the bread, apple, banana, raisins, peanuts, almonds and cheese one-half at a time in a buttered 2-quart baking dish. Pour the syrup over the layers. Bake at 350 degrees for 20 to 25 minutes. Cool for 10 minutes before serving. Serve hot or cold.

Serves 9

My grandfather Marciel Porras's recipe has been a family and friend favorite for years.

Joel Arreola
Foods Co
Lompoc, California

Pineapple Cheesecake

Barbara Holderby
Kroger
Proctorville, Ohio

2 cups all-purpose flour
1/2 cup sugar
1 teaspoon baking powder
Pinch of salt
1/2 cup (1 stick) margarine
2 eggs, well beaten
1 (20-ounce) can crushed
   pineapple, drained
4 egg whites, at room temperature

4 egg yolks
28 ounces cream cheese, softened
1 cup sugar
1/4 cup all-purpose flour
2 teaspoons vanilla extract
Juice of 1 lemon (about 3 tablespoons)
3 cups milk
Cinnamon for sprinkling

Mix 2 cups flour, 1/2 cup sugar, the baking powder and salt in a bowl. Cut in the margarine until crumbly. Add 2 eggs and mix well. The dough will be the consistency of cookie dough. Spread over the bottom and up the side of a 10x14-inch baking pan. Spread the pineapple over the bottom. Chill in the refrigerator.

Beat the egg whites at high speed in a mixing bowl until stiff peaks form. Cream the egg yolks, cream cheese, 1 cup sugar, 1/4 cup flour, the vanilla, lemon juice and milk in a mixing bowl until fluffy. Add the egg whites and beat for 2 minutes. Pour into the prepared pan and sprinkle with cinnamon. Bake at 350 degrees for 45 to 50 minutes or until the crust is brown around the edges. The cheesecake will not be firm when removed from the oven.

This recipe is also good with a graham cracker crust. To prepare using a graham cracker crust, mix 2 cups graham cracker crumbs, 3 tablespoons sugar and 1/2 cup (1 stick) to 3/4 cup (1 1/2 sticks) butter, melted, in a bowl. Spread over the bottom and up the side of the pan. Bake at 350 degrees for 8 minutes. Remove from the oven and cool. Spread with the pineapple and continue with the recipe as above.

Serves 10

Chocolate Chip Cheesecake

8 ounces cream cheese, softened

1/2 cup sugar

1 egg

1/8 teaspoon salt

1 cup (6 ounces) milk chocolate chips or
   semisweet chocolate chips

1 1/2 cups all-purpose flour

1/4 cup baking cocoa

1/2 teaspoon salt

1/2 cup vegetable oil

1 cup sugar

1 teaspoon vanilla extract

1 teaspoon baking soda

1 cup water

1 tablespoon vinegar

Combine the cream cheese, 1/2 cup sugar, the egg and 1/8 teaspoon salt in a mixing bowl and beat well. Stir in the chocolate chips and set aside. Combine the flour, baking cocoa, 1/2 teaspoon salt, the oil, 1 cup sugar, vanilla, baking soda, water and vinegar in a bowl and mix well. The batter will be thin. Pour into a greased 8x8-inch baking pan. Drop the cream cheese mixture over the batter and swirl with a knife to marbleize. Bake at 350 degrees for 50 to 60 minutes. Cool and cut into squares.

Serves 10 to 16

This dessert is very moist and rich. It also keeps well. This recipe came from A Collection of Recipes cookbook sponsored by Parents and Friends of Children in B.E.E.S. (Brandon Early Education Support) Specialized Fund-Raising Program. B.E.E.S. is a program for young children ages two through five who can benefit from support in one or more areas of their development. My son was in the program. He is now twenty-seven years old.

Mary Szymkowski
Kroger
Ortonville, Michigan

Lemon Meringue Cheesecake

2³/4 cups finely crushed shortbread cookies
   or vanilla wafers
¹/4 cup (¹/2 stick) butter, melted
32 ounces cream cheese, softened
1¹/2 cups sugar
1 cup sour cream
4 eggs
2 egg yolks

¹/2 cup lemon juice
2 teaspoons lemon zest
1¹/2 teaspoons vanilla extract
2 egg whites
¹/8 teaspoon cream of tartar
¹/4 cup sugar
1 teaspoon vanilla extract

To make the cookie crumbs, place 12 ounces of cookies in a sealable plastic bag. Press out the air and crush the cookies with a rolling pin.

Vickie Williamson
Kroger
Moneta, Virginia

Wrap the outside of a 9-inch springform pan with a double layer of foil. Combine the cookie crumbs and butter in a bowl and mix well. Press over the bottom and 1 inch up the side of the springform pan. Bake at 350 degrees for 12 to 14 minutes. Remove from the oven and maintain the oven temperature.

Beat the cream cheese at high speed in a mixing bowl for 4 minutes or until very light and fluffy. Add 1¹/2 cups sugar and beat at low speed for 2 minutes. Add the sour cream, eggs, egg yolks, lemon juice, lemon zest and 1¹/2 teaspoons vanilla and beat for 4 minutes or until smooth. Pour into the prepared pan. Place the springform pan in a large roasting pan. Add enough water to the large pan to come half way up the side of the springform pan. Bake for 1¹/2 hours, covering loosely with foil after 1 hour to prevent browning. Cool on a wire rack for 1 hour. Cover and chill for 8 to 10 hours.

Beat the egg whites and cream of tartar at high speed in a mixing bowl until soft peaks form. Add ¹/4 cup sugar gradually, beating until stiff peaks form. Beat in 1 teaspoon vanilla. Spread over the top of the cheesecake. Bake at 375 degrees for 8 to 10 minutes or until light brown. Cool on a wire rack. Release and remove the side of the pan to serve.

Serves 16

Apple Yam Delight

3/4 cup instant oats
1/4 cup all-purpose flour
3/4 cup packed brown sugar
1/3 cup butter or margarine
1 (16-ounce) jar chunky applesauce
1/2 teaspoon cinnamon
1 (16-ounce) can yams, cut into slices
1/2 teaspoon cinnamon

Mix the oats, flour and brown sugar in a bowl. Cut in the butter until evenly distributed and crumbly. Spread a little less than half of the applesauce in an 8x8-inch baking dish and sprinkle with 1/2 teaspoon cinnamon. Spoon 3 tablespoons of the oat mixture over the applesauce. Layer the yams over the oat mixture. Cover with the remaining applesauce and sprinkle with 1/2 teaspoon cinnamon. Spread the remaining oat mixture evenly over the top. Bake at 350 degrees for 30 to 40 minutes or until heated through. Serve hot. Top with whipped topping or vanilla ice cream, if desired.

Serves 8 to 12

This recipe can also be served as a side dish.

Debra Rogers
Kroger
Clarksburg, West Virginia

Paul Dowell
Kroger
Louisville, Kentucky

Berry Cream Crumble

16 ounces strawberries, trimmed and cut into halves

1 pint blueberries

1 pint raspberries

1 pint blackberries

2/3 cup all-purpose flour

2 cups sugar

4 eggs

1 cup sour cream

1/4 teaspoon salt

1 cup sugar

1 1/2 cups all-purpose flour

1 cup (2 sticks) unsalted butter, cubed and chilled

Layer the strawberries, blueberries, raspberries and blackberries in a lightly greased 9x13-inch baking dish. Combine 2/3 cup flour, 2 cups sugar, the eggs, sour cream and salt in a medium bowl and mix well. Pour over the fruit. Mix 1 cup sugar and 1 1/2 cups flour in a bowl. Add the butter and mix with your hands until crumbly. Sprinkle over the batter. Bake at 350 degrees for 50 to 55 minutes or until brown and set. Serve hot. Top with vanilla ice cream, if desired.

Serves 12 to 15

Cherry Dumplings

1/2 cup sugar
Dash of salt
1/2 cup cherry juice
1 1/2 cups sour or tart cherries
1 1/2 cups boiling water
1 cup sifted all-purpose flour
1 1/2 teaspoons baking powder
Dash of salt
1/4 cup sugar
2 tablespoons butter
1/2 teaspoon vanilla extract
1/3 cup milk

Combine 1/2 cup sugar, dash of salt, cherry juice, cherries and boiling water in the order listed in a 3-quart heavy saucepan or heavy skillet with a lid. Simmer gently for 5 minutes. Sift the flour, baking powder, dash of salt and 1/4 cup sugar into a bowl. Cut in the butter until crumbly. Stir the vanilla into the milk. Add to the flour mixture and stir to form a thick batter. Drop by teaspoonfuls into the simmering sauce. Cover and steam for 20 minutes. Serve the dumplings with the sauce.

You may use one 16-ounce package frozen cherries and reserve the juice. Peaches or apricots may be used instead of the cherries.

Serves 6

My mother, Evelyn Hawkins, made this recipe when I was growing up. She would make it in a 4-quart Presto cooker where she could steam it. I always loved this dessert. My mom was quite a cook. She passed away in November 2002.

Clarine Colliver
Kroger
Hillsboro, Ohio

Peach Cobbler with Cheese Biscuits

Great served with whipped cream or ice cream.

Donna Newman

Kroger

Kewanna, Indiana

2 quarts fresh peach slices

1 1/2 cups sugar

2 tablespoons quick-cooking tapioca

1/2 teaspoon salt

2 tablespoons lemon juice

1/2 teaspoon almond extract

3 tablespoons butter

2 cups baking mix

1 cup (4 ounces) shredded sharp Cheddar cheese

1/4 cup (1/2 stick) butter, melted

2/3 cup (about) milk

Place the peaches in a greased 9x13-inch or 3-quart baking dish. Mix the sugar, tapioca and salt in a bowl. Sprinkle over the peaches. Sprinkle with the lemon juice and almond extract. Dot with 3 tablespoons butter. Bake at 400 degrees for 15 minutes or until hot and bubbly.

Mix the baking mix and cheese in a bowl. Add 1/4 cup butter and enough of the milk to form a soft dough, stirring with a fork. Remove the peach mixture from the oven and stir to mix. Drop the dough by twelve spoonfuls over the hot peaches. Bake for 20 minutes or until the biscuits are golden brown. Top with whipped cream or ice cream, if desired.

Serves 12 to 16

Orange Mousse

1 (8-ounce) can crushed pineapple
1 (3-ounce) package orange gelatin
8 ounces cream cheese, softened
2 tablespoons half-and-half
1 (11-ounce) can mandarin oranges, drained
1 cup heavy whipping cream, whipped

Drain the pineapple, reserving the juice. Add enough water to the reserved juice to measure 1 cup. Pour into a saucepan and bring to a boil. Add the gelatin. Heat until dissolved, stirring constantly. Chill until partially set.

Beat the cream cheese and half-and-half in a small bowl until blended. Beat in the gelatin mixture gradually. Stir in the pineapple and mandarin oranges. Chill until partially set. Fold in the whipped cream. Spoon into eight individual molds or dessert dishes. Chill for 8 to 10 hours or until set. The mousse will have a creamy consistency.

Serves 8

My mother enjoyed making this recipe in her kitchen many times. And, we enjoyed eating it. Thanks, Mom.

Debbie Skarja
Kroger
Macy, Indiana

This is my favorite Christmas treat. My Mom always made it without the cherries just for me.

Coco Bill

Kroger

Indianapolis, Indiana

Paradise Pudding

1 (3-ounce) package lemon gelatin
2 cups boiling water
1 cup small miniature marshmallows (100)
6 macaroons, crushed
1/2 cup nuts
1 cup heavy whipping cream, whipped
1/4 cup sugar
1/4 teaspoon salt

Dissolve the gelatin in boiling water in a 2-quart bowl. Let stand for 15 minutes. Chill in the refrigerator for 35 to 40 minutes or until partially set. Stir in the marshmallows, cookies and nuts. Whip the cream, sugar and salt in a mixing bowl until firm peaks form. Fold into the gelatin mixture. Spoon into a serving bowl. Chill for 8 to 10 hours or until set.

For Christmas, you may add twelve red or green chopped maraschino cherries.

Serves 8 to 12

Individual Cranberry Trifles

1 (16-ounce) angel food cake
16 ounces low-fat cream cheese, softened
2 cups confectioners' sugar
1 cup low-fat sour cream
1 teaspoon vanilla extract
16 ounces light whipped topping
2 (16-ounce) cans whole cranberry sauce
2 tablespoons granulated sugar
3 to 4 teaspoons grated orange zest

This recipe can be made with other fruit fillings and also can be served in a trifle bowl. It's great for the holidays or as a summer dessert.

Shirley Ruge
Baker's
Bellevue, Nebraska

Cut the cake into 1-inch cubes. Combine the cream cheese, confectioners' sugar, sour cream and vanilla in a large mixing bowl and beat until smooth. Fold in half the whipped topping. Combine the cranberry sauce, granulated sugar and orange zest in a bowl and mix well.

Alternate layers of the cake, cranberry mixture and whipped topping mixture in parfait glasses until full, ending with a layer of the cranberry mixture and a dollop of the remaining whipped topping. Garnish each with a fresh cranberry and mint sprig. Chill until serving time.

Serves 10 to 12

40+ Year Associates

The dedication and hard work of our family of associates has been a critical factor in The Kroger Co.'s success for the past 125 years. We salute the following members of the Kroger family who had more than 40 years of service with the Company, as of December 31, 2007.

Thank you for your commitment.

Atlanta
Billy Allison
George Bills
Gary Cheatwood
Larry Claxton
James Collins
Donald Daniell
Thomas Davis
Sam Davis
Larry Edmondson
Anna Eisenberg
John Emberton
Robert Fields
Bobby Hallmark
Bobby Harbin
Jimmy Harrell
James Heintz
Jerry Hendrix
Dennis Henson
Howard Higdon
Larry Hitch
Jacqueline Holcomb
Frederick Hummel
Hugh Ikner
Joyce Jones
Gary Kuykendall
Dennis Land
Cheryl Lynn
Thermon Mann
Edgar McCaleb
Gordon Pressnell
Juanita Reep

Billy Rhea
Thomas Robinia
Jerry Seabolt
Talmadge Smith
Larry Summey
Nancy Sweat
Roger Swinford
Roy Webster
Tommy Williams

Central
Samuel Barnard
Jerry Bella
Barry Beyers
Marty Biroschik
Betty Bobo
Lydia Brinkman
Richard Burke
Jimmy Carroll
Patrick Ciesiolka
Michael Cole
Larry Cook
Robert Eha
Gordon Evans
Dorathea Everett
Michael Gaines
Carolyn Hall
David Harmon
Michael Holtkamp
Joyce Irvin
Jean Jacobs
Donald Jeffers

Stephen Kimmell
David Knauff
Kenneth Lowery
Donald Lowery
Patrick Lynch
Jerry McCartney
Brian McCord
Roger Meuleman
William Moore
Susan Mullins
Michael Murdock
Ernest Pike
John Plessinger
Walter Randolph
Larry Raudenbush
Richard Rides
Wladimir Ride
George Ringer
Wayne Rosebrock
Judy Sanders
James Sinclair
Stephen Smith
Cynthia Speakman
Leonard Swain
Terry Terwelp
Merle Tompkins
Jerry Troyer
Betsy Wable
Gene Wilcox
Robert Worley

Cincinnati
Bruce Anderson
Jeff Baker
John Biehn
Raymond Brown
Bruce Drew
Thomas French
Waitman Gobble
Kenneth Gold
Carl Grooms
Joseph Hagemeyer
Steve Hall
William Harp
Sidney Isaacs
Edward Ivers
Herman Kennedy
Paul Kline
Mary Klocke
Michael Kuntz
Derryl Pitts
Timothy Quinlan
Thomas Scherman
Ambries Taylor
Lawrence Umberg
Michael Weiskittel
Steve Wells
Joseph Wiedman

City Market
Clarke Davis
Richard Sadvar

Columbus

Delmar Allison
Lawrence Arnold
Ronald Berry
Michael Brown
Paul Brown
Ted Burden
Ronald Burkle
Lynn Carter
Claude Clayborne
Douglas Clinton
Charles Cochran
Darl Crawford
Robert Davis
Michael Dugas
Joseph Fetty
James Finfgeld
Doris Galloway
Jerold Graham
Vaughn Grubb
Jerry Hall
Kenneth Harvey
Bob Hasson
George Heckler
Wayne Hunsinger
Carolyn Ialenti
Daniel Ingweiller
Dan Johnson
James Kisker
Thomas Koepfler
James Konecny
Herbert Lehmann
William Lennex
Larry Lowery
Patrick McCraley
Steve McIntosh
Lona Meadows
Philip Morris
Karl Nachtman
Michael Newman
Gayle Nourse
Douglas Phipps
Monda Reineke
David Rings
William Robertson

Corrine Salisbury
Frank Santa
Edward Skeens
Wilma Spangler
Michael Spradlin
Edward Strohl
James Swartz
Mary Tennant
Thomas Traunero
Vincent Trovato
Carl Tutt
Gary Vance
Ronald Watkins
Mona Whipkey

Delta

Jerry Allen
Daniel Burle
John Call
Robert Cannon
Paul Cissell
Billy Curry
Timothy Davey
Jeffrey Elliott
Guy Ellis
Lauren Felder
Charles Gabbard
Theresa Garrone
William Graves
Richard Hale
Larry Horton
David Jones
Franklin Keller
Donald Lawrence
Noel Lewallen
Edmund Mahony
Randy Martin
Donald McFadden
Larry McIntosh
Ulysses Medford
J. Mentgen
Linda Mitchell
J.F. Morgan
Richard Naber
Earlene Perry

Donald Poole
Charles Smith
Michael Speaks
Danny Terry
Bobby Thomas
Charles Turner
George Weaver
Kenneth Williamson
Johnny Wilson
Charles Wright

Dillon Stores

John Bays
Danny Boyes
Barbara Bruemmer
Steven Carpenter
Alvin Collins
Billy Combs
Melvin Cowger
Allen Drennon
Dennis Elston
James Frager
Michael Franklin
Albert Garcia
Julius Gassman
Howard Hart
LaVerne Havel
Gail Huddle
Richard Hunt
Terry Loeffler
Kenneth Lovell
William Madsen
Richard Meyer
Richard Miller
Richard Piatt
Paul Schaefer
Willard Schrag
Keith Schuster
Darwin Seal
Jerome Simmons
Donald Stewart
Robert Wheeler
Jerry Young

Food 4 Less

Larry Stepp

Fred Meyer

Kenneth Bailey
George Bradley
Gail Breimon
John Brown
J. Butler
M. Campbell
Mark Carter
Matthew Chandler
Larry Cleveland
Alice Gabert
Gerald Gallagher
Ray Gee
C. Hartson
R. Hiromura
Paul Lawrence
Keith Morrison
Sharon Munkers
David Pratt
Joe Schell
F. Schuchart
Edward Seiwald
Beverly Takahashi
B. VanWinkle
David Wells
Dennis Wersch
Marvin Williams
Danny Wilson
Nancy Yee
Terry Zimmerman
David Zuercher

Fred Meyer Jewelers

Mike Lewinsky
Linda Rutger

Fry's

Robert Leets
James Nygren

Jay C

Robert Barnett
Robert Decker
Darrell Dyer
Donald Dyson
Marion Eubank
Jerry Fleenor
Oddis Freese
Jess Hendershot
David Motsinger
Marvin Rutan
Larry Trambaugh
Ronald Trueblood
John Yeary

King Soopers

Gary Beedle
Kenneth Boyes
Roger Brodzik
William Campbell
Jon Cave
Vincent Creadon
Russell Dispense
Robert Ferguson
Roger Goatcher
Michael Houghton
David Hunt
Steven Janss
Steve Katzenberger
John Kuhns
Robert Lucero
Richard Martin
Michael McBee
Byrne Miller
David Murphy
Richard Nethery
Dale Servo
Delbert Trimble
Thomas Young

40+ Year Associates

Michigan

Beverly Adams
Keith Aldrich
David Allmond
William Applegate
Frank Aretz
Margaret Atkins
William Bailey
Donald Bank
Doretha Bell
Ross Beltz
Karen Bouie
John Brandt
Richard Brighton
Nancy Brown
Michael Bruce
Charles Brynski
William Burke
Wayne Busby
Phillip Busch
Clayton Butterfield
William Cairns
Michael Calvin
William Carlisi
Carmela Catanzaro
Barbara Chauvin
Jerome Christmas
Rosalie Ciluffo
Thomas Cole
Donald Coleman
James Conley
Douglas Couture
Jack Culver
Michael Czajka
Joseph Danik
James Deck
James Decker
Richard Delvecchio
John Desmarteaux
Barbara Dorman

Walter Dubay
Rex Dubois
Thomas Dueweke
Thomas Duff
Diane Durolik
Randall Eldridge
Kent Fehribach
Alexandria Ferrari
Sue Fitzpatrick
John Fleming
Michael Fogarty
Tony Ford
Gerry Frisk
James Fulkerson
Douglas Garavaglia
Dennis Geikowski
Richard Gennari
James Gerben
Anthony Gniatkiewicz
Robert Godlewski
Karl Graham
Kenneth Griffes
Robert Guse
Kenneth Gutowski
Lavere Hake
John Hamper
Richard Hample
Janelle Hawley Myers
Gregory Hendershot
Sara Hlavin
James Hochkins
Thomas Holden
John Holmes
George Holunga
Bernard Jajko
Michael Jeziorowski
Janet Jones
Olivia Jones
Joseph Kanske
James Keathley

Jerry Kelley
Thomas Kelly
Russel Kittleson
Donald Kowalski
Terry Krohn
James Lang
Edward Langowski
Keith Lavere
Paul Leedy
Tony Lijoi
Robert Little
Pamela Lizewski
Jack Lloyd
Willaim Lloyd
Wayne Lounsbury
Marion Lozen
Lyn Lymond
Terrence Mahoney
Henry Majestic
Bonnie Maki
Bernard Makled
Gregory Malek
John Manoulian
Arlene March
Thomas Marker
Peter McGough
Peter McLaren
Paul Meck
Thomas Mesnard
Theodore Miela
Agnes Milazzo
Russell Miller
Petrina Miller
James Miller
Kenneth Moore
Ronald Morency
William Mullins
Marion Neely
Arthur Odonohue
Roger Paison

Gary Palkowski
Charlene Pantaleo
John Paul
Gene Payne
Charles Pedick
Richard Peeler
Shirley Penner
Leszek Petrykowski
Karl Petyk
John Pickelhaupt
Julian Pirog
Kenneth Pisoni
Errol Pulk
Frank Rakoczy
Richard Reaume
Robert Redlin
Frederick Reiss
Joyce Riley
Gary Ringer
Thurlo Rodgers
John Ruhl
Robert Sackett
Jake Sadik
Jack Sarcona
John Schadt
Gregory Schenk
Richard Sefcovic
Ronald Sergeichik
Paul Sesta
Ronald Shasko
Diana Sikorski
Geoffrey Simpson
Antonia Siuru
Charles Sloan
Harley Smith
Gary Spellman
Thomas Staley
Brian Steinley
Gene Stone
Frank Szostak

Lawrence Teal
David Ternes
Bernard Terwellen
Linda Tessen
Gary Thompson
Bernice Toles
Thomas Traunero
Judy Trudo
Roger Valimont
Beverly Vankuren
William Vermeersch
James Vlcek
Calvin Walker
William Weir
Curtis Wernette
Terry Williams
Marilyn Willaimson
William Winiarski
Stanley Wise
Robert Wypych

Mid-Atlantic

James Bell
James Blevins
Loren Bonnell
Joann Boone
Michael Bryant
Larry Canter
Gary Carothers
Gary Carter
Bernard Casdorph
Kenneth Connery
Owen Craig
Richard Crouse
Andrew Cutlip
Thomas Dailey
Robert Devere
Terry Evans
Gary Fox
Gregory Frazier
William Gorrell
Barry Halstead
Richard Hendrick
Danny Hicks
Robert Higginbotham

Clyde Horner
Harvey Hornish
Charles Hoy
James Hunt
Larry Lacroix
John Lucas
Jerry Mayes
Robert McAmis
Kenneth McCord
William McDaniel
Johnny McGee
John McKown
Dyan McReynolds
Hulet Montrief
Hugh Moore
Norman Moore
John Moyer
Larry Nowlin
Garry Peck
Charles Petry
Judith Pouyan
Danny Ramsey
Donald Ray
Wilton Roberts
Franklin Roetto
Gerald Salyer
Harley Sanders
Roy Sandoe
Ralph Sansom
Thomas Shifflett
Robert Shupe
George Sigler
Eugene Skaggs
Brian Smith
Harry Spencer
Lewis Stinnette
Terry Tabor
Addison Thomas
Clarence Thompson
Robert Tuck
James Utter
Don Webb
David Williams
Ernest Williamson
James Wilson

Mid-South

George Abell
Earl Adam
Sharon Almasy
Kenneth Bandy
Woodard Bowley
Charles Brumfield
Leon Buchanan
Gerald Butts
Marvin Cashman
John Cassella
Lillian Clark
Robert Collins
Patricia Cranford
Don Cummins
Stanley Davis
Radal Davis
William Davis
Claude Donithan
Doug Dugle
Stephen Easterling
Kenneth Epley
Jackie Farmer
Jim Followay
James Fulton
James Gaines
Garnett Gardner
John Goodman
Harold Goodwin
Donald Graviss
Ronald Greer
George Greer
John Hackett
Thomas Hamilton
Charles Hartley
Lawrence Hasenstab
Douglas Hayden
Charles Haynes
Daniel Hewitt
Harry Huffman
Carlos Hume
William Janes
Richard Jenkins
Ken Kaelin
Johnny King

John Krawiecki
Shirley Lewis
Robert Lockhart
Donald Maschhoff
William McCreary
Nettie McCreary
Mike McNair
Robert McPherson
James Miller
Arthur Mimms
James Moore
David Moore
Willie Murray
Andrew Neichter
Linda Nixon
Michael Osterkamp
Joyce Perkins
Anthony Pfuelb
Virginia Pontrich
William Powell
Michael Richards
Frederick Roberts
James Ryan
Michael Smith
Charles Steinmetz
Jimmy Stephens
Lawrence Stettenbenz
Tracy Thomas
Charles Tidwell
Larry Turner
Mary Vaughn
Roy Weller
Charlie Williams
Joyce Wittenback
Roy Wright

Ralphs

William Adams
Mike Aguirre
James Barton
Julie Blake
Susan Boyd
Roger Branch
Thomas Cincotta
Natt Cohan

Robert Cosgrove
Richard Fischinger
Vincent Flindt
Alan Forbush
Julee Fournier
Kay Garbizo
Steven Harshman
James Hilton
Richard Huettner
Hideko Jimenez
Dick Kawaguchi
Ted Kinoshita
Ed Kite
Carol Kumai
Harry Lee
Lawrence Lewis
John McGary
Robert Melendez
Paul Morris
James Oakes
Richard Rees, Jr.
Frank Riggio
John Rodriguez
Rick Sabin
Jim Sanders
Dave Schaub
Gary Street
Jerome Stroger
Greg Sugioka
Richard Thomas
Robert Voeltz
Charles Watson
John Weiser
David Wentworth
Chris Wyatt
Robert Wyckhouse
Marilyn Yoshihiro

40+ Year Associates

Smith's
David Cole
Glade Ely
James Hallsey
Lawrence Kirigin
Joel Kirk
Betty Lawson
Nick Mark, Jr.
Wsewolod Massen
Max Moore
Betty Nielson
John Redd
Kristine Williams

Southwest
David Becker
Danny Butler
Jerry Daugherty
Robert Dugger
Harry Fletcher
Linda Follis
Garry Forisha
Francis Howard
Steve Howell
Donald James
Ronald Jones
Charles Kaiser
James Morehead
Arthur Oden
R.R. Rodenberg
Homer Starks
John Tribo
Milton Wallace
Dorothy Wofford

Kroger Corporate
Brenda Andes
Orville Beasley
Bill Bencze
Virgil Burgess
Donald Busemeyer
Jerry Doepker
Toni Dumas
Mike Jack
Reiny Juengling
Billie Kimbrough
Graham Lee
John Lennon
Carl Markel
James Northrop
Bob Rice
Edward Schmelzle
Robert Schuermann
Paul Scutt
Rodney Sizemore
Larry Stump
Stephen Wood

Manufacturing
Joyce Anderson—State Avenue
Robert Brown—Columbus Bakery
Robert Campbell—Indianapolis Bakery
Byron Cook—State Avenue
John Cox—Columbus Bakery
Linda Faul—State Avenue
Guy Folkman—KB Specialty Foods
Evelyn Hood—State Avenue
Jerry Iven—Anderson Bakery
Floyd Kessler—Pontiac Foods
Judith Koch—Corporate Office
Gerald Lewis—KB Specialty Foods
Richard Lindner—Columbus Bakery
Veston Messer—
    Springdale Ice Cream and Beverage
Walter Murphy—Indianapolis Bakery
Jack Rasmussen—Tolleson Dairy
William Rowling—State Avenue
Allen Shaffer—State Avenue
Lawrence Stern—State Avenue
James Toy—Columbus Bakery
Alphonso Wills—State Avenue

Convenience Stores Group
Charles Frey—Turkey Hill Dairy
Larry Ibach—Turkey Hill Dairy
Gordon Kauffman—Turkey Hill Dairy
Arlis Neufeld—Kwik Shop

Index

SERVING CUSTOMERS for 125 Years

1883 Kroger 2008